THE GLAMOUR OF
NEAR EAST EXCAVATION

THE GOLDEN MASK OF TUTANKHAMEN

This portrait mask of the young Pharaoh covered the head of his mummy, within the innermost coffin. It is of beaten gold, inlaid with turquoise, carnelian, lapis lazuli, and coloured
glazes. Like the golden coffin, the mask is not only intrinsically valuable, but is also a noble
work of art. (See pp. 165 *sq.*)

(By kind permission of Dr. Howard Carter)

The Glamour of
Near East Excavation

*AN ACCOUNT OF THE TREASURE-HUNT FOR THE BURIED
ART, WISDOM & HISTORY OF THE ANCIENT EAST,
FROM THE NILE TO BABYLON, THE ADVEN-
TURES, DISAPPOINTMENTS & TRIUMPHS
OF THE HUNTERS, & THE KNOWLEDGE
THUS ACQUIRED OF THE
ANCIENT WORLD*

BY

JAMES BAIKIE, F.R.A.S.

AUTHOR OF "THE STORY OF THE PHARAOHS"
"THE SEA KINGS OF CRETE"
&c. &c.

WITH MANY ILLUSTRATIONS

London
Seeley, Service & Co. Ltd.
196 Shaftesbury Avenue
1927

PRINTED IN GREAT BRITAIN

PREFACE

THE present time is witnessing an extraordinary development of activity in the work of excavation all over the world, and naturally this has been most intense in the regions in which man first began to realise the possibilities of his nature. The interest of the general public was, no doubt, mainly aroused, in the first instance, by the wonderful romance of the Tomb of Tutankhamen ; but Babylonia and Palestine are now yielding results scarcely less remarkable and attractive than the golden wonders of the Valley of the Tombs of the Kings, and we may hope for an immense increase of our knowledge from these sources in the future. In this great work, excavators of our own nation are playing an honourable and distinguished part ; yet Great Britain is scarcely filling the place which she ought to fill, having regard to her position as a pioneer in the past. That this is so, is in no sense due to lack of skilled explorers, but simply to lack of funds to enable the men to carry out work which they are longing to do. We are lagging behind, and allowing other nations to win the prizes, because while we seem able to find any amount of money for less important things, we grudge it when it is to be spent on the acquisition of knowledge. If the following chapters succeed in arousing among our own people an interest which will lead to greater support being given to the great adventure of excavation, the purpose with which they were written will be served.

The point of view throughout the book is avowedly that which is suggested by its title. To the writer's mind, there is no more romantic story than that of the resurrection of the great historic past which has been and is being

11

accomplished by the excavators of the present, and, in accordance with this belief stress all through has been laid upon the excavator's methods, constantly developing and improving in refinement, his adventures, his triumphs and his disappointments ; but, while this is so, the need for a broad and yet accurate presentation of the results attained, and of their bearing upon our conceptions of the culture of the Ancient East, has been steadily kept in view. It must never be forgotten that unless excavation can help us to see the past as a living thing, it is the most useless of all vain labours ; and to contribute something towards this great object has been my chief aim in this, as in my other books.

In order to enable me to paint my picture of the past and its resurrection with something of that largeness of scale and sufficiency of detail without which it must remain sketchy and unconvincing, it has been necessary to limit, to some extent, the area which is dealt with. Thus the great fields of the Aegean and the Hittite cultures remain to be handled, if opportunity serve, in another volume. Egypt, Palestine, Assyria, and Babylonia form, however, a group so well-marked and familiar as to offer a satisfactory unit for treatment.

I wish to acknowledge the kindness and courtesy of Sir Flinders Petrie, Dr. G. A. Reisner, Dr. Howard Carter, Mr. C. L. Woolley, Mr. S. R. K. Glanville, The Rev. P. B. Fraser, New Zealand, the authorities of the Museum of the University of Pennsylvania (Philadelphia), the Palestine Exploration Fund, and the British Museum, in allowing me to reproduce some of the treasures which have been the result of their work, or are in their keeping, and in furnishing me with prints for reproduction. These are duly attributed to their various sources on the plates in which they appear.

JAMES BAIKIE.

CONTENTS

13

14   Contents

BOOK II. ASSYRIA & BABYLONIA

CHAPTER VIII

CHAPTER IX

CHAPTER X

CHAPTER XI

BOOK III. PALESTINE

CHAPTER XII

CHAPTER XIII

CHAPTER XIV

LIST OF ILLUSTRATIONS

THE GLAMOUR OF NEAR EASTERN EXCAVATION

(EGYPT, MESOPOTAMIA, PALESTINE)

INTRODUCTION

THE LURE OF TREASURE HUNTING ; AIMS AND METHODS OF MODERN EXCAVATION ; THE TREASURE HOUSES OF THE ANCIENT EAST

THE instinct of the treasure hunter is one of the primal instincts of human nature, and the romance of his business has made an unfailing appeal to countless generations of mankind. One has only to think of the fascination which stories like *Treasure Island* and *Dead Man's Rock* have exercised over the imagination of our generation, *The Gold Bug* over that of the generation before us, and *Ali Baba* and *Aladdin* over every generation which has lived since *The Arabian Nights* first made their appeal to a public hungering for excitement, to realise the hold which the sudden discovery of untold wealth has upon the human mind, and has had in all ages, even the most remote. At least one ancient Egyptian romance teaches us that the instinct was as strong three thousand years ago as it is to-day ; and doubtless the prehistoric man of Piltdown or Neanderthal, by his fire at night, told hair-raising tales of how some lucky ancestor had suddenly become rich " beyond the dreams of avarice " by the discovery of a hoard of chipped flints or mammoth ivory. The fact that every one of the countless tales of buried treasure is nothing more than another variation, and sometimes very little of a variation, on a single theme, seems to make as little difference to the interest with which it is followed as the companion fact that everybody knows from the start that the story will end with the well-earned enrichment of the noble hero, and the discomfiture, if not the extinction, of his miserable rivals and enemies.

The modern pursuit of knowledge, however, has led to the development of a form of treasure hunting whose story ought to be still more fascinating than that of any mere search for gold or jewels. Its scene is laid, not in some unnamed and undistinguished island of an uncharted sea, but in the most richly storied lands of the romantic Orient. If it has not for its background the tossing ocean, with the black schooner hove to in the offing, it has the endless sand-waves of the desert, with all the wizardry of that immemorial nurse of romance ; and if it lacks the romantic figure of the pirate, who was actually the dirtiest and least romantic of rascals, it has the rivalries of excavators, which have sometimes been almost as dangerous as the pirate's endearing little ways, and often a good deal more amusing.

Above all, the modern treasure hunt has all the undying charm of the unknown. The treasure seeker of romance looks, with wearisome repetition of the same theme, for nothing but sordid gold and jewels, and the only possible variations of his success concern nothing more vital than the quantities and proportions of the filthy lucre, of one kind or another, for which he slaves. The excavator may find gold and jewels, sometimes in amazing quantity, as our own age has seen ; but these things are merely a by-product of his search. What he is really seeking is something whose price is above rubies ; and the object of his search may reveal itself to him in any one of a thousand different ways. He knows nothing of the narrow limitations which beset his rival of fiction. He may find anything, from a mighty king lying " in glory, in his own house," as the Hebrew prophet puts it, among his golden splendours, to a bit of potsherd with a few almost illegible words scratched upon it, or a dingy scrap of papyrus with a half-effaced verse or two from a lost

Gospel or an almost forgotten poet ; and while the world may gape and go crazy over the first discovery, the finder himself may very likely have a far deeper joy over the second, because it may enable him to add something to the sum of human knowledge concerning an almost unknown period or train of incident. The treasure hunting of the scientific excavator, unlike that of his brother of fiction, can never pall, though it is often one of the hardest and least remunerative jobs on earth, because there is no end to its possibilities, and no monotonous certainty about them. The founder of the modern science of excavation, to whom archæology owes more than to any other living man, has summed up the prospects of the excavator in something like the following fashion. Out of every ten objects which may occupy the mind of an excavator at the start of his work, the chances are that only one will be realised ; but that one will probably bring in its train ten other results, of which several may prove to be far more important than any of the original ten which prompted the search.

It ought to be manifest, therefore, that the man of science, who lives laborious days (how laborious the general public, which glances casually at his little paragraphs tucked away at the foot of more important news, little imagines) in the attempt to add another page or chapter to the wonderful history of human life through the ages, is not only, on the whole, a more respectable member of society than his illegitimate brother of the spade and pick ; he has also a much more varied and fascinating stock-in-trade to deal with. Instead of the threadbare business of pieces of eight, mingled but scarcely varied with diamonds, rubies, and emeralds, he has to handle the romance of kings and empires, made actual. If fortune should lead him to buried gold, it is not the sordid hoard of Kidd, or Roberts, or Teach that he unearths, but the gems that sparkled on the brow of a mighty Pharaoh, or the tiara which crowned the locks of a princess of Thebes or Babylon ; while his less glittering finds may have a value yet more priceless because they may open a window into the mind and the life of a great people of five thousand years ago. It is reasonably certain that there are few men who work so hard for so little material reward as does the scientific excavator ; but it is also certain that there are few men who, during the lifetime of this generation and its predecessor, have added so much to the total of human knowledge, or (it may be surmised) have enjoyed themselves so much in the doing of it.

As a rule, the ordinary world knows nothing, and cares less, about the things which rejoice the heart of the excavator. Once in a while, however, it wakes up, or rather turns uneasily in its sleep. Some wonderful discovery is made, and the news of it is flashed round the world, and even takes pride of place in the headlines of the newspapers. A Pharaoh is found lying in state in his rock-hewn tomb, with gold and jewels and infinite miracles of craftsmanship around him ; or perhaps some great statue, a wonder of artistic skill, comes to light. The public rubs its eyes, and excavation becomes a nine days' wonder. Strange and uncouth names become familiar under the quaintest metamorphoses ; and everyone who desires to be thought in the know acquires for the nonce as much picturesquely inaccurate information about the subject of interest as can reasonably, and without undue effort, be attained in the time. Then a new marvel of another type—probably a thrilling murder, or a spicy divorce case—claims attention. The glamour fades away, and the public turns once more to its peaceful slumbers, having acquired in the interval, however, two fixed ideas about the excavator : first, that his sole object is the discovery of dead royalties ; and, second, that excavation must be a most extraordinarily exciting and paying business.

Both of these ideas, of course, are just about as utterly wrong as they can be, and as one would expect from the conditions under which they were acquired. Finding dead royalties is just about the least important part of the job. They may turn up, and, if they do, the excavator welcomes them, and treats them with more respect than if they were alive, since they are in a much more fragile condition ; but he is seeking for something far more valuable than dead royalties. Within the last half-century there have been three finds of Pharaohs—in 1881, 1898, and 1922. Each of these, and especially the first and the last, has created a considerable sensation, and has both directly and indirectly benefited archæology, though by no means in proportion to the fuss which was made about the matter ; but it would be quite safe to say that in the same period one could match each find of Pharaohs with half a dozen other discoveries of which the public scarcely heard at all, and of which it took not the least notice, which yet were of far greater importance.

For the aim of modern excavation is not to unearth dead kings, and so to enable us to see over again what we knew already—that kings of old could command the most gorgeous funerary equipment, and that the art of some periods was capable of rising to a wonderful level ; it is to recreate for us the life of those long-dead days, and to show us how living men and women, not kings and queens and nobles only, but far more the common people of the time, lived, what they thought, what they hoped for in this life and the life to come, and how, under such inspirations, they wrought their part in the long story of human progress. Finding all the Pharaohs who ever reigned will not tell us that, though it may help us a little to one aspect of the subject ; but it may very well be that an excavation which has yielded nothing at which the ordinary visitor to a museum would look a second time may yet have given us something which will make all the difference to our conception of a whole age, or will breathe new life into the dry bones of the puppets of history. To do this is to accomplish something infinitely more worth doing than the mere unveiling of golden coffins or jewelled pectorals, fascinating though the less important discovery may be to minds which judge values by the cash standard. It is even more worth doing than the discovery of the most notable treasure of the art of any period otherwise well known ; though here the question of artistic values complicates the comparison.

Before me, as I write, there stands a cast of what is perhaps the loveliest thing that Egyptian art ever created—the world-famous limestone head of Akhenaten's beautiful queen, Nefertiti ; and beside it lies a cast of one of the Tell el-Amarna Tablets, coming from the same period and the same city which gave us the brilliant bust of the young queen. There is all the difference in the world in the attractiveness of the two casts. The charm of Nefertiti makes an instant appeal, and one feels that here is another heroine of romance, worthy of a place with Helen of Troy, Cleopatra, or Mary of Scotland ; while the dingy and chipped clay tablet looks like nothing so much as an ancient dog biscuit in an imperfect state of repair : but it is really the insignificant-looking object which is by far the more important discovery of the two. That Queen Nefertiti was beautiful, and that the Egyptian sculptor of the Amarna Age was a master of his craft, we knew from a score of examples before this bust, for whose beauty the world ought to be duly thankful, was discovered ; but the Amarna Tablets have been a searchlight cast upon the whole inner history of the ancient East during the decisive crisis of that old world.

Accordingly, the methods of the modern excavator have entirely changed, in accordance with the change in his aims, from those which characterised his predecessor. " Archæological research," says one of the most distinguished of its modern exponents, " consists principally in the discovery and the classification of the common things of daily life— houses, personal ornaments, domestic utensils, tools, weapons, and the like." Such a definition is calculated to appal and disgust the man who thinks of the past only in terms of kings and colossi, for it seems to reduce the romance

of excavation to a very humble and prosaic business of rum-
maging in the debris of a nation's back-kitchens instead of
exploring the state-rooms of its palaces ; but there can be
no doubt that it comes far nearer to the truth about the
business, and points the way to a far more fruitful line of
investigation. For, after all, a moment's reflection will reveal
the doubtless humiliating but quite certain fact that the
back-kitchens are decidedly more important features of any
nation's life than the state-rooms. The nation could get on
quite well without the state-rooms ; but the back-kitchens
are absolutely essential ; and if you wish to form a picture
of how the nation lived—its average standard of well-being,
its habits and customs, and the ways of thought which ruled
these—it is to the humble national domesticities, and not to
the exceptional splendours, that you must turn.

The great lesson which the modern excavator has had to
learn, and which the public, in its turn, will slowly have to
learn about the work of excavation, is simply this—that it
is the little things of ancient life (as of modern) which are
of infinite importance. You can learn far more about ancient
Egypt from its potsherds than from its pyramids ; and a
crock may be more valuable than a colossus. This point of
view, of course, was denied to the great pioneers of the
movement of research into the treasure house of the past.
Men like Botta and Layard, in Mesopotamia, and Belzoni
and Drovetti, in Egypt, sought, and quite naturally and
justifiably, from their own point of view, for conspicuous
and arresting evidences of the past greatness, historical and
artistic, of the races with whose treasures they were dealing.
It was only by such discoveries that they could justify their
enterprise, and still more the expenditure which it involved,
in the eyes of the public which, in the long run, had to
furnish the funds, and which then, as now, craved a good
return for its money, and was, quite naturally, far more
impressed by a huge statue in granite or alabaster than by
any amount of broken earthenware. That is why the visitor

to any of the great European museums will find that the bulk of the large and impressive specimens of each collection belongs to the early period of excavation ; while the results of the more modern workers, less impressive in magnitude, and less immediate in their appeal, deal far more with the intimate life of the age in question. Probably the excavator of to-day, as he surveys the imposing results of his predecessors, the gigantic winged bulls and lions of Kalah, or the colossal calm of the granite head of Thothmes III, is not so much impressed either with the enterprise or the good fortune of Layard or Belzoni, as filled with a kind of rueful wonder as to how much priceless material, which he would give his ears to light upon, was sacrificed by the rough and ready methods of work which brought the great statues to their present resting-place.

To say this is not, of course, to impute blame to the early explorers. They were pioneers, and the pioneer cannot be expected to work with the delicate regard for relative values, and the patient appreciation of the importance of trifles, which we expect of the worker who builds on the site which the pioneer cleared for him. It is enough if he fulfils his function of clearing the forest and driving the beast, though much that is beautiful and precious may perish in the process. Moreover, with all the wealth of an old world, new from its very ancientry, suddenly disclosed to him, who can wonder if he were too overwhelmed with the majesty of the colossal works around him to be able to appreciate the value and the significance of the smaller things which we have slowly learned to prize ? The pioneers of excavation did, in their day, the work which was necessary to arouse that interest of the modern world without which such work could not be carried on with any continuity ; they did it, perhaps, roughly and wastefully, as all such work will be done, until the true principles which should rule its methods are gradually determined ; but we owe them too great a debt for what they did accomplish to feel that we are in a position to criticise them for the way in which they accomplished it.

Nevertheless, the methods of the early explorers, on the whole, belong to the past, and, it may be hoped, will never be used again in any investigation of importance. Even in their day of the beginnings, when you never knew what new wonder might be awaiting you, there were men who had some dawning idea of the value of the small game of the archæologist, and the necessity and the supreme importance of not only finding an object, but of being able to give an absolutely clear account of where and in what conditions and surroundings it was found. But, even with this qualification, the wastefulness of the old way of working must have caused the loss or the overlooking of an immense quantity of material which the present-day worker would know how to appreciate, but which he is never likely now to see. Most of the early work in Mesopotamia, for instance, and a good deal of that in Palestine, was carried on mainly by processes of tunnelling which has been described as " the most unsatisfactory of all excavation processes." There are, of course, conditions under which tunnelling is inevitable, owing to the existence on the surface of buildings which cannot be removed or tombs which are sacred ; but no modern excavator would dream of using tunnelling unless it was impossible to attain his object by other and better means. Tunnelling is costly, slow, and dangerous ; moreover, it multiplies, on the one hand, the difficulties of effective supervision of the workmen employed ; and, on the other, the opportunities for the concealment and subsequent surreptitious sale of articles which may be of the utmost value to the excavator. The Oriental workman is a past master in the art of " conveying " such articles ; and tunnelling gives him every possible advantage. Finally, tunnelling touches only a small fraction of the ground which it is supposed to have investigated, so that the greater part of the huge mounds which have been subjected to this

process remains still unsearched, awaiting the efforts of
excavators, who, along with the better methods of modern
work, will be fortunate enough to possess means sufficient
to enable them to carry out these methods on an adequate
scale, and patience enough to put up with the long waiting
which thoroughness involves.

Roughly, it may be said that the main principles by which
the modern excavator guides his operations are principles
which did not rule his predecessor's work to anything like
the same extent. They are these : First, that there is
nothing so small or so apparently unimportant as that it
can be safely neglected ; or, to put the same truth in a more
positive fashion, that the very smallest thing may be, and
ought to be, dealt with as though it were of infinite importance ; second, that no object can be said to have been
properly dealt with unless its discoverer has not only preserved, but noted and measured and portrayed, either by
photograph or otherwise, the position in which it was found,
and its relation to the stratification of its surroundings and
the other objects which accompanied it ; thirdly, that pick
and spade are not the final implements of the excavator, but
only the means of preparing his subject for the real and
thorough search by which, so to speak, he must go over his
ground with a small-tooth comb or its equivalent, a fine
sieve. These are perhaps " the first and the great command-
ments " of the excavator ; but there are others, of scarcely
less importance, all tending to impress his mind with the
infinite value of the least of things, with the conviction that
the unpardonable sin, in the case of an investigator, is to
neglect or to overlook anything, no matter how insignificant
it may seem to him, or how unrelated to his main purpose,
and with the faith, scarcely less momentous in comparison
with the outlook of the past, that the best clue to the story
of a nation's life is to be found in its broken earthenware.

On the whole, this is perhaps the quaintest, as it is also,
to the uninitiated, the most surprising and unexpected of

the results which the change of outlook as to the methods
and aims of the archæologist has brought about ; yet a
moment's consideration will show that it is entirely reasonable and, indeed, inevitable in a world which has wakened
up to the fact that the history of nations does not consist
of lists of kings and warriors and chronicles of their deeds
and battles, but in the recording and making visible of the
actual life of each successive age and race, in all its classes,
from " Pharaoh that sits on his throne unto the captive that
is in the dungeon." As aids to the accomplishment of this
great and most worthy task, the things which constituted the
main object and the great reward of early excavation, colossal
statues and ranges of bas-relief, and lengthy inscriptions
recording the wars and conquests of monarchs, still have
their own importance ; but they are no longer the only
important things ; they take their place merely as one single
source of information among many, and the type of information which they convey by no means holds the position which
it once held in the picture of ancient life which we seek to
paint. Modern thought does not necessarily bestow less
consideration upon Pharaoh that sits on his throne ; but it
has learned to give a great deal more to the unconsidered
item at the other end of the scale, the captive that is in the
dungeon, and to all the ranks of the social order between the
one and the other.

Consequently it will value each ancient object, great or
small, intrinsically costly or valueless, in direct proportion,
not to its scale or its material, but to the contribution which
it makes to the picture ; and naturally, as the bulk of life
is made up of common things, whether it be the life of a
prince or a beggar, it will be common things which will contribute the most numerous and the most generally effective
touches to our sketch. " The true function of archæological
research," says Dr. R. A. S. Macalister, " is to discover the
conditions amid which lived such heroes of old as we have
mentioned ; to show them no longer as solitary, more or less

idealised or superhuman figures, but as men of like passions to ourselves, moving with other men in a busy world engrossed in its secular interests, and making use of the common things of life." When you get to this point of view, you can see at once that a big statue of Rameses II, of whom we have so many statues already, or even a long inscription of the same veracious monarch, who has told us quite a lot about himself, not always with the strictest regard to the truth, may actually be of far less value, as an addition to our knowledge of human life in his age, than a broken bit of pottery which adds something to our knowledge of the manner of life of " the maidservant that is behind the mill." And so we get back to the supreme importance of a nation's broken crockery, as material for reconstructing the picture of its past, and find a great excavator rebuking the false ideals of the man who, dominated by the passion for inscriptions, " has neglected the pots and pans, which are essential if he is to fill in the picture of the ancient life of the past."

Obviously, to the casual observer who has debauched his imagination by pictures of the explorer as a modern Aladdin, wandering through mysterious underground chambers, and revealing by the light of his electric torch the golden coffins of long-dead emperors and the glittering heaps of gold and jewels which made their provision for the Underworld, this modern view of the duties, the aims, and the responsibilities of the explorer must seem somewhat dingy and unromantic. To see the dream of gorgeous palaces, millenniums old and yet magnificent in their splendour of superb material and rich adornment, vanish into thin air and be replaced by the sordid reality of a heap of broken crockery, while the dazzling pageant of mighty kings and fair queens dissolves into one of the toiling myriads whose unremembered labours sustained the golden thrones of the ancient East—all this may appear a sufficiently bitter disillusionment. Actually it is not so. I believe that it is only now that the true romance of the excavator's work is beginning to become manifest and to be truly appreciated. For we have come now to understand in some measure the fact that he is not a mere warlock, who calls up from the past dim, gigantic shadow-figures of its heroes and potentates, to thrill our fancy for a little ; but a man to whose patience and instructed industry it is wonderfully given to abolish for awhile the dominion which Time has over us all, and to make the past live again before us, so that we may enter into the life of those long-past centuries and understand the conditions under which men lived, whether in the palace or in the hovel, and be able in a measure to look out on the ancient world with the eyes of the men who were shaping its destinies, and to think the thoughts which ruled their lives. Properly understood, it is by far the most romantic business in the world ; and the only misfortune about it is that Providence so seldom sends us a man who, along with the gifts of the born excavator, has also the gifts of the born interpreter, and can convey to the world something of the thrill and fascination of his own experiences. Men like Layard and Maspero have at least somewhat of the double gift ; while Breasted has one side of it in a high degree ; and the result is that the great books of these men are far more arresting than ninety-nine out of every hundred professed romances.

The object of this volume is to tell, as simply and straightforwardly as may be, the story of some of the work which has been done since the time, not so long ago, when the world began to wake up to the interest and value of the treasures of the past which had lain concealed for ages beneath the sands or the mud of the Classic East—work which is being carried on at the present moment with greater energy than ever before, and with that new spirit and new standpoint which I have tried to indicate in the preceding pages. It is impossible, of course, to cover in a single small volume anything like the whole ground even of excavation in the Near East ; for the number of sites involved, and the wealth of material attained, is so great that the attempt to deal with it would result in the book simply becoming a catalogue, incomplete at the best. We have to limit our survey at present to the great storehouses of what has been called above, and elsewhere, " the Classic East," whose history nevertheless belongs almost entirely to that pre-classical period when Greece and Rome had not yet risen above the horizon, leaving the area occupied by the wonderful civilisation of the " Mediterranean Race " and its successors to form the subject of a further study. The limits of our survey, then, are Egypt, Babylonia, Assyria, and Palestine ; and it may be worth while to glance for a moment at the general characteristics of each of the various lands concerned, as these have largely determined the conditions under which excavation work has been carried on, and also, to a great extent, the character of the results attained.

Egypt, the richest by far of all the treasure houses of the ancient East, has attained this pre-eminence largely because of the character of her soil and climate. She is simply a ribbon of exceedingly fertile alluvial soil deposited by her great river, the Nile, between two deserts. Her climate is one of the driest and also one of the healthiest imaginable, and rain, while not markedly infrequent in Lower Egypt, especially near the Mediterranean, becomes of rarer and rarer occurrence as the upper reaches of the Nile Valley are traversed, until at Thebes, and south of it, rain is an unusual phenomenon. This atmospheric dryness, and the corresponding dryness of the desert soil, in which alone, according to Egyptian custom, burials took place, have acted as natural preservatives for articles of all sorts, and especially for things of fine substance or workmanship. Thus it has come about that there is no other land of the ancient East which can for a moment compete with Egypt in the abundance of its relics of the past. Articles of the most delicate texture or composition—fine linen, papyrus, ivory, which in moister climates and damper soils would long ago have inevitably perished—have been preserved in the dry air and soil of Egypt in such a condition that the finest details of workmanship or carving have survived in a manner almost miraculous.

Further, Egypt's great richness in building stone of all kinds, from the granites of Aswan, and the porphyries and other volcanic stones of the Arabian hills, to the limestone of Turrah and the sandstone of Silsileh, has resulted in the development of methods of construction of a peculiarly solid type, and on a scale which seems destined for eternity rather than for time. It is in this respect that Egypt presents the most marked contrast with the next land which we have to survey, Babylonia. Babylonia is, equally with Egypt, a great riverine state, and in ancient times rivalled Egypt, if it did not surpass it, in fertility. The surface strata of Babylonia, however, were entirely composed of alluvium, deposited in the course of millenniums by the great rivers Euphrates and Tigris ; and hence much of the small and fine material representative of racial culture which would have been preserved in Egypt has been entirely lost in Babylonia, whose conditions much more nearly resemble those prevailing in the Egyptian Delta, from which next to no small or fine material has survived. Babylonia's practically complete lack of building stone, the result of its alluvial character, has resulted in the development of a form of building as characteristic as that of Egypt, but unfortunately by no means so enduring ; and in the course of many centuries the mud-brick buildings of the land, huge though many of them are, have weathered down and lost their distinctive outlines and have been submerged under the invading sands of the desert in a fashion quite unknown in Egypt. The typical styles of Babylonian architecture were as directly the native growth of the natural material of the land as the colossal column and architrave style of Egypt was the outcome of her possession of noble material with which to work.

The third of our areas, Assyria, was also a riverine land, watered by the same rivers which had created Babylonia, but lying much more upland, and with a much higher general elevation and a corresponding difference of climate. The land appears to have been finally colonised, before the dawn of its history as an important state, by Semites of Babylonia, who superseded the inhabitants of Sumerian stock who had previously possessed it. Accordingly the Babylonian tradition survived all through the history of the Assyrian culture, which displayed no originality, though it reached a high level of skill in the working out of the motives which it derived from its original. The most notable instance of the dominance of the Babylonian tradition in Assyrian practice is the fact that though good building stone, and especially fine alabaster suited for the purposes of sculpture, was available, the Babylonian practice of mud-brick construction was invariably followed, though the alabaster was used freely for decorative purposes. The land was one of fierce animals and fiercer men, and the constant use of the horse and the dog in the chase of the great beasts of the field made the Assyrian intimately familiar with all the characteristics of animal structure and motion, and resulted in the development of a school of animal sculpture scarcely equalled elsewhere, and certainly never surpassed until the rise of the great modern masters of animal form in the plastic art.

Historically and geographically subsidiary, but in many respects of prime importance, and from some points of view most important of all, is Palestine, a land which, geographically merely the bridge, and historically merely the war road, between the Asiatic and the African centres of culture, has yet played a part of such supreme importance in the spiritual history of the world that its historical and cultural insignificance is forgotten in view of the greatness of its legacy to the world in other respects.

With the story of excavation in these lands we must now proceed to deal, taking first of all that land where it began first, and where it has always met with its richest rewards—Egypt.

BOOK I

EGYPT

CHAPTER I

THE LAND, ITS EARLY VISITORS, AND THE BEGINNINGS OF EXCAVATION

" EGYPT," says Herodotus, in words often quoted, " is acquired land, and a gift of the river." One could scarcely find a terser or fitter description of this wonderful country than is given in these words of the old historian. The Nile made Egypt in the beginning, and the life of the land is only maintained by the ceaseless gifts which the great river bestows by means of the annual Inundation. This is not the place in which to deal with the processes and results of the Inundation ; what we have to notice, in connection with it, is the extraordinary influence which it exercised upon the development of the race which was called upon to deal with it. It is by no mere chance that the two earliest developments of high civilisation which we know in the world, the Babylonian and the Egyptian, both take place in riverine lands, subject to periodic inundations of the great rivers which watered them. Such inundations must have seemed at first little less than unmitigated disasters to the early races which were subjected to them ; and it is more than likely that we find a survival of the incredibly ancient times, in which the annual overflow of the river was a matter of dread and destruction, in the primitive Egyptian belief in which Osiris, who was not only the god of the Resurrection, but also the god of the overflowing river, was regarded as an object of dread, against whom protection had to be sought.

Manifestly, however, it would not be long before the

fertility caused by the inundation would be noticed, as well as its destructive effects ; and the dwellers in the Nile Valley would learn not only that they must find a way to bridle the inundation or else perish, but also that there were almost unlimited possibilities of advantage in the inundation, once bridled. Self-interest, on both accounts, prompted immediate association and organisation of all the scattered units of population in the land for the common advantage ; and thus, at an extremely early stage, we have the attainment of a highly organised and cultured community. The two habits, of admirable organisation and of dealing with difficult engineering problems on a big scale, which the early Egyptians thus acquired, were never lost, but continued to be the heritage of the dynastic Egyptian people throughout their long history, as is evidenced by the wonderful works which they accomplished. In Babylonia, similar conditions were producing similar results, with the natural modifications due to variations of environment and climate.

The people or peoples who developed the earlier stages of the Egyptian culture (Sir Flinders Petrie traces five different races of pre-dynastic people preceding the arrival of the dynastic Egyptians) were not the people with whom we are familiar in the historic period of Egypt, though they doubtless contributed elements of greater or less importance to the common stock of culture and racial characteristics, as all superseded races have succeeded in doing, modifying often to a very considerable extent the race which has superseded them. This conquering race, in the case of Egypt, seems to have entered the land from Upper Egypt, and Semitic origins or connections have been suggested for it ; but certainty on this point has not yet been reached. In any case, our main concern is with the dynastic race, though modern research has done much with regard to pre-dynastic Egypt which will have to be noticed in its due place. The early dynasties, whose relics we shall also have to deal with, were succeeded, during a period of, roughly speaking, three

thousand years (3500 B.C. to the Persian Conquest in
525 B.C.) by four great flowerings of the human genius,
separated by gulfs of darkness and misfortune. These outstanding epochs may be distinguished as the Period of the
Old Kingdom, or of the Pyramid-Builders, the Period of
the Middle Kingdom, the Period of the Empire, and the
Period of the Saite Renaissance. Each of these periods has
left relics more or less abundant, and excavation has worked
on all the periods with most astonishing success, not least
so in the case where success was, on ordinary grounds of
reason, least to be expected—that of the earliest state.

The ordinary idea, that it is only within comparatively
recent times that Egypt and its ancient civilisation has become an object of general interest, is quite wide of the mark.
Egypt has been what might almost be called a great tourist
centre for considerably more than two thousand years, and
some of the greatest names of the ancient world are written
in its visiting book. Five hundred and seventy years at least
before Christ, Solon, the great Athenian lawgiver, came to
the land of the Nile in the palmiest days of the Saite Renaissance, when the wise Pharaoh Amasis was gradually
accustoming his ancient land to the breaking down of its
old conventions and prejudices ; and at Sais the great Greek
learned from a priest of Neith that legend of the Lost
Atlantis which has intrigued the imagination of the world
ever since. Solon was followed by one to whom we owe a
deep debt of gratitude for the manner in which he exercised
a temperament of restless inquisitiveness and a wonderful
gift of picturesque narration ; for the vivid pages of Herodotus are never more vivid than when he is dealing with
that ancient Egypt which so awakened his candid wonder.
Even the blunders of the old historian are such as to show
that he was no mean judge of what he saw—witness his
apparently amazing misplacement of the pyramid-building
Pharaohs, a mistake which, however hopeless historically, is
actually a witness to his appreciation of the resemblances

between Old Kingdom art and that of the Saite period, which was based on conscious imitation of the older work. Behind these two great figures comes a host of others, famous and otherwise, from Greece and Rome ; and they exhibit their interest in what they saw in ways very much akin to those of their modern followers.

The colossal statues of Amenhotep III, on the west bank of the Nile opposite Thebes, were supposed in classical times to be statues of Memnon, the warrior son of Eos, or Aurora, and Tithonus ; and the northern statue, which had been wrecked in its upper part by an earthquake, was one of the stock objects which no self-respecting globe-trotter of the early Roman Empire could afford to omit from his itinerary. The curious musical sound which the broken stone used to emit on being first warmed by the rays of the rising sun was the wonder which drew them ; and they have left numerous comments on Memnon's performance, scribbled, in prose and verse, upon the legs of the great figure. This vulgarity was not confined in those days to the equivalents of Brown, Jones, and Robinson, for the inscriptions include those of eight governors of Egypt and three district-governors of the Thebaid ; while one of the worst offenders is the court poetess Balbilla, who visited the place in the suite of the Emperor Hadrian, and who might have known better. Septimius Severus patched Memnon up in the clumsy fashion which is still to be seen, apparently with the idea of honouring the hero ; but the result was disastrous. Memnon was struck dumb, and has remained dumb ever since.

Modern excavation has given us a gem which we should be sorry to have missed, in the shape of a letter on papyrus from a high official at Alexandria to an official in the Fayum, warning him of the approach of a globe-trotting Roman Senator, in preparation for whose advent he is instructed to have everything about the show-places in apple-pie order, and especially to have tit-bits provided which the big man might throw to the sacred crocodiles ! So that the modern

custom of giving " nuts unto the monkey, and buns unto
the bear," dates as far back as the early days of the Roman
Empire and a good deal farther, since the custom of feeding
the crocodiles obviously did not grow up in a day, and is,
indeed, described by Herodotus. Another discovery of
recent date is the letter of a gentleman who has gone up
the Nile to Aswan to see the sights, and who informs his
correspondent that he has " engraved the names of his
friends on the sanctuaries for perpetual remembrance," with
a prayer. So that, just as the lady who spring-cleans is
actually repeating the ancient spring rite of driving out the
spirits from the house, so the tourist who scribbles his undistinguished name, or those of his friends, upon monuments and rocks is really offering a prayer for himself and
those whom he commemorates. He certainly needs it,
though he is not conscious of offering it. All the same, we
owe a good deal to some of these ancient tourists, for our
only information as to some of the great wonders of Egypt,
which we would fain have seen, but which have absolutely
vanished, comes from the writings of some of them. The
most notable instance, of course, is the Labyrinth, of which,
were it not for the descriptions of Herodotus and Strabo,
we should know next to nothing, though it was the vastest
building ever reared, even by the Egyptians.

During the early part of the eighteenth century of our
own era it began to become quite the fashion to " do "
Egypt as an addition to " the Grand Tour," not, it may be
feared, with any great advantage either to Egypt or the
tourists, if their researches were carried out in the spirit
which Addison has satirised in the first number of the
Spectator. " Nay, to such a degree was my curiosity raised,
that having read the controversies of some great men concerning the antiquities of Egypt, I made a voyage to Grand
Cairo on purpose to take the measure of a pyramid ; and
as soon as I had set myself right in that particular, returned
to my native country with great satisfaction." Other tourists,

fortunately, did more, and some of the records of Pococke
(1743) and Bruce (1769) are still of value. Perhaps the most
unlucky of all these early modern visitors to Egypt was Lord
Charlemont. His journey to Egypt has immortalised him
indeed, but scarcely with the kind of immortality which he
would have desired ; for it merely served as a text on which
Dr. Johnson might hang his sermon on the trifling value of
travel. " How little," observed the sage, " does travelling
supply to the conversation of any man who has travelled . . ."
Boswell : " What say you to Lord Charlemont ? " Johnson : " I never but once heard him talk of what he had
seen, and that was of a large serpent in one of the pyramids
of Egypt." Boswell : " Well, I happened to hear him tell
the same thing, which made me mention him." But better
things were preparing for Egypt, though in strange fashion.

The father of all modern interest in Egypt, and so of all
excavation there, is Napoleon. The great expedition of 1798
may have been a disastrous failure as regards the objects
which Napoleon really had at heart ; but at least he deserves
the credit of having made his own ambitions serve other and
more lasting interests. Few conquerors, save himself, would
ever have conceived the idea of cumbering an army with the
troop of learned men whom he carried with him to Egypt ;
and perhaps few learned men, save the French scholars of
the Revolutionary period, would have carried their enthusiasm for learning to the point of being ready to face the
dangers and hardships which Vivant Denon so vivaciously
describes in his *Voyages dans la Basse et la Haute Egypte,*
pendant les Campagnes de Bonaparte. It was Denon's vast
Description de L'Egypte, twelve mortal volumes of plates,
with twenty-four of text ! which first opened the eyes of the
European scholars to the incredible wealth of Egypt in
treasures of the past, though, of course, the glories of ancient
Egypt had never suffered an eclipse so complete as that which
had descended on those of Babylonia and Mesopotamia. The
work of Denon and his brother savants no doubt lies open

to the criticism which has been passed upon it by one of his own countrymen : " Il n'est pas nécessaire de faire un livre colossal parce qu'on y décrit des colosses." But its very bulk drew the eyes of the whole world to the land which it described. A country which needed twenty-four volumes to describe its marvels must be worth some attention !

Accordingly, it is from Napoleon's invasion that modern interest in the Land of the Nile must be dated ; and had it been for nothing else than the discovery which an officer of the expedition made at Rashid of the now world-famous slab of basalt which we know as the Rosetta Stone, the venture would have been amply justified. No doubt the perseverance of scholarship would in course of time have found out the secret of the hieroglyphics in any case ; but it was the Rosetta Stone, in company with the Philæ Obelisk over which Belzoni had so many adventures and misadventures, which furnished Champollion with the key to the mystery, so that as early as 1822 Egyptology was in possession of the *Open Sesame* to all the treasures of Egyptian literature. Since then, the work of building up a complete knowledge of the structure of the Egyptian language has been a long and laborious one ; but its success has been such that Egyptian grammar is now as thoroughly understood as the grammar of any other Oriental language, and the refinements of Egyptian style which distinguish the various periods of the history of the language are becoming more and more exactly appreciated.

Napoleon's Expedition was followed by a period of considerable activity in the exploration of the Egyptian treasure house ; but, unfortunately, the zeal of the explorers of the opening years of the nineteenth century was not, in the main, according to knowledge, but was, in many cases, simply a matter of personal gain or notoriety, and was often spurred on, not so much by interest in Egyptology and the desire to increase human knowledge of the past, as by the malicious desire to get ahead of someone else who was working in the interests of some other nation. International rivalries, one would imagine, ought to be hushed in the presence of relics whose battered antiquity proclaims only too surely that—

> " The glories of our blood and state
> Are shadows, not substantial things."

But, on the contrary, the story of early excavation, not in Egypt only, is too often simply the story of how the representative of Britain wrangled and squabbled with the representative of France or Italy for the possession of some statue or relief whose presence in the national museum might give his country some occasion to crow over its less fortunate rivals, who, of course, acted in precisely the same manner when their chance came. " Those were the great days of excavating," writes Mr. Howard Carter, in *The Tomb of Tut-ankh-Amen*. " Anything to which a fancy was taken, from a scarab to an obelisk, was just appropriated, and if there was a difference with a brother excavator, one laid for him with a gun."

There were, indeed, a few more enlightened spirits among the gang of tomb-robbers (one can scarcely call them anything better), to whom there had been granted some Pisgah-view of the real aims and methods which should inspire and guide the work of excavation ; and a man like Passalacqua is honourably distinguished by a remarkably close approximation to the ideals of the modern worker, however far he may have come short in the carrying out of them ; but, in the main, Mr. Carter's terse description is not an exaggeration in the least, but a literal statement of truth. Here is the fashion in which Belzoni, who was acting partly for Mr. Salt, the British Consul-General, and a good deal for himself, was treated by the agents of Signor Drovetti, who represented the French Consul. Mr. Belzoni is approaching Luxor, having returned from securing the Philæ Obelisk, which Signor Drovetti had marked for his own. " I was at about three hundred yards from the great propylæon, when I saw a group of people running towards us ; they were

about thirty Arabs, headed by two Europeans, agents of
Mr. Drouetti. On their approaching, Mr. Lebulo was first,
and the renegade Rossignano second, both Piedmontese and
countrymen of Mr. Drouetti. Lebulo began his address to
me by asking what business I had to take away an obelisk
that did not belong to me ; and that I had done so many
things of this kind to him, that I should not do any more.
Meanwhile he seized the bridle of my donkey with one hand,
and with the other laid hold of my waistcoat and stopped
me from proceeding any farther : he had also a large stick
hung to his wrist by a string. . . . At the same moment, the
renegade Rossignano reached within four yards of me, and
with all the rage of a ruffian levelled a double-barrelled gun
at my breast, loading me with all the imprecations that a
villain could invent ; by this time my servant was disarmed,
and overpowered by numbers, and, in spite of his efforts,
took his pistols from his belt (Mr. Belzoni's grammar is
agitated, which is perhaps not surprising ; but his meaning
is quite plain). The two gallant knights before me, I mean
Lebulo and Rossignano, escorted by the two other Arabian
servants of Mr. Drouetti, both armed with pistols, and many
others armed with sticks, continued their clamorous imprecations against me, and the brave Rossignano, still keeping
the gun pointed at my breast, said that it was time that I
should pay for all I had done to them. The courageous
Lebulo said, with all the emphasis of an enraged man, that
he was to have one-third of the profit derived from the
selling of that obelisk, when in Europe, according to a
promise from Mr. Drouetti, had I not stolen it from the
island of Philæ. My situation was not pleasant, surrounded
by a band of ruffians like those, and I have no doubt that
if I had attempted to dismount, the cowards would have
dispatched me on the ground, and said that they did it in
defence of their lives, as I had been the aggressor."

One takes the liberty of doubting whether Mr. Belzoni,
who had been a professional strong man in his not far past

youth, was altogether so lamb-like in his bearing under such provocation as his narrative makes out ; but the picture is convincing as a representation of the picturesque conditions under which excavation was carried on in the early years of the nineteenth century by the agents of highly respectable official gentlemen. Was it not said, a little back, that the ways of early excavators were almost as dangerous as the little ways of the treasure-hunting pirate, and a good deal more amusing ? Even to-day the disagreements of Egypt-ologists are reputed to have an edge and a bitterness quite unknown in other studies, whose representatives are notori-ously courteous in their most pronounced differences. But the strongest language used by one Egyptologist towards another (and it is sometimes pretty strong) is always to be interpreted in a strictly Pickwickian sense ; while pistols and double-barrelled shot-guns have quite gone out of date as controversial methods.

The point is, however, that the gentlemen whom we see here raving and cursing at one another before the pylon of Luxor are specimens, not of the worst, but of the best work that was being done in Egypt in 1818, when this little un-pleasantness took place. Italy owes one of the noblest of Egyptian statues, the black granite Rameses II at Turin, to this same Signor Drovetti whose scallywags we have just seen assaulting their fellow-explorer ; and London owes the colossal head of Thothmes III and that of Rameses II, both in the British Museum, and the wonderful alabaster sarco-phagus of Seti I, in the Sir John Soane Museum, to say nothing of other treasures, to the long-suffering Mr. Belzoni, whose character one would like to have heard from the point of view of Messrs. Lebulo and Rossignano. If they did these things in a green tree, what would be done in the dry ?

It may be worth while to pursue the activities of Mr. Belzoni a little further, for he is thoroughly representative of what is far from the worst, and not far from the best, work of those bad old days. Moreover, he has told us the story of his deeds and misdeeds in a style and with a vivacity for which Egyptology has not been half grateful enough ; so that the comely quarto which he published in 1820 can now be obtained for a price of which the purchaser ought to be ashamed. Mr. Howard Carter has described this volume as " one of the most fascinating books in the whole of Egyptian literature," and he does it no more than justice. It is a narrative of achievements and crimes, like the auto-biography of its author's fellow-countryman, Benvenuto Cellini, a book which Belzoni perpetually brings to one's mind ; and it is hard to determine whether Egyptology has greater reason to bless its author for the remarkable work which he actually accomplished in very difficult conditions, or to curse him for the wholesale destruction which must have accompanied his triumphs.

Mr. Carter has said that " we must give Belzoni full credit for the manner in which his excavations (in the Valley of the Kings at Thebes) were carried out." This is high and generous praise from one whose work on the same ground is as typical of the modern method as Belzoni's was of the ancient lack of method ; and perhaps, in a sense, it is deserved. For Belzoni possessed in ample measure what is precisely one of the most precious and incommunicable gifts of the explorer. He had the instinct, so to speak, for a likely site, and sniffed antiquities in what seemed to his rivals an impossible place, as a pig scents truffles. Moreover, though he reveals himself as one of the vainest and most petulant of men, ready to quarrel with his own shadow if he could find nothing else to quarrel with, he had also what seldom goes along with such a temperament, a patience almost un-fathomable. The man who spent months in the stifling air of the depths of the great tomb of Seti I, modelling all the figures of its reliefs in wax, had little to learn, in the way of patience, at all events, from the most careful of modern excavators. The work was done partly during the heat of an Egyptian May and June, when most moderns would think such work impossible, and its laboriousness must be judged from Belzoni's own words : " The greatest difficulty was to take the impression of the figure without injuring the colours of it. The figures as large as life I found to be in all a hundred and eighty-two : those of a smaller size, from one to three feet, I did not count, but they cannot be less than eight hundred. The hieroglyphics in this tomb are nearly five hundred, of which I took a faithful copy, with their colours ; but they are of four different sizes, from one to six inches ; so that I have been obliged to take one of each size, which makes nearly two thousand in all."

But having said so much, one has said almost all that can be said in praise of his methods. " On the whole," says Mr. Carter, " the work was extraordinarily good ; " but one imagines that anyone who attempted to follow Belzoni's methods under Mr. Carter to-day would receive extraordinarily short shrift. Here is the misguided man's description of how he opened a tomb in the Valley of the Kings : " The following day I caused a large pole to be brought, and by means of another small piece of palm-tree laid across the entrance, I made a machine not unlike a battering-ram. The walls resisted the blows of the Arabs for some time, as they were not Romans, nor had the pole the ram's head of bronze at its end ; but they contrived to make a breach at last, and in the same way the opening was enlarged. We immediately entered, and found ourselves on a staircase, eight feet wide and ten feet high, at the bottom of which were four mummies, in their cases, lying flat on the ground, with their heads towards the outside. Farther on were four more, lying in the same direction. The cases were all painted, and one had a large covering thrown over it, exactly like the pall upon the coffins of the present day."

The mummies whose rest was thus disturbed in a fashion calculated to turn a modern excavator's hair white were apparently those of royalties, which had been rewrapped and reinterred, as so many royal mummies were at the time of

the scare of tomb robbery in the Ramesside period, for
Belzoni mentions that one mummy had new wrappings put
on over the " old rags," as he irreverently calls the earlier
wrappings.   What became of them, and of the pall which
he mentions—the earliest mention of the funeral pall of
Egyptian royalty of which Tutankhamen's tomb has provided the finest specimen—Belzoni does not condescend to
tell us ; but we may form our own opinion, from his own
account of the way in which he treated two other mummies
which he discovered in another tomb on the same day :
" They were females, and their hair pretty long, and well
preserved, *though it was easily separated from the head by
pulling it a little !* "   His account of the various tombs which
he visited in the Valley of the Kings, imperfect as it is, and
cumbered with all kinds of guesses, some of them pretty
wild, helps one to realise a little of the wealth of material
which, even so late as between 1815 and 1820, was lying
almost untouched at Thebes and elsewhere in Egypt.   How
much of it perished through such handling as Belzoni gave
his mummies, how much was uselessly dispersed among the
private collections of tourists, to be thrown on the rubbish
heap when the taste for it had worn off, who can tell ?

The case of Belzoni may be taken as typical of almost the
best work which was being done in Egypt at this time ; and
one may judge from it what the worst was like !   His serious
contributions to Egyptology, along with the colossal statues
already mentioned and those of two of the queens of
Rameses II, which are also in the British Museum, were the
opening and investigation of the chambers of the Second
Pyramid, the transport of the small obelisk of Philæ, whose
bilingual inscription was part of the material which afforded
to Champollion the key to the mystery of the hieroglyphics,
the discovery and partial clearing of the tombs of the
Pharaoh Ay, the Prince Mentu-her-khepshef, Rameses I, and
Seti I.   His supreme triumph, which he describes with a
pride for which he had perfect warrant, was the discovery

of the last-mentioned tomb, which still remains by far the finest and most beautifully decorated, though not the largest, of the royal tombs in the Valley of the Kings. We have already seen with what faithfulness he discharged his task of making a facsimile of the reliefs in the tomb—a task which occupied him altogether for more than a year. His account of the reception which his discovery got from the Turkish local governor, Hamed Aga of Keneh, is typical of the attitude of Turkish officialdom to such work, not only in 1818, but up to a much more recent date. "After a long and minute survey, the Aga at last ordered the soldiers to retire, and said to me, ' Pray, where have you put the treasure ? ' ' What treasure ? ' ' The treasure you found in this place.' I could not help smiling at his question, which confirmed him in his supposition. I told him that we had found no treasure there. At this he laughed, and still continued to entreat that I would show it him. ' I have been told,' he added, ' by a person to whom I can give credit, that you have found in this place a large golden cock, filled with diamonds and pearls. I must see it. Where is it ? ' I could scarcely keep myself from laughing, while I assured him that nothing of the kind had been found there. Seeming quite disappointed, he seated himself before the sarcophagus, and I was afraid he would take it into his head that this was the treasure, and break it to pieces to see whether it contained any gold ; for their notions of treasure are confined to gold and jewels. At last he gave up the idea of the riches to be expected, and rose to go out of the tomb. I asked him what he thought of the beautiful figures painted all around. He just gave a glance at them, quite uncon- cerned, and said, ' This would be a good place for a harem, as the women would have something to look at.' At length, though only half persuaded there was no treasure, he set off with an appearance of much vexation."

A quarter of a century later Layard found much the same standard of intelligence in the officials with whom he had

to deal in Mesopotamia ; while even in 1922 the generally
accepted idea among the natives of Luxor, on the discovery
of Tutankhamen's tomb, was that " three aeroplanes had
landed in the Valley, and gone off to some destination
unknown with loads of treasure."

During this early period of excavation, almost infinite
damage must have been done by the excavators, native and
European, who simply ransacked tombs for the purpose of
obtaining the papyri, copies of the Book of the Dead or of
some of its variants and abridgments, which were com-
monly buried along with the dead of the Empire. Belzoni
himself candidly admits that the object of his " researches,"
as he gravely calls his looting of mummy pits, " was to rob
the Egyptians of their papyri," and apparently he cared
nothing for the destruction of the mummy itself or its case,
so long as he succeeded in carrying off a papyrus or two.
He speaks with the utmost calm of sitting down upon a
mummy : " But when my weight bore on the body of an
Egyptian, it crushed it like a band-box. I naturally had
recourse to my hands to sustain my weight, but they found
no better support ; so that I sunk altogether among the
broken mummies, with a crash of bones, rags, and wooden
cases, which raised such a dust as kept me motionless for a
quarter of an hour, waiting till it subsided again ! " Such
was excavation as conducted in the first quarter of the nineteenth century, by one of its most enlightened practitioners.
One may imagine what happened when the least enlightened,
the native digger who knew nothing about the matter except
that papyri had a marketable value, got loose in a tomb !
The contrast between this shocking and reckless waste of
priceless material, and the precision and scrupulous care
which characterise modern methods, is sufficiently striking ;
and we should probably not be exaggerating in the least were
we to say that for every article of interest that was secured
by these early methods, a score of equal interest were utterly
destroyed ; while even the things which were preserved lost

half their value to the archæologist by the fact that in most cases next to no care was taken to note the surroundings of the find and the relative positions of its component parts.

This wasteful period, to which, however, we owe many of the most striking treasures of the great European museums, was more or less closed by the appointment of the brilliant Frenchman, Auguste Mariette, as the first Director of the Service of Antiquities in Egypt, an event which took place on June 1, 1858. One has to say " more or less " for the simple reason that Mariette's own methods of excavation were by no means above reproach. Gruesome stories are still in circulation as to the drastic methods which the impatient Frenchman did not hesitate to adopt when things were not progressing as fast as he wished, and as to the means which he took to prevent even the remains of any of his finds falling into the hands of other people ; and the mere mention of his name is in some circles sufficient to call forth a volley of execration on the man and his ways. How could it be otherwise, in view of the fact that he allowed no one but himself to excavate in Egypt, and that he attempted to carry on excavation at no fewer than thirty-seven sites during his tenure of office ? Obviously it was impossible to exercise proper supervision over even a fraction of his wide-spreading excavations ; and consequently, while he accumulated an enormous mass of fine material from his diggings, the most of it was never properly catalogued and dealt with at all. No complete and satisfactory account of his work was ever given to the world ; nor can such an account ever now be given. Consequently, the undoubtedly great work which he did has been deprived of more than half its value.

At the same time, Mariette did at least establish two positions which are the very foundation of the business— first, that excavation in a land like Egypt (or indeed any-where) is far too important a thing to be left to the indiscriminate zeal or cupidity of anyone who chooses to embark

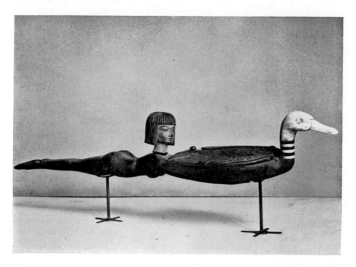

THE EGYPTIAN ARTIST AT PLAY—AN OINTMENT SPOON FROM
THE LOUVRE

The dainty taste of the Egyptians of the Empire is well shown by this and the many
similar specimens of toilet objects which are extant. The swimming girl and the
goose form a favourite combination for such ointment spoons.

(By permission of the Curator, The Louvre.)

THE EGYPTIAN ARTIST AT PLAY—A FAIENCE HIPPOPOTAMUS
AMONG AQUATIC PLANTS

The thing is a mere trifle, thrown off in sport ; but the characteristics of Behemoth
are admirably suggested, and the whole conception reveals the spirit of gaiety and
humour so often stupidly denied to the Egyptian race.

upon it, but must be regulated by definite rules laid down by the Government of the land in question ; and, second, that the proper place for the bestowal of the results of excavation is not in the private collections of individuals, but in the care of the nation whose land has yielded them, if that is possible. His first rule was pushed to extremity under his management of the Service of Antiquities by his mania for allowing nobody to excavate but himself ; and, of course, it was evaded by the native poachers of antiquities, who had no intention of allowing their profitable trade in their dead ancestors to be hindered by any mad foreigner ; but the rule was in itself a sound and good one, and though it has often been vexatiously interpreted, as it is at the present moment, to the great hindrance of work which clamours to be done, it is obviously better that there should be an authority responsible for the regulation of all such work than that each man who wishes to excavate should do what is right in his own eyes, as in the happy days when Belzoni, Drovetti, and Company squabbled and fought like ghouls over the plunder.

The second rule is even more obviously right, though here again its application is subject to qualifications. It is manifestly better that interesting objects of antiquity should be retained as nearly as possible in their original setting, or, if that is impossible, at least in some central position in the land which produced them, and under conditions of surroundings and climate which are natural to them. An object loses half its interest and importance when it is divorced, so to speak, from its context and preserved in isolation, in an alien land, and under conditions totally different from those which originally surrounded it. This principle Mariette sought to establish by the creation of the great museum at Cairo, for which he laboured and fought during all his tenure of office ; and it is now generally recognised as right and fitting. We acknowledge that it is a scandal that in Egypt, the land of obelisks, there should

D

now be left only five standing ; while Rome possesses
nine over 29 feet high, besides smaller specimens of these
wonders of Egyptian craftsmanship. We recognise that
when the tomb of a Pharaoh like Tutankhamen is discovered, the ideal completion of the matter would be that
the dead king should be left, after science has learned all
that can be learned from his funerary equipment, lying in
state as his mourning subjects left him three thousand
years ago, though access might be provided for the continuance of reverent and respectful study. Pharaoh in his
own tomb in the lonely Valley is a bit of the mighty past
made visible ; even in the museum at Cairo he is only a
museum specimen.

Yet, desirable as it may seem to have such a rule observed
in its entirety, the thing is not altogether possible. Even in
our own land it has not proved a simple matter to secure
that valuable objects of antiquity, if left in their own setting,
shall be respected and safeguarded ; much less is it easy to
secure such an end in a land like Egypt, where for three
thousand years at least there has been a well-established
tradition of tomb-robbery as one of the normal trades of the
land, and where interference with the laudable custom of
pillaging the graves of one's far-away ancestors is regarded
as an intolerable restriction of the liberty of the subject.
The most humorous touch in connection with the discovery
of the tomb of Tutankhamen was the protest on the part
of native Egyptians against the sacrilege committed by
Westerners in intruding on the tomb of an Egyptian king.
To anyone familiar with the Egyptian literature on the
subject of three thousand years ago, and with the present-
day practice of the descendants of the tomb-robbers of the
Ramesside period, the protest was delightful ; but had the
tomb been discovered by a native Egyptian it would have
been another story ! The tragedy of the tomb of Amenhotep II is sufficient warning against trying to force the
observance of a counsel of perfection upon a land which is

not ready for it as yet. You have first to educate the land
to the point of being able to safeguard its treasures before
you can leave them in its care ; and neither in Egypt nor
in Mesopotamia, nor in any other land of the Near East, has
that point of education been attained. Yet Mariette's rule
is the goal at which the efforts of archæology must be
directed, and the excavator has not only to think of the
discovering of the antiquities of a nation, but also of endeavouring to secure that the nation shall at last become
capable of taking care of its antiquities when discovered.

To Belzoni, Drovetti and Company, with their palm-log
battering-rams and their disrespectful pulling of the hair of
mummies, succeeds Mariette, with his thoroughly good rules
and his wasteful and haphazard methods of working ; and
to Mariette, in the fulness of the time, succeeds the modern
excavator, with his elaborate apparatus of preservatives, his
acres of cotton-wool, his fine sieve, and, above all, his carefully acquired knowledge of the *differentia* of all the various
periods of Egyptian art and the arts of all the surrounding
nations which were in contact with Egypt. The most typical
representative of the modern period would be the man who
has indeed every right to the title which has been given to
him by a well-known excavator, " the father of scientific
excavation in Egypt." To Sir Flinders Petrie, Egyptology,
and indeed archæology in general, owes more than to any
other living man, or half-dozen of men, for it was he who
first established and exemplified in his own practice the
laws by which modern excavation is guided ; he, in especial,
who first showed the supreme importance of tracing the
sequence of a nation's pottery as a clue to its historical
development.

The contrast between the past and the present cannot be
better exhibited than by comparing Belzoni's well-meant
and industrious methods, described in the earlier part of
this chapter, with those of a modern practitioner, trained in
Petrie's school and working under his supervision. Here is

part of Mr. Guy Brunton's description of how he dealt with the Treasure of Lahun· (the earlier find, February, 1914), which yielded some of the most remarkable specimens of Egyptian craftsmanship which have ever come to light. " The recess was so low (only 40 inches to the roof) that I could not even kneel in it, and had as a rule to work lying flat and resting on my elbows. Of course, the continued succession of finds, day after day, was amazing and utterly unexpected. *The whole of the clearing, except in certain areas where the mud contained no remains whatever, was done with a small penknife ; or with a pin when there was a chance of finding small beads in position.* The work of picking out the minute beads (there were over 9500 of them) was so laborious, that eventually any detached scraps of mud were examined in camp." One can imagine the strain of such work, continued for day after day, and only varied by the labour of trying to reconstitute the dismembered articles thus patiently extracted from their mantle of ages. The result, however, was well worth the pains, as the collections of the Cairo Museum and the Metropolitan Museum of New York abundantly show.

Mr. Howard Carter tells us that among his first purchases at Cairo, after the discovery of the tomb of Tutankhamen, were " thirty-two bales of calico, more than a mile of wadding, and as much again of surgical bandages " ! Such is the care with which the treasures of the past are handled by the modern archæologist. We have travelled a long way in a century, from Belzoni, with his battering-ram, to Brunton and Carter, with the penknife and the pin, and the miles of wadding and bandages. One cannot help speculating rather ruefully on the amount of priceless material which might have been preserved to the world had the earlier excavators been inspired by the same spirit and guided by the same principles which govern the activities of their successors of to-day. Yet it would not be fair to blame the **pioneers** unduly. They did their best, according to the lights of their time ; and, however much they may have wasted in the doing of it, they at least created, by their energetic and patient work, that interest in things Egyptian which has never since died away. For this their names deserve to be held in honour ; and even their misdeeds to be covered with a merciful oblivion.

CHAPTER II

HALF a century ago, or even considerably less than that, our knowledge of Egyptian civilisation and history practically began with the Pyramid-building Pharaohs of the IVth Dynasty, say about 3000 B.C. (Petrie's date for the beginning of the Dynasty is round about 4750 B.C.). This may seem early enough for all practical purposes, giving us a continuous stream of history for five thousand years ; but it is certain that the story of Egyptian culture was in the full current of its course at a period as far before the IVth Dynasty as the latter is before the Christian era. Of all this early activity, however, we knew next to nothing until its traces were revealed by the extraordinarily fruitful and interesting work with which Egyptology rounded off the century of active life which commenced, as we have seen, with Napoleon's Expedition. Before the discoveries at Hierakonpolis, Abydos, Bet-Khallaf, Naqada, and elsewhere, early Egyptian history was veiled in clouds among which moved dim, gigantic figures of the past, to whom Manetho, the ancient historian of Sebennytus (third century B.C.), had given names coupled with some scraps of romantic legend, but who were still nothing but shadows. Manetho himself was very generally regarded as quite unreliable, though his thirty dynasties were recognised as a convenient framework within which the known facts of Egyptian history might be assembled. Apart from Manetho and what were considered his fairy-tales, the only sources of information were the bare and late lists of kings at Abydos and Sakkara, the torn scraps of the Turin Papyrus, and the scattered fragments of the

54

Palermo Stone. The fate of the Turin Papyrus, which, had it been preserved intact, would have been of absolutely priceless value for the reconstitution of the historical outline of early times, is typical of that of much precious material in the beginnings of Egyptological study. " It was discovered in Egypt somewhere about the time of Bonaparte, and came into the possession of the King of Sardinia. It was then sent to Turin, in a box without packing ; and, when it arrived, this most precious and unique document was found to have fallen into scores of dry and brittle little pieces which lay in a heap at the bottom of the box. It was put together, more or less by guesswork, in 1826 . . ." since when scholars have spent no end of time and labour in the effort to undo the mischief done by the carelessness of its early transmitters and the misguided zeal of its restorer, and to make the Turin Papyrus once more a reliable source for the earliest history of Egypt. Almost as heartrending is the condition of the other great authority, known as " The Palermo Stone," from the fact that its largest fragment is in the Museum at Palermo. It was originally a great stone tablet, about 9 feet long, inscribed with the Annals of the first five dynasties ; but no one knows where it came from, and though there are five other fragments of the tablet, or of a duplicate of it, in existence, besides the Palermo fragment, four at Cairo and one at University College, London, these only represent a small portion of the original inscription.

So far as written sources go, therefore, we are in a pretty hopeless position when faced with the problem of the reconstruction of the life and history of these far-off times. Fortunately, however, while we are still very much at a loss, in spite of the labours of Borchardt, Weigall, and others, as to the actual order of succession of the somewhat shadowy Pharaohs who figure in the scraps of the Turin Papyrus and the fragments of the Palermo Stone, and seem likely to remain so until our difficulties are resolved by the discovery of a more complete source of information, the case is by no means so hopeless as regards the reconstruction of the life of ancient Egypt in these incredibly early days. During the closing years of the nineteenth and the opening years of the twentieth century there has been a very remarkable resurrection of the detail of what in strictness we must still call " prehistoric " Egyptian life, so that, while we are still unable to provide our information with its framework of dates and reigns with the strictness of detail which is desirable, we are able to form a picture of Egyptian life in these far-off days upon whose correctness, at least in its broad general outlines, we can rely with considerable confidence. The work which has given us our information with regard to the general life of the people of pre-dynastic Egypt has been carried on at many different centres and by many different excavators. Quibell at Hierakonpolis, and Petrie and Quibell at Naqada and Ballas, Reisner at Naga-ed-Der, Randall-MacIver and Mace at El-Amrah, Ayrton and Loat at El-Mahasna, Peet and others at Abydos, have all, with others, made considerable contributions to our knowledge of the dawn of Egyptian culture.

To enter in detail into the story of their work would more than occupy all our volume ; and we must be content with a general summary of what has been learned as to the level of civilisation reached in Egypt in pre-dynastic days. With many differences of detail, the results of the excavation of the pre-dynastic cemeteries show a general uniformity of custom and a general level of culture of a quite definite type prevailing throughout the land. The pre-dynastic tomb (we are excluding in the meantime the question of royal tombs) is a flat-bottomed pit, either oval or oblong ; and the body is laid in it usually on its left side, in the contracted or " embryonic " posture, with the hands placed in front of the face, and the knees drawn up towards the chin. In the earliest burials the body is wrapped in a skin, which is replaced, in later instances, by a woven fabric, and beneath it is placed a mat of plaited material. In the hand, or close to it, is a slate palette for grinding green malachite for face-paint, and a supply of the malachite lies near in a little bag. Weapons of flint and bone accompany the dead warrior, to enable him to defend himself against his enemies, or to secure for himself further supplies of food when the provision which had been made for him by the piety of his friends was exhausted. This provision was stored in jars of pottery or stone, finely wrought in many instances, and sometimes, in the case of pottery, painted with pleasing, if elementary, decoration. In addition, the dead man was often supplied with clay models of objects which might prove useful to him in his journey through the underworld, and especially with boats to enable him to cross the various rivers, canals, and lakes which he might meet with on his path. In a number of instances the body is protected by a big pottery jar, which is inverted over it in the pit.

Thus modern excavation has revealed to us the evidence of the stage of culture to which the Egyptian had attained at a period which may be roughly put down as about 5000 B.C. or earlier. A certain quite clearly defined level of civilisation is indicated, with an attainment in the simpler arts of civilised life which is by no means to be despised. The pottery is often of good quality and design, and the working of the stone vessels is admirable ; while the flint tools and weapons reach a standard attained by no other race. The beginnings of a national art are indicated by the designs carved on some of the slate palettes, and on the ivories which have been found in many graves, and also by the primitive, but often highly pictorial, paintings which occur on some of the pottery. Perhaps the most interesting suggestion from these pre-dynastic tombs is given by the mere fact of all this provision being found ; for it indicates that already this people had formulated a certain theory about the after life, and believed that the death of the body was not the end of the man's life, but that he had a further destiny awaiting him in which he would have needs and faculties, as in the existence which had terminated. We learn also certain other very interesting facts from the pre-dynastic tombs about the ancient Egyptian race. It may have been a very mixed breed, as has been alleged by various Egyptologists ; but " the anatomical evidence shows that the oldest peasant inhabitant of the Nile Valley was, in build and stature, very much like the fellah of to-day." Two other points which have emerged from these excavations, and are perhaps more curious than important, may be noted. The first is that the inhabitants of prehistoric Egypt suffered terribly from rheumatism and rheumatoid arthritis, the majority of the burials showing signs of this affliction, while in many cases the bones are shapeless and distorted from the effects of the disease. This condition does not appear in later ages, when the Nile had been bridled and the swamp area reduced ; and it is much what one would have expected in these early days when there was no regulation of the inundation. " People must have lived in damp mud and undrained marshes for a great part of the year—not much wonder they had rheumatism ! " The other point is still more curious, and far more intriguing. In several of the prehistoric cemeteries the women habitually have the left forearm broken ! " The only explanation as yet suggested for this," says Mrs. Quibell, " is that they got them broken by endeavouring to protect their heads from the blows of their male relatives, and one hesitates to attribute such un-pleasant conduct to people who could make such delightful pottery." Possibly the breaking of the forearm was done after death in accordance with some obscure ritual necessity, the memory of which has perished from the records of Egyptian religion. This suggestion would at least relieve the prehistoric Egyptian from the reproach of having been a habitual wife-beater ; but it is highly improbable that we shall ever find a satisfactory explanation of this curious feature of the prehistoric interments.

The main interest of the excavations which have dealt with the early period centres, however, upon those researches at Abydos, which have revealed to us the highest point reached by early Egyptian culture through the evidence derived from the tombs of the kings of the earliest dynasties. Abydos was, throughout the whole of Egyptian history, emphatically *the* Holy City of Egypt. It shared with thirteen other cities the distinction of being one of the sites at which Isis buried one of the members of the body of Osiris after the dismemberment of the body of the dead god by his brother Set ; but it was supreme among its peers in that it claimed to have been the place where the head of the god was buried. At a very early stage of Egyptian history it became the centre of a cult of which one feature was the periodical representation of a kind of Passion Play, in which the death, resurrection, and final triumph of Osiris were enacted before vast crowds of pious worshippers ; and from the dawn of the dynastic period to its close every devout Egyptian craved, as the supreme blessing of his life, to be buried as near as possible to the sacred tomb which held the head of the god, or at least to make a pilgrimage, dead or alive, to the holy site ; or, if even that was denied him, to send a votive offering, in the shape of a piece of pottery, to be laid upon the sacred tomb, or as near it as might be. It was probably the prevalence of this belief in the actual presence of the head of Osiris at Abydos which determined the creation of the Royal Cemetery of the Kings of the earliest dynasties there, as it was the continuance of the tradition which made the royal cemetery, and in particular the one royal tomb which was erroneously identified with that of the god, the recipient of such a wealth of votive pottery that the place now goes by the Arab name *Umm el Ga'ab* (" Mother of Pots ").

On this obviously most important site Mariette had already worked for a considerable time and had accumulated an immense mass of material from the great necropolis, whence

he exhumed over fifteen thousand monuments of one kind
or another. Unfortunately his work at Abydos was marred
by the same hasty and slapdash methods which so often
impaired its value elsewhere, and only the slightest records
were attempted of the huge accumulation of valuable
antiquities which resulted from his labours. Still, Mariette's
work here was by no means fruitless ; and it ought not to
be forgotten that it was he who prophesied the discovery of
the tombs of the Ist Dynasty Pharaohs and that of the
underground " Pool of Osiris " (so-called), which has been
one of the notable results of M. Naville's work from 1913–14
onwards. " The excavations," he said (*Monuments of Upper
Egypt*, p. 124), " may furnish us with valuable tombs which
become more and more ancient the further we penetrate into
the sides of the mountain, so that it is not unreasonable to
hope that in time we may come upon some belonging even
to the Ist Dynasty. In the second place, they may any day
lead us to the discovery of the still unknown entrance of the
divine tomb, if indeed it were ever a subterranean vault."
In less than twenty years this prophecy was in process of
fulfilment. In the face of these facts it is futile to say that
Mariette " never recognised the real antiquity of the site nor
even suspected the existence there of antiquities belonging
to a period earlier than the VIth Dynasty " (Budge, *Hist.
of Egypt*, I, 11). Mariette's sins as an excavator may have
been many ; but that is no reason for denying to him the
credit which is justly his due.

Modern excavation at Abydos began with the work of
the Mission Amélineau, which opened work at the Holy
City in 1895–6 and continued its operations in 1896–7 and
1897–8. M. Amélineau's earliest results were several primitive graves similar to those already described ; but more
striking discoveries came with the campaign of 1896–7, when
the first of the great royal tombs was discovered. His most
striking find, however, came in the winter of 1897–8, when
he opened a large royal tomb belonging to a Pharaoh whose

name he believed to be Khent. As this tomb, on account
of the controversy which followed its discovery, and the
intrinsic interest of the material found in it, is one of the
most important of the tombs of Abydos, we may take it as
a typical specimen of these earliest royal tombs of Egypt.
It was originally a great square pit, about 28 feet across in
each direction, floored with brick and lined with wood, with
brick buttresses projecting from the walls, and forming a
series of cells around the chamber. The total measurement
of the pit over all was about 43 feet by 38. It was surrounded by a series of seven rows of shallower graves,
manifestly those of members of the royal household who
were buried near their royal master. From these graves
came more than seventy steles, mostly belonging to women,
so that it appears that the burials were mainly those of ladies
of Pharaoh's harem ; and the probability suggests itself that
they may have all been slain at the tomb of their master,
to accompany him on his journey through the Underworld.
At the north-west angle of the tomb a staircase of bricks
had been inserted at a later period to give access to the tomb.

The main point of the discovery, however, in M. Amélineau's view, was that the tomb of a king named Khent could
only be the tomb of the being who came to be known as
" Khenti-Amenti " (" The First of the Westerners "), and
with whom the god Osiris was later identified. Accordingly,
he announced that he had discovered the tomb of Osiris.
His faith in this unique discovery was confirmed when, on
January 2, 1898, he discovered a skull which could surely
only be that head of the dead god which was buried at
Abydos, and when on the same day a grey granite bier came
to light which he believed to be " the Bed of Osiris." The
announcement of these unique discoveries brought about a
vigorous and somewhat acrimonious controversy, in which
sides were strenuously taken in support of the supposed
solitary case in which a dead god had been traced to his last
resting-place, and in opposition to this unprecedented idea.

Judgment finally inclined to the less romantic view, propounded by the late Sir Gaston Maspero, that the tomb was not that of a god, but of a Pharaoh of the Ist Dynasty, and that the Egyptians of the New Empire had mistaken it, for the same reasons which had misled M. Amélineau, for the tomb of Osiris, had reverenced it as such, and had inserted into it, in the time of the XXth Dynasty or later, the granite bier which was a copy of an earlier one. This somewhat curious chapter in the history of excavation and of the origins of religion, supposed till recently to be closed, has to some extent been reopened by Mr. Weigall's reassertion of Amélineau's position. " The identification of this king with Osiris," says Mr. Weigall (*Hist. of the Pharaohs*, Vol. I, p. 111), " is regarded by Egyptologists as an ancient mistake ; but actually, I believe, it was perfectly correct, and I think that the famous story told of the murder of Osiris by Set is historical, and is a narrative of events which took place. . . ." Mr. Weigall, however, seems to be practically alone in his faith in what would be the most interesting of all possible discoveries in Egyptology ; though only time can decide whether he is or is not justified in it.

Abydos thus had produced apparently more heat than light, and M. Amélineau, probably disgusted by the unbelief of the scientific world, and labouring under the mistaken idea that he had exhausted the treasures of the site, abandoned his work there. Fortunately, he was succeeded, in 1899, by the explorer who has done more than any other man for the recovery of the relics of Egypt's earliest age. Sir Flinders Petrie's work on the site which Amélineau had left with the remark that " all the fellahs know that it is exhausted," was speedily to prove that not even the fellahs know everything about excavation, though they have practised it from time immemorial, and that the material still left on the exhausted site was absolutely priceless, as well as abundant in quantity.

The royal tombs, which were now compelled to yield up

what remained of their ancient treasure (for they had all
been rifled in ancient times, and some of them subjected to
the action of fire), conformed, in the main, to a single type
such as has been already described in connection with the
tomb of Osiris, or King Zer ; though there were many
variations in detail and in size. Some of the variations are
of interest as marking definite stages of advance in methods
of construction. Thus the tomb of King Den-Setui
(Usaphai of Weigall's list), who was probably the fifth
king of the Ist Dynasty, attains to the unprecedented magnificence of being not only lined with brick, but also floored
with blocks of granite—the first instance known of the use
for constructional purposes of this splendid material of
which the Egyptians later made such admirable use in the
adornment of their temples. This tomb also, like that of
King Zer, was surrounded by rows of graves, 137 in number,
in which the courtiers of the dead monarch rested beside
their lord. From the royal tomb itself came fragments of
vases, boxes, and tablets, of which the most interesting was
a piece of the lid of a box, inscribed with the words, " The
Golden Seal of Judgment," evidently the box in which the
Lord Chancellor of Egypt, in those far-off days, kept the
Great Seal of the Two Lands. Perhaps the most remarkable tomb, from the structural point of view, was that of
King Khasekhemui (" Chennere "—Weigall), the ninth king
of the IInd Dynasty, who may have reigned about three
hundred years after King Den. It measures 223 feet in
length by 54 feet in breadth at its widest part, and it consists of three separate sets of chambers, with a central
chamber for the royal interment, 10 by 17 feet, and 6 feet
deep, built entirely of stone—the earliest known example of
such construction. In this tomb, along with other treasures,
were found the fragments of the royal sceptre of King
Khasekhemui, of sard and gold.

The tomb of King Zer, already famous, yielded to Petrie's
patient search material which, if not so sensationally attrac-

tive as the skull and bed of Osiris, was of far more value as
an aid to the reconstruction of a picture of Egyptian life in
the earliest days of the monarchy. While the workmen were
clearing the tomb, one of them noticed a piece of the arm
of a mummy, still encased in its wrappings, thrust into a
hole in the wall of the tomb chamber. When the wrappings
were removed, four bracelets of gold, turquoise, amethyst,
and lapis lazuli were disclosed, still encircling the bones of
the arm of the great lady who had doubtless been King Zer's
queen. How this treasure had escaped the greed of the
robbers who had plundered the tomb at a very early date,
the pious restorers who made trouble for future archæologists in the middle of the XVIIIth–XXth Dynasty, the
iconoclastic zeal of the Coptic Christians who had destroyed
all that they could find in the ancient shrine, and the somewhat hasty methods of the Mission Amélineau, is one of
those mysteries which ought perhaps to be ascribed to a
special guiding Providence. It was probably during the
XVIIIth–XXth Dynasty restoration that the mummy of the
queen was rifled and broken up. " One workman hastily
put this forearm in the hole in the wall, and then either got
so much more plunder that he ran away, or else perished
in a squabble. This hole never seems to have been disturbed when building the stairway close by it ; and for more
than a thousand years offerings continued to be made here,
and visitors passed within a few feet of the arm without
looking at it. The Copts then destroyed the shrine and all
that they could find, but never touched the arm. The
Mission Amélineau cleared the tomb, but still the arm lay
in the hole in the wall. Lastly, my men eyed the gold, and
preserved it with all care." Such are the vicissitudes and
dangers through which a notable *antika* may come to its
resting-place in a great museum, there to bear its witness to
the standard of culture attainèd by the ancient Egyptians
five thousand years ago !

The bracelets themselves are more than sufficient

THE EGYPTIAN ARTIST AT PLAY—THE CROUCHING NEGRO AND
THE OINTMENT POT

This is one of the treasures of the Liverpool Free Public Museum. The artist has
admirably caught the essential characteristics of the negro, bending under the
weight of the lotus-wreathed ointment pot. This is a fine example of the humour
and delicacy with which the Egyptian often handled his material.

(By permission of the Keeper of the Liverpool Free Public Museum)

justification for the providence which has preserved them. Design and execution are alike masterly ; and the Egyptian goldsmith who wrought these simple and beautiful pieces of ornament for his royal client had nothing to learn in the detail of his craft from any succeeding age. But the supreme value of the pieces lies in their testimony to the level of taste and skill to which the Egyptian community of the Ist Dynasty had attained. The small and intimate details of a national culture, such as these articles of personal adornment, are often a surer gauge by which to judge of the general level of attainment than its great public monuments. Judged by this standard, the Egyptian of the Ist Dynasty ranks high indeed.

The tomb of Zer furnished us, along with the queen's bracelets, with another relic which may have belonged to the same royal lady, and which suggests that the period was not only cultured to a high degree, but had reached already that stage of culture in which artificiality has begun to creep in. Curiously enough, Zer's name is associated by Manetho with a tradition that, being a physician, he caused books on anatomy to be written ; and in the Papyrus Ebers there is preserved a recipe for a hair restorer which was prepared by his queen Shesh. The restorer was made from the claw of a dog, the hoof of a donkey, and some boiled dates ; but, alas ! the excavation of the royal belongings raises the suspicion that this notable prescription, like some other restorers of later date and greater pretensions, was not successful in arresting the ravages of time even in the case of its originator ; for one of the finds in the tomb was a plait and fringe of false hair, which in all probability had belonged, as well as the bracelets, to Queen Shesh, and doubtless supplied deficiencies better than the brew of dogs' claws and donkeys' hoofs had done ! When we get to prescriptions for hair restorers and false fronts we are obviously in a state of society which is not only civilised, but hypercivilised ; and, says Sir Flinders Petrie, " the fringe of locks

E

is exquisitely made, entirely on a band of hair, showing a long acquaintance with hair-work at that age." We are dealing with a matter of some five thousand years ago ; but manifestly we are far removed from a state of primitive simplicity.

Such matters, of course, are trifles, though even trifles have their own importance in such a connection ; but more serious evidence was not lacking in the royal tombs of the fact that the earliest Egyptian state, judged by any standard, was far advanced in civilisation and in the arts of civilised life. When we meet the Egyptian of five thousand years ago he is no rude barbarian, but a highly cultured man, of refined and sure taste, who could already read and write, who loved to have beautiful things around him, whether for use or for the mere pleasure which they gave to his eye, who used for his daily lustrations, or for the adornment of his rooms, vessels of copper, alabaster, diorite, and breccia of the most satisfying design and of the most wonderful perfection of workmanship, who slept at night on a bed of carved ivory, adorned his woman-kind with the most exquisite work of the goldsmith, moved in the midst of a society where ranks and classes were already as definitely marked out as in any modern community, and was possessed of a definitely formulated creed which regulated his relations with Deity in this life and expressed his hopes for the life to come.

The beautiful hieroglyphic writing of Egypt is represented by tablets of ebony and ivory, and history is beginning to be written in the shape of records of royal victories and lists of captives ; while more peaceful records recount the founding of new temples, the breaking of ground for a new canal, or the establishment of a new festival in honour of a god. The ebony label of Aha-Mena contains hieroglyphics which, though of archaic form, are intelligible. By the middle of the Ist Dynasty hieroglyphic is in regular use ; by the end of the dynasty the forms of the figures are beginning to suffer degradation. Considerable progress had been made in the direction of substituting a true alphabet for a series of phonetic signs, each standing for a whole syllable ; but, unfortunately for his own convenience, the Egyptian of a later date did not carry this process to its logical conclusion.

The Court of the Pharaoh of these early days was as stiffly organised and officialised as at any subsequent period of Egyptian history. The records recovered from the royal tombs show us that a Court Chamberlain existed in the very first reign of the Ist Dynasty, that of Narmer-Mena. Two reigns later, in the days of King Zer, we have the Commander of the Inundation making his appearance—a proof of the early date at which the Egyptians organised the national resources for the purpose of dealing with this vital feature of the life of the country. Somewhat later comes the Commander of the Elders ; and, curiously enough, the functionary who is more familiar to us than any other, from early Scriptural associations, " Pharaoh's Chief Butler," makes his bow first during the reign, not of a king, but of a queen, Merneit. He is followed by the Royal Seal-Bearer, the Keeper of the King's Vineyards, and the Royal Architect ; while the names of the Leader of the Peers and the Master of Ceremonies witness to the growth of a regular aristocracy. Plainly the minute ritual of Court etiquette which marked Egyptian society in a later period was already in process of growth ; and it was accompanied by the development of a regular bureaucracy which controlled for purposes of State all the resources of the land. The Provision Office dealt with the payment of taxes in kind throughout the land ; while the division of the department of the Treasury into two sections reflects the actual state of things in the pre-dynastic period, when there were two kingdoms of Egypt, Lower and Upper Egypt, whose kings wore the Red and the White Crown respectively. The Red House was the Northern Treasury, and the White House the Southern.

The site of the royal cemetery from which Petrie's

" conscientious and arduous devotion " has recovered such priceless treasures of the past is in itself a striking one. " The site selected for the royal tombs was on a low spur from the hills, slightly raised above the plain. . . . The situation is wild and silent ; close round it the hills rise high on two sides, a ravine running up into the plateau from the corner where the lines meet. Far away and below us, stretches the long green valley of the Nile, beyond which for dozens of miles the eastern cliffs recede far into the dim distance." About the actual tombs, however, there is nothing striking ; for the Egyptian had not yet conceived the idea of converting the universal grave-mound into a mountain of stone, as in the case of the Pyramids. The first glimmer of the dawn of such a thought may be traced in the two huge tombs of Zeser of the IIIrd Dynasty, the Step Pyramid of Sakkara, and the great mastaba of Bet-Khallaf ; but at Abydos, the process which was to result in the gigantic cairns at Gizeh is seen only in its very humblest beginnings. " The tombs as they were left by the kings," says Petrie, " seem to have been but slightly heaped up. The roofs of the great tombs were about six or eight feet below the surface. . . . But there does not seem to have been any piling up of a mound. . . . On the flat, or almost flat ground of the cemetery the graves were marked by stone steles set upright in the open air. . . . Each royal grave seems to have had two great steles . . . standing up side by side, on the east of the tomb. Around the royal tomb stood the little private steles of the domestics placed in rows, thus forming an enclosure round about the king."

Thus the earliest royal tombs of Egypt offer to us something quite distinct either from the vast erections of the pyramid-building Pharaohs, or the elaborate rock-hewn corridors and chambers of the New Empire. The earliest Pharaonic burying-place must have presented an appearance more resembling a modern cemetery than anything of Egyptian practice. A bleak sand-strewn area, dotted with mounds of low elevation, each adorned with a group of gaunt headstones ; such was the resting-place of the mighty dead of the great empire of the world's childhood. It has nothing of the wonder and romance which attach to the vast piles of Gizeh or the dark galleries of the Valley of the Kings ; nor do the pitiful fragments of ancient splendour which are all that have survived the neglect, the malice, and the greed of five millenniums bear comparison for one moment with the glittering magnificence of the treasures from the tomb of Tutankhamen. What was found at Abydos was simply the refuse of the original stores, the little which had escaped the hatred of Pharaoh's enemies, or which even the greed of tomb-robbers had not deemed worth carrying away. All the same, it may be questioned if the broken fragments of ivory, the scraps of gold-work, and the pottery and stone-work of Abydos are not of greater importance than all the magnificence which has come out of the Valley of the Kings put together ; for these things have held up a light where before all was dark, and by its glimmer we can discern a whole age which once was blank to us, only dimly, indeed, yet not uncertainly. In our age there has been no more momentous conquest over the destroying power of Time than that which has been won by the work at Abydos and the kindred discoveries which preceded it and have followed it.

CHAPTER III

THE MIGHTIEST BUILDERS OF THE WORLD AND
THEIR WORK

OF all buildings which the hand of man has reared on earth, the most famous, as well as the vastest, are the Pyramids of Egypt. Perhaps one should rather say the Pyramids of Gizeh, for the great IVth Dynasty group there so far exceeds all the other groups which Egypt possesses that hardly anybody ever thinks of any others, and when the Pyramids are mentioned, the mind naturally turns at once to the giant group which squats on the Libyan plateau, and has watched for nearly fifty centuries the glory and the shame of Egypt. The three great mausoleums of Khufu, Khafra, and Menkaura are, to nine people out of ten, the characteristic feature of Egypt, and the most alluring mystery of that mysterious land. Around no other buildings in the world has such a tissue of wild and absurd fancies been woven ; and it would be hard to set any limit to the nonsense which seems to find credence whenever the Great Pyramid, in particular, is mentioned. No fancy appears to be too wild to be believed, and worthy folk, presumably sane in most respects, have spent years of what might have been useful life in demonstrating to their own complete satisfaction that the Pyramids were created for purposes for which no sane human being would ever have dreamed of creating them. Thus it has been proved, at successive periods during the nineteenth and twentieth centuries, that the Pyramids were the storehouses which Joseph built to store up grain against the coming of the seven years of famine ; that they were meant (the Great Pyramid in particular) for astronomical observatories ; that they contain Divine revelations of the standard measures of length, weight, and capacity ; and finally, of late days, that they contain the embodiment of the Divine will concerning everything that is in heaven above, and in the earth beneath, and that is in the waters under the earth, together with prophecies of all events, past, present, and future—the Almighty having seemingly nothing better to do than to play a childish game of hide-and-seek with His creatures by concealing all these interesting matters where it was a million to one against anyone ever finding them ; until, of course, the inspired interpreters of the mystery appeared and proclaimed their wondrous discoveries by advertisement and otherwise.

All this is, of course, absolute moonshine ; and the various and totally inconsistent theories which are the symptoms of the disease which we might call " Great-Pyramiditis " may be left to devour one another. The plain truth about the Pyramids is far simpler, and infinitely more impressive than any of them. They are the most wonderful and the most pathetic evidence ever given of man's craving for immortality. The ancient Egyptians cherished, with a passionate insistence known to no other race on earth, the belief that the great change which we call Death was not the end of human existence ; and that, given the observance of certain conditions, life might continue, and become practically unending, and correspondingly blessed. Of these conditions, one of the most urgently important was the preservation, if not for all time, at least for as long a period as possible, of the actual body in which the dead man had spent his earthly life. With the object of securing this from one point of view, the practice of mummification grew up ; to obtain security in another direction, the mummy, when science had done all that was possible to protect it against natural corruption, had to be protected against the chances of violent destruction by ill-disposed persons ; and with this object in view there came that development of the tomb in which Egypt has so strangely excelled all other nations. Naturally, as Pharaoh was infinitely greater than all other men, being god, in fact, as well as man, it was infinitely more to be dreaded that he should undergo the second death which resulted from the destruction of the body than for this to happen to any mere man ; therefore Pharaoh's tomb must afford infinitely greater protection to his body than that of any other man. It is this belief which leads to all the different forms of Egyptian royal tombs, from the great brick-lined pits of Abydos to the long rock-hewn galleries of the Valley of the Kings. The particular form which this cult of the tomb as *the* necessity of continued life took for a period of, roughly speaking, fifteen hundred years of Egyptian history was the Pyramid, and there is no more sense in seeking Divine revelations in one particular pyramid than in seeking them in any other of its scores of more or less important companions, or in the long pictured corridors and chambers of the tombs of Seti I or Rameses III. All, from greatest to smallest, whether pyramid or rock-tomb, existed simply to serve the one purpose ; and whatever their other distinctions, of size, material, or decoration, no valid distinction can be drawn, or will ever be drawn by anyone who knows the elements of Egyptian faith, in respect of the purpose for which they were created.

In dealing with the excavation of the Pyramids, and the results which have followed upon the work in and around them, we have first to realise that the Gizeh group, though by far the most imposing set of examples of this form of tomb-building, is only one group among the many which exist in Egypt and its former dependencies. Further, it is by no means the oldest group, and, from some points of view, it is not the most interesting. Actually there are still scores of pyramids in Egypt and the Sudan, and the number must originally have run well into the hundreds. There are two main pyramid fields, of which the first, and the most important, extends from Abu Roash, at a point due west of

Cairo, to Hawara, at the mouth of the Fayum, a matter of sixty miles farther south.   The second field lies far south in the Sudan, around Napata and Meroë, the ancient cities of the Ethiopian Pharaohs of the XXVth Dynasty, who ruled Egypt in the eighth century B.C. and later.   These Sudanese pyramids are, of course, practically out of the reckoning of the ordinary visitor to Egypt, though their existence has been known for a long time ; and it is only within the last few years that they have been scientifically examined by the American Expedition (Harvard Boston) under Reisner.   In addition to these two great fields, we know that there were formerly other groups of pyramids in Egypt, notably at Thebes.   We have, in the records of the Abbott and Amherst Papyri, accounts of the plundering of some of these ancient tombs of the Pharaohs of the XIIIth and subsequent dynasties, in which ten pyramids are mentioned ; while the base of the pyramid of Mentuhotep III of the XIth Dynasty still stands, surrounded by his pyramid-temple, side by side with Hatshepsut's terraced temple at Der el-Bahri.

All these more southerly pyramids, however, seem to have been of comparatively small size, and almost all the interest lies in the great pyramid-field which stretches from Abu Roash to Hawara.   Even within this sixty-mile stretch there is an astonishing amount of material of which the popular mind never takes account.   At Abu Roash stands the pyramid of the Pharaoh Razedef of the IVth Dynasty, the successor to the " Big Three " of the Dynasty—Khufu, Khafra, and Menkaura.   Four miles south of this lies the great Gizeh group, where the kings just named once lay in state, surrounded by the lesser pyramids of other members of the royal family, and by regular streets of the oblong mastabas, where the courtiers and officials of " the Good Gods " slept their long sleep beside the masters whom they had served in life.   The next stage, a little further south still, is Zawiyet-el-Aryan, where the unfinished pyramid of Neb-ka-ra of the IIIrd Dynasty, in spite of, or perhaps because of, its incomplete condition, is one of the most interesting and astonishing examples of the gigantic simplicity of this early period which Egypt has to show. Next comes Abusir, with its brick pyramids of three kings of the Vth Dynasty, and the remains of the remarkable temples which they reared to the Sun-god ; and a stage further south we reach Sakkara. Here we are met with a double interest, for it is at Sakkara that King Zeser of the IIIrd Dynasty built the first real pyramid, and, indeed, the first great stone structure in the history of the world (*c.* 3000 B.C.)—the Step Pyramid of Sakkara. Despite the claims of Zeser's great tomb, however, the ruined pyramids of the kings of the Vth and VIth Dynasties, which stand close to the more famous tomb, have proved of still greater importance, for the walls of the chambers of those of Unas, of the Vth, and of Teti, Pepy I, Merenra, and Pepy II, of the VIth Dynasty, are covered with long religious inscriptions, which have the double value of furnishing the most priceless store of information which we possess concerning the early religious ideas of the Egyptians, and also the earliest specimens of any length of early Egyptian writing.

Still travelling southwards, we reach Dahshur, where the pyramid-field in which some of the great monarchs of the XIIth Dynasty, the Senuserts and Amenemhats, found their resting-place, is famous as the scene of the discovery of the Treasure of Dahshur, which includes some of the most beautiful examples of the skill of the Egyptian goldsmith of the time of Abraham in existence. A slightly longer interval brings us to Lisht, where lay the founder of this great line of kings, Amenemhat I and his son and successor Senusert I. Lastly, at the mouth of the Fayum, we have the pyramids of Senusert II and Amenemhat III, at Lahun and Hawara respectively. Lahun is famous as the scene of the discovery by Sir Flinders Petrie of the Treasure of Lahun, consisting of the jewellery of the princess Sat-hathor-ant, another of those exquisite series of examples of the taste and skill of the Egyptian craftsman of 2000 B.C. Slightly to the north of these XIIth-Dynasty tombs stands one of the most famous of the pyramids, that of Seneferu, the last king of the IIIrd Dynasty at Medum. Seneferu's pyramid, though it is called " The False Pyramid " by the Arabs, has some claim to be actually the first true pyramid, for it appears to have been originally cased from peak to base, as Zeser's pyramid never was, in smooth limestone. At present, in its stripped and mutilated condition, it exhibits very impressively the stages of its evolution from the original mastaba form.

Such, then, is the mass of material with which we are presented in Egypt proper ; for the comparatively trifling remains at Thebes may be left out of account, and the Ethiopian pyramid-field, interesting as have been many of the results of the Reisner Expedition, does not command the same attention as if it had been purely Egyptian. It is plain that even in the sixty miles from Abu Roash to Lahun we have quite enough to deal with. For our purposes we may divide the pyramids of this great field into four groups, of which we shall only have to deal with three in this chapter. In the first group come the earlier pyramids—that of Zeser at Sakkara, that of Seneferu at Medum, with the unfinished work at Zawiyet-el-Aryan. The second is the Gizeh group, the most imposing of all. In the third group come the pyramids of the Vth and VIth Dynasty kings, notable, not from their structure, but because of their inscriptions. Lastly, we have the pyramids of the XIIth-Dynasty Pharaohs at the mouth of the Fayum ; but, as these will fall to be noticed when we deal with the period of the Middle Kingdom, we need not include them in the present survey. The oldest of all the pyramids, that of Zeser, was excavated in 1819 by the Prussian General Minutoli. It ought here to be noted, once for all, that in dealing with such enormous structures of hewn stone as the pyramids, and the greater temples of Egypt, the word " excavation " is used in a strictly limited sense. The gigantic buildings of Egypt were

never so completely entombed in sand, like the palaces of
Assyria, as to require excavation to make them visible. They
were always manifest to the eye, even though the sand had
crept a certain distance up the sides of the pyramids or the
columns of the temples. What is meant, in such cases as
that of Karnak and the pyramids, by excavation, is simply
the clearing away of the sand which encumbers the building,
so that its complete structure may be discerned, with its
subsidiary buildings, if such exist ; and, in the case of the
pyramids, the opening out of its interior passages and
chambers, where these have been blocked, either by sand
or stones, in the course of centuries of neglect.

Excavation, in the case of the Step Pyramid, revealed that
the subterranean portion of the pyramid consisted of a great
rock-cutting 77 feet deep and 24 feet square, which was
approached by a sloping passage and stairway and paved
with granite blocks. Upon this pavement two chambers
were erected, their walls being lined with beautiful tiles in
blue glaze. Between the two rooms was a doorway, inscribed
with the king's titles. These chambers were bedded in
masonry, and around and over them a flat rectangular
structure, resembling the familiar " mastaba," the typical
tomb of the early dynasties, was erected. This formed the
first stage of the pyramid, and five others of diminishing
area were subsequently added, until the building assumed
its present form. The Step Pyramid was never cased, as
were the others, with hewn stone, to bring it to a smooth
uniform slope, and therefore is not so truly a pyramid as
Seneferu's pyramid at Medum, though the latter, since the
loss of its casing, does not look nearly so like a pyramid as
Zeser's tomb. Zeser was not content even with this stately
mausoleum, but built another for himself at Bet-Khallaf in
Upper Egypt. This second tomb was in the form of a
gigantic mastaba, and has been excavated in modern times
by Professor Garstang. The habit of having two tombs was
not confined to Zeser, as several Pharaohs followed the same

practice, whether with the view of making it more difficult for their enemies to destroy their mummies, or of providing a tomb for the royal " Ka," as well as for the actual body.

The Medum pyramid was excavated by Sir Flinders Petrie in 1891, and was again investigated by the same explorer in 1910. The notable result of the work was the discovery of the tiny little pyramid-temple on the east side of the building —the first complete Egyptian temple known. The extreme simplicity of the little building, with its twin steles and its little courtyard, and the total absence of any attempt at decoration, point to its early date. At the same time, as the later excavations proved, the whole system of the pyramid complex which we shall meet again at the Gizeh group was already in existence at Medum. The causeway leading down to the plain was traced, and at its foot, though the portico-temple had been destroyed, the foundation deposits were discovered, proving that the temple had actually existed. In the tomb-chamber beneath the pyramid the explorer found fragments of a wooden coffin, and of a wooden jar. The king's mummy had perished or been destroyed, nor were any inscriptions found which might have determined the original ownership of the pyramid. This, however, was fortunately established by the chance that the tourist in the days of the ancient Egyptian empire was of the same reprehensible habit as some of his successors of to-day, and was wont to scribble his opinions on the walls of ancient buildings just like Tom, Dick, or Harry on a holiday. Seneferu's little temple had not escaped their attentions, and the walls were scribbled over with remarks from visitors, some of them from the time of the Old Kingdom, others from that of the XVIIIth Dynasty. Five of these inscriptions mention Seneferu as the owner of the pyramid. So that for once the wandering tourist's itch for scrawling his foolishness on every available surface has proved of some use.

The most interesting member of this ancient pyramid group, however, is the amazing work at Zawiyet-el-Aryan, where one can see all the preliminary work for a pyramid which was never carried further, lying as the workmen left it nearly five thousand years ago. The site was excavated in recent years by Barsanti, and scarcely anything, even the Grand Gallery of the Great Pyramid, makes such an instant impression of tremendous power as does this first sketch for a great tomb. " A huge rectangular pit, 73 feet deep, has been laboriously cut down into the limestone bed of the desert plateau, like a monstrous tank, 82 feet long and 46 feet wide, with precipitous sides of sheer hewn rock, approached at one end by a magnificent stairway, 28 feet broad and 360 feet long. The floor of this pit was paved with great rectangular blocks of dressed granite, each weighing some 9 tons, while the middle block is so large that it must weigh at least 45 tons. . . . Sunk into this tremendous pavement there was an oval sarcophagus or cistern, having a lid of polished granite cemented to it." . . . " The impression it makes," says the late Sir G. Maspero, " when one goes down into it is unforgettable. The richness and the cutting of the materials, the perfection of the joints and sections, the incomparable finish of the basin, the boldness of the lines and the height of the walls all combine to make up a unique creation." Neb-ka-ra's unfinished tomb is the fitting preparation for the most astonishing group of buildings that the world has ever seen—the group of the three great pyramids at Gizeh.

It is quite needless to enter into detail with regard to the structure and dimensions of the Great Pyramid and its two smaller but still gigantic companions. They are perhaps the best-known buildings in the world, and all the facts with regard to them are common property. What we have to do is to consider whether these mighty mausoleums adequately fulfilled the purpose for which they were created, of protecting the bodies of the kings who built them from greed or hatred ; and if not, how, when, and by whom the great tombs were entered and rifled, whether in ancient or modern

times. No doubt Khufu and his successors imagined that
the vast mountains of stone which they had piled above the
chambers where they hoped to sleep for ever undisturbed
rendered their resting-places absolutely secure ; and the
complicated machinery of plug-blocks of granite and pivot-
ing doors of solid stone, which was devised to render access
to the inner passages and chambers absolutely impracticable,
save to the priests of the pyramids, must have increased
their sense of security. The probability is, however, that
the very scale of their precautions defeated the end for
which they had been devised. If such care was taken to
protect the treasure, there must be a correspondingly
precious treasure to protect. Such, no doubt, was the
reasoning of the ancient tomb-robbers who disturbed the
rest of the great Pharaohs at a very early date. It is probable
that the tomb-chamber in the Great Pyramid was rifled,
and the dust of the greatest builder of the world scattered
to the four winds of heaven, before Khufu had lain for more
than a century or two in his granite sarcophagus in the heart
of the pyramid, " Yakhet-Khufu " (" The Horizon (Burial-
place) of Khufu "), as it was called. It was probably somewhere in the closing days of the Old Kingdom, between the
decline of the VIth Dynasty and the rise of the Middle
Kingdom, that the pyramid was first penetrated and rifled ;
and thereafter, through the classical period, the secret of
the entrance passages was well known. By the time of the
Arab conquest, however, it had been lost, and when the
Khalif Mamun, in the early part of the ninth century A.D.,
lured on by stories of life-sized cocks made of gold and
jewels, ewers cut from a single emerald, and heaps of coined
gold, succeeded, after a huge expenditure of money and
energy, in breaking through into the interior, he found
nothing to reward him for all his labours but an empty
sarcophagus without a lid. The tunnel by which he managed
to break through into the passage still goes by the name of
" Mamun's Hole."

Mamun was followed at intervals by various other investigators, among whom Captain Caviglia (1817) was the most successful. Lepsius, Perring and Vyse, and Petrie, all in turn added to our knowledge of the great building, and Petrie's careful survey in 1881–2 brought out many interesting facts with regard to the accuracy with which the work had been laid out, among them the curious point, somewhat disconcerting to the theorists, that almost the most inaccurate piece of workmanship in the whole vast structure is the very piece which, if theory is right, ought to have been the most accurate—the very sarcophagus of Khufu. " The kernel of the whole, the sarcophagus, has much worse work in it than in the building, or than in other sarcophagi of the same period."

The Second Pyramid, that of Khafra, was first opened in modern times by Belzoni, who has left us an account, in his usual vivacious manner, of his achievement. It was in the early spring of 1818 that he began his somewhat unpromising task, undeterred by the statement of Herodotus that the pyramid contained no subterranean chambers, but no doubt much incited by the report that some of the Europeans in Egypt, headed by his deadly enemy Drovetti, were trying to raise a subscription of £20,000, with a view " to force their way into the centre of this pyramid by explosions, or any other means that could be suggested." Belzoni had only £200 wherewith to match his enemy's anticipated £20,000 ; but he would have attacked the pyramid with his bare fingers sooner than see Drovetti forestalling him. His first attempt ended in a disappointment ; but Belzoni was not easily discouraged, and after a day's meditation on the likenesses and unlikenesses of the First and Second Pyramids, " hope," as he says, " returned to cherish my pyramidical brains," and he made a second assault. His Arab workmen thought him mad, but were quite prepared to accept his pay as long as he was fool enough to pay them. " As to expectation that the entrance

BOAT-PIT OF AN EGYPTIAN QUEEN OF FIVE THOUSAND YEARS AGO

This great pit, on the south face of the northern Queen's Pyramid, beside the Great Pyramid of Khufu, once held the funerary boat which was buried with the Queen to ensure her a passage over the rivers and lakes of the Egyptian Underworld. The roughly built partitions seen in the picture are not of the same age as the rest of the structure. (See p. 86.)

(Photo by kindness of Dr. G. A. Reisner)

might be found, they had none ; and I often heard them utter, in a low voice, the word ' *magnoon*,' in plain English, madman." There was, however, method in his madness, and, thirty days from the start of his venture, on March 2, 1818, the indomitable explorer had the satisfaction of crawling under the granite portcullis with which the passage to the sarcophagus chamber had been closed, and finding himself and his companion, the Chevalier Frediani, in the great rock-hewn chamber under the pyramid in which Khafra had been buried. The granite sarcophagus was sunk into the floor of the chamber ; but if Belzoni had cherished any hopes of finding Pharaoh in his last abode, he was quickly disillusionised. The lid of the sarcophagus lay by its side, displaced and broken, and the great granite coffin, 8 feet long, 3 feet 6 inches wide, and 2 feet 3 inches deep, held nothing but rubbish ; while an inscription in Arabic on the western wall of the chamber informed the excavator that one of the Egyptian Khalifs had anticipated him by about a thousand years. What became of Drovetti's subscription, history does not record ; and perhaps it is as well that entrance was obtained by less drastic means than " explosions, or any other means that could be suggested."

Colonel Howard Vyse, who in 1837 succeeded in penetrating to the heart of the Third Pyramid, was also " a day behind the fair " in respect of priority of entrance, for Menkaura's tomb had been opened in A.D. 1226 by treasure-seekers. " After passing through various passages, a room was reached wherein was found a long blue vessel (Menkaura's sarcophagus), quite empty. . . . They found in this basin, after they had broken the lid of it, the decayed remains of a man, but no treasures, excepting some golden tablets inscribed with characters of a language which nobody could understand." Vyse discovered in the tomb-chamber some human bones, some portions of a wooden coffin, which purports to be that of " the King of the North and South, Men-kau-Ra, living for ever," with the splendid basalt

F

sarcophagus which had originally held the inner coffins of the king. Part of the broken lid of the sarcophagus was also found ; but the great stone casket itself was unfortunately lost in transhipment to London. It was taken out of the pyramid with great difficulty, and was put on board a merchant ship at Alexandria. The vessel touched at Leghorn, and left that port on October 12, 1838 ; since that date she has never been heard of. Some wreckage of her was picked up off Carthagena, and we may conclude that the great basalt sarcophagus of the just king whose days, according to the story of Herodotus, were cut short because of his justice and mercifulness, rests now somewhere off the Spanish coast, at the bottom of the Mediterranean.

The wooden coffin, or rather its fragments, together with the human remains, had better luck and are preserved in the British Museum. Some doubt has been cast upon the genuineness of the coffin, and it has been suggested that it is a restoration of the time of the XXVIth Dynasty, and that the bones are not those of Menkaura, but of one of the treasure hunters who perished in the attempt of 1226 ; but, on the whole, the weight of authority seems on the side of the authenticity of the relics. Still it cannot be said with certainty that Vyse's finds disprove the rule that no Pharaoh has ever been found in any of the pyramids.

On the whole, therefore, the record of pyramid-excavation seems singularly blank, so far as regards the quantity and quality of the relics discovered within these greatest of all tombs. Knowledge as to the structures themselves has been attained with such exactitude that we may say that no buildings on earth are more thoroughly known in all their proportions than the pyramids of Gizeh ; but while the husk has been studied with such minuteness, the kernel for which the husk was created has eluded all search, and the pyramid-building Pharaohs, with all the splendour which surrounded them when they were laid to rest within their mighty mausoleums, have vanished as though they had never existed.

The simple reason, of course, is that too ostentatious pre-cautions defeat their own end. We need not suppose that Khufu and Khafra were the ruthless and sacrilegious tyrants whom Herodotus depicts, and that their pyramids were invaded, and their remains scattered to the winds by an outraged people. Anyone who knows the normal attitude of the native Egyptian of all ages towards the tombs of his ancestors and their treasures will realise that the pyramid builders were putting before their subjects a temptation such as the most loyal Egyptian could not be expected to resist when they reared tombs of such unparalleled magnificence. They were simply asking for trouble, and they got it.

But, though pyramid-excavation at Gizeh has not been rewarded with any such glittering treasures as have been found in the Valley of the Kings, it has reaped other rewards, perhaps quite as important in another way. Excavation at the pyramid-field of Gizeh has been directed in recent times, with remarkable success, in two directions. The first of these has been the tracing out of the whole complex of buildings belonging to each pyramid, on the lines established by the German Expedition which excavated the Vth Dynasty pyramids and temples at Abusir. The second has been the excavation of as much as possible of the great town of tombs of the IVth Dynasty nobles, who were buried around the pyramids of their liege lords at Gizeh. In both these undertakings, Dr. G. A. Reisner, who has been in command of the American Expedition (Boston-Harvard) which has carried on the work, has had notable success, and his results have markedly added to our knowledge, both of the pyramid structures and of the streets of mastabas which lie beneath the shadows of the pyramids.

It has long been known, of course, that each of the three giants of Gizeh had a temple standing at its base on the eastern side. Belzoni, for instance, describes what was visible in his time of the temple of the Second Pyramid and the causeway leading down from it towards the Great

Sphinx, and notes the huge blocks of which the core of the
temple walls was formed ; and he realised quite accurately
that pyramid, temple, and causeway must all have been
erected at the same period, and that the Sphinx also belonged to the same time.   The results of the German
excavators at the Vth Dynasty pyramids at Abusir have
enabled us to understand that we are to expect to find these
features associated with every royal pyramid ; and Reisner's
excavations have laid bare a considerable portion of the
remains of the temples and causeways associated with the
Gizeh group.   We can realise now something of the aspect
which the pyramids of Gizeh must have presented in the
days when they stood complete, each with its staff of priests
attached to its service, and surrounded, not as now by
tourists and their attendant Arabs, but by devout worshippers.

The pyramid, as we see it now, is only a fragment of what
was once a complete organism designed and elaborated with
the view of serving one single purpose, the attainment of
eternal welfare for the dead Pharaoh whom it commemo-
rated.   At the foot of the plateau on which it stood, at the
edge of the cultivated land to which the waters of the
inundation reached, stood a comparatively small and simple
temple, with a platform in front of it which served as a quay
in inundation-time.   From this portico-temple or valley-
temple a paved causeway, sometimes covered in, led up to
the eastern face of the pyramid, terminating at the doorway
of the actual pyramid-temple.   The base of the pyramid was
surrounded by a flat pavement of considerable extent, and
the whole complex was enclosed by a girdle-wall marking
out the sacred *temenos*.   To us, at present, the Pyramids
seem just about the last word of stripped and austere
majesty, with an indescribable dignity in their absolute
simplicity, and it seems, perhaps, something of a loss to
have to substitute for this the idea of a complex religious
structure, with its vivid colour and its crowd of worshippers.

But it is a loss which is more than compensated for by the fact that the results of excavation now permit us to form with our mind's eye a picture, of whose accuracy there can be no reasonable doubt, of what the Pyramids actually looked like to the men of forty-five centuries ago. We see the giant bulks, not roughly stepped, as at present, but cased from peak to base in smooth white limestone, standing in the midst of their spacious enclosures. Beneath their eastern faces crouch the temples, with the long paved causeways stretching down to the portico-temples on the margin of the flood-water. At the quay of one portico the galleys of one procession of priests and nobles are being moored, while another white-clad throng is making its way down another causeway to the portico where their boats are waiting for them. The whole picture is alive, as it was meant to be, seeing that its whole *raison d'être* was to insist on the triumph of life over death. Such were the Pyramids as their builders conceived them, and as they continued to be for hundreds of years ; for priests of the pyramid-temples of Khufu and Khafra existed still in the XXVIth Dynasty. It ought to be superfluous to point out the bearing of all this accumulation of evidence as to the actual structure and use of the pyramid system on all the crazy theories, which will, however, in all probability, still continue to be held by their originators, if by no one else.

Dr. Reisner's results at Gizeh, however, have been by no means confined to the increase of knowledge as to the main structures of the pyramid-field. During the last few years he has been engaged, as already indicated, in exploring the great cemetery of Old Kingdom nobles which lies around the Great Pyramid. The great gathering of ancient notabilities beneath the shadow of Khufu's vast tomb one may imagine to have taken place as a kind of continuation of the barbarous custom of more ancient days, when there was a regular slaughter and entombment of the dead king's favourites at his interment, so that he should not lack for company in the Underworld. By the time of Khufu, that hideous custom had doubtless passed out of use in Egypt proper, though Dr. Reisner's excavations at Kerma in Ethiopia have shown that it continued in the less civilised southern land to a much later date. But the old sentiment of personal devotion, whether in life or in death, evidently persisted, and Khufu's reputation was evidently such (contrary to Herodotus's tale of his evil repute among his people) that courtiers of a much later period still chose to be buried near to his pyramid rather than beside the kings of their own time.

The Great Pyramid is surrounded by a perfect town of mastabas, of which a number belong to members of Khufu's own family, or to prominent courtiers of his reign ; but some of the most notable specimens of these most interesting Old Kingdom tombs belong to the period of the VIth Dynasty, roughly a matter of four hundred years later than the time of Khufu. East of the pyramid, stand three small and partially ruined pyramids, which belonged to the three queens of Khufu ; and between the middle one and its northern neighbour Dr. Reisner's excavations have revealed the great rock-hewn boat-pit, 60 feet in length, which held the funerary barge in which the dead queen would sail along the river of the Underworld in company with Ra, the Sun-God, or would voyage across the Lily Lake to the abode of the Blessed. Pharaoh himself had a similar boat-pit beside the causeway leading down from his temple to the portico-temple on the edge of the plateau. The barge of the queen was not found ; but we already have a specimen of such a vessel in the barge of Senusert III, which was found at Dahshur, and is now in the Field Columbian Museum at Chicago. Senusert's barge was only 30 feet long ; but evidently the king, in all ages, had no intention of trusting his sacred person, or those of his wives, to the flimsy models of boats which were deemed sufficient for the needs of commoner folk, but insisted on a decent workmanlike vessel being provided, both for himself and for those who were dear to him.

The clearance of the eastern cemetery in 1925 revealed five streets of mastabas. At the northern end of each street was a huge mastaba, double the length of the others, and arranged for the accommodation of husband and wife in each case, the wife taking the northern, and the husband the southern half of the great tomb. These had belonged either to a prince of the royal family and his wife, or to a princess and her husband. In one case it was impossible to identify the prince to whom the mastaba belonged. Some deadly enemy had chiselled out from his tomb the prince's name, with all the figures and the offering formulæ, so that his *Ka* should suffer hunger and thirst through all eternity.

Even more interesting than the princely tombs, however, were some of the private tombs of the great court officials, such as those of the Senezem and the Qa'ar families. These tombs show us at an early date the Egyptian tradition of great courtier families, in which office tended to become hereditary. Thus Qa'ar, whose mastaba was one of the VIth Dynasty intrusions already alluded to, was not only " Chief gardener of the pyramid of Pepy," the Pharaoh of his own time, but also " Mayor of the pyramid-city of Khufu," " chief purifying-priest of the pyramid of Khafra," " Mayor of the pyramid-city of Menkaura," and " writer of the King's letters in his presence," or, in other words, personal scribe to Pharaoh. His son Iduw, whose tomb lay beside that of his father, inherited the priestly duties attached to the three great pyramids, and was also personal scribe to Pharaoh, like his father. The interesting reliefs in the chapels of these two tombs followed, in general, the traditions of the Egyptian tomb-decoration of the time ; but the stela of Iduw gives a break with tradition in that the lower half of it not only represents the royal scribe looking out upon the offerings in his chapel, but depicts him with hands outstretched to receive the offerings, and with a broad smile of satisfaction on his plump and somewhat homely countenance.

During the clearance of this eastern cemetery the appearance of a rectangular strip of plaster of Paris on the rock near one of the three small pyramids already mentioned led the explorers to suspect the existence of a tomb beneath. Following this hint, they found a stairway which led to a low tunnel cut in the rock and packed with masonry ; and this in turn led to the side of a great vertical shaft, also packed with masonry. At a depth of 50 feet the shaft had a niche in its western wall, and this was found to contain, not the burial, but a deposit of the bones of a bull, a mat, and some beer jars. The real burial-chamber was discovered at a depth of 90 feet, and it contained an alabaster sarcophagus, vessels of alabaster and bronze, and a mass of furniture of gilded wood—this last find being, unfortunately, terribly decayed. The sarcophagus was covered with a gilded mat, bearing the names of the famous Pharaoh Seneferu, of the IIIrd Dynasty, the immediate predecessor (possibly) of Khufu. The importance of the burial, as evidenced by the remarkable depth of the shaft, together with the presence of the titles of Seneferu in the burial-chamber, led to the idea that possibly the burial was that of the great Pharaoh himself. Such a discovery would, of course, have been an event of the first magnitude in Egyptology, as no Pharaonic remains of anything like such an antiquity, let alone of such historic interest, have been found ; but it is extremely unlikely that a great monarch like Seneferu, who had already two stately pyramids, one at Medum and one at Dahshur, could be buried in a comparatively insignificant tomb in a pyramid-field whose glory belonged to his successor, and not to himself. The tomb has now been proved to be that of the otherwise unknown royal lady Queen Hetepheres, who was one of the wives of Seneferu, and the mother of Khufu, which explains both the presence of her tomb in the neighbourhood of her son's pyramid and

THE TOMB OF PHARAOH'S CHIEF GARDENER

The principal chamber of the tomb of Qaʿar, a high official of the VIth Dynasty, "Chief Gardener of the Pyramid of Pepy," of that royal line, and also Mayor of the Pyramid Cities of several of the greater Pharaohs of the IVth Dynasty. (See page 87.)

(Photo by kindness of Dr. G. A. Reisner)

the occurrence of the names of Seneferu in the burial-chamber. Even on this footing, the discovery is one of great interest and value, as no such find of funerary furniture has come down to us from such an ancient date ; though it is to be feared that the extremely decayed condition of the articles will make the task of the restorer a heart-breaking one. Unfortunately, the alabaster sarcophagus, when opened on March 3, 1927, proved to be empty.

The last group of pyramids with which we have to deal at present is that of the kings of the Vth and VIth Dynasties at Sakkara, where, not far from the Step Pyramid of Zeser, the first suggestion of this form of tomb, stand the pyramids of Unas of the Vth, and Teta, Pepy I, Mer-en-ra, and Pepy II of the VIth Dynasty. Externally, there is nothing remarkable in these small pyramids of the declining days of the Old Kingdom. It is not only their size, but their manner of construction, which tells us that the great days of the first period of Egypt's splendour are drawing to a close. Instead of the magnificent construction of the pyramids of the Gizeh group, with their huge blocks of fine limestone, and the superb fitting, which scarcely admits of the insertion of a knife-blade between one great block and its neighbour, we have rough and hasty methods and poor materials. " The body of the masonry, instead of being of hewn stone, is merely built of walls of flakes, filled in with loose chips." The precautions adopted to block the passages against un-authorised entry are indeed elaborate and skilful ; but the feeble construction of the mass of the pyramids has rendered all precaution unavailing. Indeed, the manner in which these pyramids have been wrecked seems to show that the Old Kingdom passed away in a sea of troubles in which the rage of the enemies of the royal house found vent in a fashion against which no precautions would have availed. " The spiteful destruction . . .," writes Sir Flinders Petrie, " is far beyond what would be done by treasure seekers." The feebleness of the scale and fabric of these five pyramids tells us that Pharaoh no longer had at his disposal the whole resources of the nation ; the malicious wrecking of the buildings tells us that the forces of rebellion had gained the upper hand.

Yet these ruined and insignificant piles have an interest of their own not inferior to that of their gigantic compeers at Gizeh ; while, from every point of view save that of mere structural splendour, they are far more important than the Gizeh group. The Great Pyramid and its companions bear absolutely no inscriptions—not the least remarkable feature of these wonderful buildings. There may have been inscriptions, of course, on their smooth outer casing, which has now almost entirely vanished ; and, indeed, Herodotus tells us that there was an inscription on the Great Pyramid which his interpreter read to him ; though it is hard to believe, as he tells us, that it merely gave information as to the amount that had been spent on radishes, onions, and garlic for the workmen employed in building the pyramid. Whatever may have been the case in this respect, no trace of any inscription remains. The pyramids of Gizeh are dumb ; and Mariette did not hesitate to affirm that in his opinion all the pyramids would be found to be as dumb as the greatest members of the family had proved to be, and that the attempt to find inscriptions on or in them was a mere waste of time and labour.

In spite of this conviction of his, however, one of his last official undertakings was the opening of the smaller pyramids of Sakkara ; and he was on his death-bed, and only half-conscious, when Emil Brugsch came in from Sakkara and brought with him preliminary copies of the texts which he had found in the two pyramids which he had opened, those of Pepy I and Mer-en-ra. It was a fitting close to a life which, whatever the mistakes of Mariette's methods of excavation, had been given whole-heartedly to the cause of Egyptology, and which ended amidst dreams of the completion of that ideal museum to the establishment of which

he had given so much of his strength. His successor, the
late Sir Gaston Maspero, one of those expatriated Italians
who have done so much to add to the fame of France,
carried on the work which Mariette had initiated, and after
Mariette's death, in the beginning of 1881, the other three
pyramids named—those of Teta, Unas, and Pepy II—were
also opened, and were found, like the first two, to contain
long religious texts which are cut into the stone of the
chambers, and filled in with coloured paste. The copying
of more than four thousand lines of hieroglyphic text, and
its subsequent translation and publication, occupied Maspero
from 1882 to 1894 ; but when the work was complete it
was found that these insignificant-looking pyramids of the
Vth and VIth Dynasties had furnished students with by far
the earliest and most interesting religious texts extant ; and
since that time, all studies of Egyptian religion have had to
begin with what are now universally known as " The
Pyramid Texts." The religious ideas revealed by these
primitive Scriptures are, as might be expected, very different
from those of the later periods, which are preserved for us,
as regards the Middle Kingdom, in what are known as " The
Coffin Texts," and, as regards the New Empire, in " The
Book of the Dead " and its abridgments and variants.
Here we have survivals from the incredibly early days when
the Egyptian was still a primitive savage, mingled with ideas
of a later and more cultured though still very early period—
the whole set down in language which has a wild and fan-
tastic power, quite alien from anything to be met with in
the later and more stilted and decorous texts of the Empire.
Such passages as those in which the dead Pharaoh is
described as hunting, lassoing, and devouring the gods in
the abode of the Blessed, or triumphantly silencing the
challenging voices which dispute his entrance to the realms
of the sky, have a weird and savage fire which ranks them
infinitely higher than ninety-nine hundredths of the amazing
jumble of childish nonsense and high morality which makes

up the bulk of later Egyptian religious writing. The Pyramid Texts, crude as they may be, are literature ; most of the later texts are little more than priestly drivel, in spite of the conscientious efforts of modern believers in the super-human wisdom of the Egyptians to read into them wonderful hidden meanings which would have astonished no one so much as the old priests to whose spiritual insight they are attributed, but whose own pathetically helpless glosses upon the obscurities of their religious texts show how little they understood them. In short, the discovery of the Pyramid Texts must rank with that of the Tel el-Amarna Letters as one of the two events which, more than any other discoveries of modern times, have added to our knowledge of Egyptian thought and history. The excavation of the Pyramids may not have given us anything which in romance and splendour can compare for a moment with some of the discoveries in the Valley of the Kings ; but it has given us what is far more important than any amount of the works of the hands of the ancient Egyptian—an insight into the inmost thought of the man who wrought the works.

CHAPTER IV

THE GOLDEN AGE OF EGYPT : THE MIDDLE KINGDOM AND ITS
WONDERS OF ART AND CRAFT

SOME of the most remarkable specimens of Egyptian luxury
and skill in the arts and crafts have rewarded the excavators
who have dealt with the sites which are linked with that
period of the Middle Kingdom which is now coming to be
regarded as the true Golden Age of Egyptian History.
Greek legend preserved wonderful traditions of a great
Egyptian king named " Sesostris," who, among his quite
apocryphal conquests, achieved also the real conquest of
Ethiopia, and left steles with vainglorious and insulting
inscriptions in each country which he conquered. In later
days, and until comparatively recent times, this Sesostris
was generally supposed to be a legendary version of the
great self-advertiser among the Egyptian Pharaohs, Rameses
II. It is, indeed, quite possible that some of the fame of
Rameses II was added to that of other kings to build up
the legend of an imaginary Pharaoh, and that Sesostris
cannot be identified absolutely with any single Egyptian
monarch, as he is certainly not to be identified with
Rameses II ; but, at the same time, if the Greek legend
has to find its ground in any particular period, it is in the
period of the Middle Kingdom when the three Senuserts
may well among them have furnished the tradition of a
great Pharaoh whose name is not too unlike theirs.
Examination of the legend of Sesostris, as Heredotus gives
it, reveals features which seem undoubtedly to refer to the
exploits of Senusert III. Senusert's conquest of Ethiopia,
and his setting up of his statue on the boundary, " not that

ye should worship it, but that ye should fight for it," with his insulting remarks about the unmanly qualities of the conquered Ethiopians, are the obvious originals of the fairy-tales which Herodotus tells about Sesostris (ii, 102-110), however much the lively fancy of the Father of History may have adorned his narrative with details which certainly never existed in actual fact ; while the achievements of the XIIth Dynasty of Senuserts and Amenemhats, as modern excavation and research have revealed them, are perhaps ground as solid, though not as wide-reaching, for a great historic reputation as the wider conquests of the Thothmes and Amenhoteps of the XVIIIth Dynasty.

These great Pharaohs were of Theban origin, like the Mentuhoteps of the XIth Dynasty, whom they succeeded, and from whom they may have been descended, more or less directly ; but the time when Thebes could be made the permanent seat of government had not yet arrived, and the new line of kings found it necessary to shift their administrative centre from the southern city to a point nearer to the centre of gravity of the Double Kingdom. The spot selected was not Memphis, though the ancient fame of that great city might have suggested it as the suitable seat of the new dynasty ; but it was near enough to Memphis to overawe the city, and was also well placed for the purpose of exercising control over both Upper and Lower Egypt. It was on the west bank of the Nile, about thirty miles south of Memphis, and almost as far north of the mouth of the depressed area which is now the fertile district known as the Fayum. With this area the kings of the dynasty were to be closely associated all through, and their most important works, as well as their pyramids, were all connected with the district.

It was in 1888 that Mr. Flinders Petrie (now Sir Flinders Petrie) began at Hawara, at the mouth of the Fayum, a series of excavations which were to prove marvellously fruitful, not only as regards the period with which they were immediately concerned, but also as regards later times. His immediate object there was the brick pyramid of Amenemhat III, the great Pharaoh who was known to Greek story as Moeris, and to whom the creation of the great irrigation-lake system known as Lake Moeris was said to be due. As a preliminary exercise, on his way to the main task at Hawara, the explorer settled the question of what Herodotus meant by saying that in this neighbourhood were two statues of a Pharaoh standing upon pyramids in the midst of the water. The remains of colossi 39 feet high were found. They had stood upon tall pedestals, within a courtyard with sloping walls, and when viewed across the water from a distance by Herodotus, who evidently did not go near enough to see details, they appeared to be perched upon the tops of small pyramids.

Finding the way into the centre of the pyramid proved a long and tiresome job, which was not completed till the next season. The XIIth Dynasty pyramids are humble structures compared with the vast Gizeh group ; but the complexity of the devices with which they were provided to defeat the tomb-robbers is even more remarkable than anything to be found in connection with the Great Pyramid or any of its companions. Petrie's description of the arrangements reads something like the story of a tomb-robber's nightmare ; and one scarcely knows which to wonder at most—the ingenuity which devised such safeguards for the dead king, or the patience of the robbers which rendered all the precautions futile. " A new system was elaborated here, of dumb chambers, with gigantic sliding trap-doors in the roofs leading to further passages. The explorer who had found the entrance, in the unusual place on the south side, descended a long staircase, which ended in a dumb chamber. The roof of this, if slid aside, showed another passage, which was filled with blocks. This was a mere blind, to divert attention from the real passage, which stood ostentatiously open. A plunderer has, however, fruitlessly

mined his way through all these blocks. On going down
the real passage, another dumb chamber was reached ;
another sliding trap-door was passed ; another passage led
to a third dumb chamber ; a third trap-door was passed ;
and now a passage led along past one side of the real
sepulchre ; and, to amuse explorers, two false wells open
in the passage floor, and the wrong side of the passage is
filled with masonry blocks fitted in. Yet by some means
the plunderers found a cross trench in the passage floor,
which led to the chamber. Here another device was met.
The chamber had no door, but was entered solely by one
of the immense roof-blocks—weighing 45 tons—being
left raised, and afterwards dropped into place, on closing
the pyramid. This had been mined through, and thus
the royal interments were reached. They had been entirely
burnt ; and only fired grains of diorite and pieces of lazuli
inlaying showed the splendour of the decorations of the
coffins."

There must have been some furious passion, either of
the greed of gain, or of venomous malice, at work in this
desecration of the tomb of one of Egypt's greatest and most
beneficent monarchs. The spoilers, whoever they were,
knew perfectly that in thus destroying by fire the mummies
and all the funerary offerings in the chamber which they did
not carry away, they were dooming the great king and his
daughter, who was buried beside him, to annihilation, or an
eternity of misery and starvation ; and one would be
tempted to believe that such was their object, and that it
was malice and not greed which was the spur to all this
destruction, were it not for the fact that the confessions of
the Ramesside tomb-robbers show them doing exactly the
same thing to the mummies of the Pharaoh Sebek-em-saf
and his wife Nub-khas, and burning " the august mummy
of this god," as they reverently call the poor corpse which
they had been spoiling of its treasures, as soon as they had
finished pillaging it. One pictures a weird scene in the

heart of the pyramid, on the night when the robbers had at last triumphed over all King Amenemhat's defences, and dropped through the pierced roof-block to the floor of the burial-chamber—the hasty pillaging of the dead bodies of the great king and his young daughter, interrupted again and again, as the robbers listened for any sound that might tell them that the priests of the pyramid, or the guards, had been aroused, and were coming through the long passages to trap the men who were desecrating the sleep of a god. Then the twirling of the fire-drill, and the touch of the glowing wood to the mummy-wrappings, and the sudden roar of fire, as the flame caught the natron-soaked linen. No doubt a death of curious and ingenious torture would have awaited the robbers if they had been caught ; but, no doubt also, they had taken steps to secure that they would not be caught, and had squared the pyramid-priests, if indeed, the priests themselves were not the robbers, as we know them to have been more than once.

However it may have been, the job was well and truly done, and all that was left were the broken fragments of things which the thieves had not thought it worth while to burn or to carry away. There was enough, however, to identify the pyramid, pieces of alabaster vases bearing the name of Amenemhat, Maat-en-ra, and some broken dishes and an alabaster altar, inscribed for " the king's daughter, Ptah-neferu," whose sarcophagus stood between that of her great father and the wall of the chamber. The wonderful thing about the whole place was the sepulchral chamber itself. Not even Khufu, in his vast dwelling-place of eternity, had so stately a sleeping-chamber. It was hollowed out of a single block of glass-hard yellow quartzite, cut and polished with the most exquisite truth. The block measures 22 feet long, and the chamber scooped out of it is 8 feet wide inside, with walls two feet thick, so that the mass, in its present condition, must weigh about 110 tons. King Amenemhat's burial-place leaves the death-chamber of

G

the kings in *King Solomon's Mines*, and all the other imaginations of the tellers of treasure-hunting stories, far behind.

Close to the pyramid, Petrie found the pitiful traces which were all that remained of the most gigantic building which the Egyptians ever reared to the glory of the gods— the world-famous Labyrinth. The Egyptian Labyrinth has not shared the good fortune of its Cretan rival, which was beginning to take shape about the same time. It served for centuries, apparently, as a quarry ; but the indications of its foundations which Petrie found show that in its time it was a building big enough to have held all the existing temples of Karnak and Luxor put together !

But the pyramid and temple of Hawara proved to be the lesser part of the work there, and the greatest surprises and rewards awaited the excavator in what looked the least promising part of the site. This was the cemetery, whose ancient tombs had all been ravaged and ruined ages ago, leaving nothing of earlier date than the time of the XXVIth Dynasty. Now to the Egyptian explorer, to say XXVIth Dynasty is to say a thing of the day before yesterday, while to say Ptolemaic and Roman, the periods to which the bulk of the remains of the Hawara cemetery belonged, is to say yesterday morning and evening ; so that it was with no great expectations that Petrie began his work at the cemetery. Fortune had in store for him, however, one of the most wonderful finds of the Saite period which have ever rewarded an excavator ; while the Roman part of the cemetery was to yield a series of discoveries of absolutely priceless value for the history of ancient art. Strictly speaking, of course, these discoveries belong to a much later point of our story ; but they are so much part of the work at Hawara that it will be more convenient to deal with them here.

In the north-east corner of the cemetery the explorers came upon a fine tomb shaft which had belonged to a great local family of the latter end of the XXVIth Dynasty. In the work of the first season the shaft was followed until it led into a great chamber cut in the hard limestone rock, where stood two plain stone coffins. The chamber was flooded, two feet deep, with infiltrating water, and the only access was by being slung down the deep shaft at the end of a thin and untrustworthy rope ; so the exploration of the tomb was left for a subsequent season, only the canopic jars being brought away. No one dreamed of the treasure awaiting resurrection at the further side of that rock chamber.

The following season the work was resumed, with two rope ladders to give safer access ; and the first Arab boy who entered the chamber came rushing back at once with a gold-covered amulet in his hand. Mummy after mummy proved to carry upon it a full armoury of these weapons for the defence of the soul in the Underworld. The explorer realised that he had, so to speak, " struck it rich " ; but the work was by no means all pleasure, and Sir Flinders Petrie's own description of it so aptly suggests the difficulties with which the most successful excavation may have to contend that the best way will be to let him largely tell his own story of his conquest. " However delightful such results may be, the circumstances were not attractive. The tomb-chambers were very large . . . and the length of fifty feet was nearly all dark. . . . There was still water nearly waist-deep remaining in the tomb ; and to reach the sarcophagi it was necessary to wade cautiously among the fragments of slippery woodwork which lay about under the water, and to avoid breaking one's shins on floating coffins, while skulls bobbed around on the waves." The results already mentioned repaid the discomfort ; but the triumph and the difficulties of the tomb were only beginning.

On the north side of the long chamber the excavator noticed a small recess, and on examining it carefully, he noticed marks of trowelled mortar, and concluded that something or somebody of importance was walled-up in the recess. When some of the blocks had been removed, one of the Arab boys came running to Petrie's tent crying in great excitement that there were " images as long as a candle " in the recess. The removal of a few more stones allowed the excavator to see the whole of the recess. In the midst of the space stood a stone sarcophagus, on one side of which was a shelf on which stood range after range of beautifully moulded ushabtis. " At the sight of all these the lad who worked this tomb yelled with frantic delight in the echoing chamber, dancing about in the water, and snapping his fingers, beside himself with joy. It was a fascinating view indeed, the two hundred bewigged heads and placid faces all rising out of the water which more than half filled the hollow." . . . " In a few days a boy came up once more, with the news of ' more images,' and a significant nod. On going down I found a recess on the other side of the sarcophagus with a similar garrison of ushabtis."

These are the joys of excavation ; but they were not reached without risks and pains. " Going down Horuta's tomb always reminded me of the descent of Ishtar into Hades ; first I left my coat at the top, then took off my hat last thing before descending, then at the bottom of the shaft I had to leave my trousers and boots, and last of all I often had—as for these ushabtis—finally to part with my shirt, and get under the water to reach the work." The ushabtis, of course, were only the preliminary whet for the great *pièce de résistance* of the tomb—the sarcophagus of Horuta himself. How to handle this great mass of stone in the confined space was a difficult problem. The lid alone of the sarcophagus weighed about seven tons, and could only be moved after it had been cut in two—a process which occupied two masons for six weeks of constant work. At last the lid was shifted so far as to render the inner coffin accessible. " But to stir the inner coffin was beyond all our efforts. It was set tight in a bed of sand in the sarcophagus ; and was so deep beneath the water that only the lid could be reached, the body of the coffin being scarcely touchable at all, even when my head was all but submerged in the salt and acrid water. Of course, I had to sit under the water, on the coffin, to do anything at all ; and the lid of the sarcophagus, weighing three or four tons each piece, could only be tilted just enough to leave room for my head about the middle of one side, between the water and the inside of the large stones. Thus the greater part of the coffin could only be reached by the feet. In this way I cleared out much of the sand packing by scraping with my feet, and lifting out the sand very quietly, for the least current in the water carried it all down again. Still we could not stir the coffin.''

Finally, after iron bolts had been painfully fastened in its sides, and ropes attached to these, with a crowbar to get a purchase on them, a colossal pull was made. '' There was a slight shift. On hearing of this the Arabs pulled more lustily, and howling and hauling, up the coffin came inch by inch, and at last rose, a vast brown mass, out of the water, ' like a buffalo ' as the Arabs said.'' Then came the unveiling of Horuta, whose resurrection had cost so much pains. He proved to be well worth it all. '' On the breast of the mummy, outside all the bandages, was a superb gold *ba* bird, with human head, and outspread wings, all encrusted with minute mosaic of lazuli. Then, after carefully removing all the beads of lazuli, beryl, and silver, which had formed a network over the mummy, we towed the mummy out to the mouth of the tomb, and at the bottom of the well I cut him up. . . . As I cut away the pitch and outer bandages, one after another of the gold amulets came in sight, and our men must have wondered to see me leave them all untouched, as I went on exploring in the wrappings, until the whole group of chest amulets were all exposed in position, and we could note all their relative places as a whole. These were the most gorgeous of all such amulets, a dozen being in solid gold, exquisitely chased and finished, and several of these inlaid *cloisonnée* with minute pieces of lazuli and other stones, all cut exactly to fit the gold ouches, and polished. Lower on the body long strings of hearts and eyes, and scarabs, curved round, with the groups of figures of gods, all delicately carved in lazuli, in the midst. A hundred stone amulets finely wrought and polished lay upon this body, besides the gold ones mentioned, gold plates on fingers and toes, gold bands on the wrists, and a gold sheath between the legs. The whole of this unparalleled series is now in the Cairo Museum." . . . " I only wish," says the explorer, " that every official there could have taken his share of the days of subaqueous work which it cost me to obtain it."

The finding of Horuta has been told in detail not only because it is an outstanding example of the toil which often accompanies excavation, and which is not always rewarded by a find so rich, but also because it gives a notable illustration of the extreme care with which the results of excavation have to be handled if they are to yield the maximum of information. The complete series of Horuta's amulets, with the position in which each one was found carefully noted, was an hundredfold more valuable for the study of Egyptian beliefs than a score of similar series would have been had they been gathered together, without order or system, by a careless discoverer. It was fortunate that the funerary toilet of a great magnate, so amply provided with all that could be needed in the Underworld, should have fallen into the hands of a competent observer.

Horuta, however, priceless as he was, was only one of the prizes, and by no means the most notable, of the Hawara cemetery. The tombs in the cemetery were largely, as we have seen, of Roman times—a period inconceivably modern to the true Egyptologist, and almost beneath his notice, unless he happens to be a hunter of papyri from the Greco-Roman period. " I was going to give it up as not worth working," says the explorer, " when one day a mummy

was found with a painted portrait on a wooden panel placed
over the face. This was a beautifully drawn head of a girl,
in soft grey tints, entirely classical in its style and mode,
without any Egyptian influence. More men were put on
to this region, and in two days another portrait-mummy
was found. . . . Generally three or four were found every
week, and I have even rejoiced over five in one day.
Altogether sixty were found in clearing this cemetery, some
much decayed and worthless, others as fresh as the day
they were painted." The value of this wonderful find was
not in the intrinsic quality of the paintings, though that
was in some cases surprisingly good, when one thinks that
these pictures were only the work of undertakers in a small
provincial town ; it was in the light which was cast upon
Greek painting, of whose methods we were, up to this time,
almost entirely ignorant. Now we are in possession of a
body of material, which, slight though its artistic value
may be, is of infinite value as a revelation of the processes
by which the great Greek painters, Zeuxis, Apelles,
Polygnotus, Parrhasius and the rest, obtained the results
which the Greeks prized as highly as they did the matchless
Greek statuary. To enter into details of the methods of the
Hawara painters would take up more space than we can
spare. We need only note that the painter did his work in
colour mixed with melted wax. It is not strictly encaustic
painting, but a cross between that and the tempera method
of the early Italian painters. " In looking at these portraits,"
says their discoverer, " we must remember that they are only
the work of a remote provincial town, surrounded by
desert, and belong to the latest age of great art, some four
or five centuries after it had reached its zenith. We can
dimly see in them what the great paintings may have been,
as in portraits painted to-day in Nigeria or Mauritius we
might find traces of the methods of Titian or Botticelli.
We can only be thankful that we have anything at all."
The survival of these relics of ancient art we owe to a

curious custom of the time. Apparently the good folks of
Hawara had the habit of having their portraits painted,
while they were living, by the local performer, on canvas,
or more generally on panel. These little pictures, about
15 inches by 13, were then framed in Oxford frames, glazed,
and hung up in the house. When the subject of the picture
died, the portrait was taken down, sent to the embalmer,
trimmed down to a size suitable for insertion in the mummy-
case above the face, and fastened in its position. The
mummy, with the portrait attached, was then brought
home, and stood for a generation or two in one of the rooms
or a lobby of the family house. Eventually it became shabby,
or the family wearied of seeing it standing about. " After
it had become damaged or dirty it was then sent off without
any ceremony, often in a cartload of ancestors, and buried
in the cemetery." The habit seems rather a gruesome
compound of misplaced affection and disrespect ; but we
may be thankful that it existed, for without it we should
have had little or no evidence as to the methods of the ancient
painter.

From Hawara, the explorers turned to Lahun, where
another king of the XIIth Dynasty, Senusert II, had built
the pyramid which now presents an appearance more like
a shapeless Babylonian mound than a pyramid. Such as it
was, however, Lahun was to prove, once and again, one of
the most fruitful of Egyptian sites, unpromising as the
shapeless mound might appear. Twenty-five years later,
the place was to yield one of the memorable treasures of
Egyptian excavation ; but the chief result of this earlier
work (1889-90) was the discovery of the Pyramid-town,
" Hat-hetep-Senusert," " Senusert is satisfied," where the
workers lived while they were building the Pharaoh's
pyramid. Obviously it was impossible to transport workmen to and from this remote site day by day for the long
period during which the pyramid and its complex of temple
and sacred enclosure were being built. The solution was

BACK OF THE PECTORAL OF SENUSERT II, FROM THE TREASURES
OF LAHUN

At Lahun, in 1914, Sir Flinders Petrie and Mr. Guy Brunton discovered a treasure of
Egyptian jewellery of which this breast ornament, in gold and inlay, is one of the
most beautiful pieces. It was suspended round the neck by a necklet of precious, or
semi-precious stones, and was held in position by a counter-weight, also beautifully
wrought. It dates back to XIIth Dynasty (c. 2000 B.C.). (See pp. 109 sq.)
(*Photo by kindness of Sir Flinders Petrie*)

EGYPTIAN USHABTI OR SHAWABTI FIGURES

These little figures of the God Osiris supplied, during the period of the New Empire,
the place taken in pre-historic times by the servants who were slain at the tomb of
their master, and in the Middle Kingdom by models of slaves engaged in various
kinds of labour. (For the description of a notable find of such figures, see pp. 98 sq.)
(*Photo by kindness of Sir Flinders Petrie*)

to establish a small town for them on the spot. Once the
work was over, the need for the maintenance of the town
ceased ; and accordingly excavation revealed at Kahun,
as the place is now called, a practically unaltered town of the
XIIth Dynasty. The walls of the houses, being of crude
brick, had suffered such denudation that it was only the
plan that survived, in general ; but, even so, it was possible
to plan the complete town, covering an area of 18 acres,
with a total of over two thousand rooms, to trace the narrow
streets, or rather alleys, the crowded hovels of the common
workmen, and the more spacious mansions of the foremen
and other officials, and generally to gain an insight into
the conditions of life and work in Egypt two thousand
years before Christ such as one would scarcely have believed
to be possible. The soil of and beneath the floors yielded
specimens of almost every conceivable tool of the Egyptian
workman, from the bow-drill with which he kindled his
domestic fire in the morning to the basket in which he
carried his tools to his work on the pyramid, and the hoe
with which he cultivated his plot of vegetables. Bronze
hand-mirrors showed that his wife did not lack for the
means of adjusting her dress and doing up her back-hair ;
and a pair of ivory castanets suggested that life in Kahun
was not all toil, but that there were music and dancing in
the evenings when work was over. There were manifestly
plenty of children in the little town, and one of the most
vivid helps to the realising of that long-dead life is the
group of children's toys, whip-tops, tip-cats, dolls, draught-
boards, and clay crocodiles and hippopotami, with a clay
boat in which to hunt them. Life in ancient Egypt four
thousand years ago did not differ very much in its essential
elements from life to-day. The charmingly carved ivory
baboon, sitting on the top of an ivory cluster of palm-leaves,
no doubt adorned the walking staff of the pompous clerk
of works, when he went out to take his walks abroad,
and bully his underlings ; or perhaps the staff may have

belonged to the doctor who looked after the health of the town, and who has left us some scraps of a medical papyrus. Altogether a wonderful glimpse into the past, reversing for a little while the current of the " ever-rolling stream " of Time.

Two of the kings of this dynasty, Amenemhat II and Senusert III, had their pyramids at Dahshur, and it was around these that M. J. de Morgan, the famous French excavator, discovered, in the middle of the last decade of the nineteenth century, a cluster of royal tombs belonging to the queens, princes, and princesses of the royal house of this time, which yielded a treasure of goldsmith's work which remained unique until it was matched, twenty-five years later, by the treasure of Lahun. For quantity, of course, both of these treasures have been surpassed by the stores from the tomb of Tutankhamen ; for quality and for delicacy of workmanship and daintiness of design, they have never been matched, nor does it seem likely that anything that Egypt may yet yield will ever surpass them.

De Morgan's wonderful find came to light in two sections, nearly a year elapsing between the two discoveries. On March 6th, 1894, the workmen who had been engaged in clearing the vault of the princesses Sat-hathor and Sent-senb noticed that the soil by the side of the sarcophagus of Sat-hathor had been disturbed, and that a cavity had been dug there in ancient times. A few strokes of the pick brought to view a number of articles of jewellery which had once been stored in a wooden coffer ornamented with gold and silver. The wood, of course, had rotted, and the treasure lay in a heap on the earth. Next day a similar deposit was unearthed a few yards away, close to the sarcophagus of Sent-senb. The following season, ten days' work among three tombs of princesses on the western side of the pyramid of Amenemhat II yielded to M. de Morgan the rest of an amazing treasure-trove.

The find consisted of necklaces of all sorts of precious

and semi-precious stones—jasper, carnelian, green felspar, amazonite, and lapis lazuli, with gold settings, bracelets of gold, enamel and precious stones, golden vases for holding *kohl*, amulets of all sorts in gold and semi-precious stones, the constituent parts of several hand-mirrors in silver or bronze, and innumerable fragments of metal and stone and enamel work which had once belonged to articles of jewellery. But the gems of the collection were the three pectorals or breast-ornaments bearing the cartouches of Senusert II, Senusert III, and Amenemhat III, and the two diadems of the Princess Khnumit. The three pectorals are of gold plate *cloisonnée*, with coloured stones set in the cloisons. The workmanship in all is marvellous in its accuracy ; but it is curious to trace the rapid degeneration of design, even in a period which from first to last does not cover more than fifty years. The pectoral bearing the name of Senusert II is as admirable in design as in execution, simple, dignified and restful ; that of Senusert III, the next in point of date, begins to be overloaded and elaborated, though still by no means a bad design ; the latest in point of time, that of Amenemhat III, is by far the worst, too busy and complicated to be at all satisfactory, however admirable in workmanship.

These pieces are all characteristically Egyptian, and could never be mistaken for anything else. The curious and peculiarly Egyptian charm of balance and formality is very noticeably felt even in regarding the least satisfactory of them. But the diadems of the Princess Khnumit have the beauty which is independent of any associations of time and place, and would be recognised as masterpieces of design and execution in any company. The simpler design is purely formal—a golden band, composed of convention-alised flowers, each pair bearing between them a golden rosette, set with red jasper, carnelian, lapis or green felspar. Between the pairs of flowers are other golden rosettes inlaid with precious stones, and from each rosette another conventionalised flower rises vertically. The whole is a design of singular simplicity and dignity, conceived with a thorough appreciation alike of the possibilities and limitations of the materials employed.

The second diadem is of a totally different quality, as naturalistic as its companion is formal. A light network of golden wires carries on its threads little florets and berries of coloured stone. At six points the threads are gathered up and fastened to Maltese crosses, each of which has a carnelian stud at the joining of the arms, while the four arms of the cross are inlaid with blue. Strictly speaking, perhaps the design is too naturalistic to be quite so satisfying as its more formal companion ; but it is difficult to criticise in the presence of so beautiful a creation, and one feels that Petrie's verdict is justified : " The floret crown is perhaps the most charmingly graceful head-dress ever seen."

The total impression left by such a mass of evidence is overwhelming. We have to realise that to the ancient Egyptian of, roughly speaking, four thousand years ago, our modern civilisation could teach nothing either in design or in executive ability, so far, at least, as the artistic crafts which minister to the love of beauty and luxury are concerned. The Dahshur jewellery puts to shame most of what passes for good work in the same kind at the present day. The implications of such a fact are pretty obvious. There is no surer evidence as to the average level of culture and taste in a community than the character of the less important things which minister to its taste for the beautiful in the small intimacies of life. Judged by such a standard, it is difficult to see how we can deny to the Egyptian of 2000 B.C. the right to be considered at least as highly civilised as the European of the present day—if not to be considered more highly civilised.

Other evidence of a similar character to that from Dahshur came to light in February, 1914, from Lahun, where Professor Petrie, Mr. Guy Brunton, and others were working

at the pyramid of Senusert II, which had already been surveyed, as we have seen, in 1889-90. At the south-east
corner of the pyramid, several tombs, apparently belonging
to members of the royal family, were discovered. They
had all been rifled in ancient days, and proved on the whole,
singularly unproductive. One of the tombs, however, was
to yield a treasure of hitherto unparalleled importance and
value. The tomb itself offered nothing remarkable. It
had been thoroughly plundered by tomb-robbers, who had
pushed back the lid of the red granite sarcophagus as far as
possible, and had then battered away the under edge of the
lid until a hole was made sufficiently large to admit a small
boy ; and by this means everything had been removed.
Nothing was left which seemed worth taking away. On
one side of the sarcophagus, however, there was a small
recess in the rock-wall, which in still more ancient times
had been filled with mud ; and this the robbers evidently
did not think worth investigating. Modern tomb-excavators,
however, are more thorough, or perhaps less hurried, in
their methods than was the ancient plunderer. Stuffed
with mud though the recess was, it had to be searched ;
and on February 10, 1914, some gold beads were discovered
among the mud. Mr. Brunton was at once put on the work
of personally extracting whatever might be concealed in the
recess ; and we have already seen the minuteness of care
with which his task was carried out. When it was completed
Egyptology was in possession of another treasure of XIIth
Dynasty workmanship almost as extensive in quantity as
that of Dahshur, and, if possible, of even superior quality.

The jewellery had belonged to the Princess, Sat-hathor-ant
whose name also occurred at Dahshur, and who may
possibly have been the youngest daughter of Senusert II,
and the wife and queen of Amenemhat III, who was also
her nephew, and whose cartouche appears on one of her
pectorals and on her bracelets. The chief constituents of
the treasure were two pectorals, one bearing the cartouche

actual divine serpent which glittered above the brow of one
of the mightiest of Egypt's Pharaohs, and flashed destruction
on his enemies.

The richest treasures which excavation has brought to
light from this Golden Age of Egyptian history have been,
as is natural, those which have been derived from royal and
princely tombs ; but the great amount of knowledge which
has been accumulated with regard to the conditions of
social life during the period, and the development of religious thought and belief, is mainly due to the excavation
of a large number of Middle Kingdom tombs belonging
to the great nobles and provincial governors, and to the
members of the upper middle class, which was now beginning to provide a large number of recruits for the growing
bureaucracy of Egypt. One of the outstanding characteristics of the Old Kingdom was, as we have seen, the habitual
grouping of the members of the aristocracy around their
king in death, as they had been closely associated with him
in life. The pyramid, with its streets of mastabas, is the
typical feature of the period. In the Middle Kingdom,
this is entirely changed. The national aristocracy is no
longer concentrated at the Court, under the immediate eye
of the Pharaoh, but is dispersed to a great extent over the
land. Each province has its own local magnate, responsible,
indeed, to the Pharaoh at the seat of government, and
perhaps also to a local representative of the royal Treasury,
but bearing this responsibility rather as a dignity added to
that which already belonged to him as virtually a prince in
his own domain. The great baron of the Middle Kingdom
had his own little court, commanded his own little army of
retainers, could set up, on occasion, his own colossal statue
to the glory of his name, and altogether was a notable
specimen of the great country gentleman and feudal
potentate. Having his main interests, not at court, but in
the district where he was the local providence, known and
revered by everybody, probably, with more practical

THE QUEEN'S CROWN FROM THE TREASURE
OF LAHUN

This 4000 years old diadem, beautiful in design and workmanship, is simple when compared with some of the other
discovered diadems, but in its exquisite simplicity is more
satisfying as an example of the refinement of Egyptian
design. (See pp. 110, 111.)

(Photo by kindness of Sir Flinders Petrie)

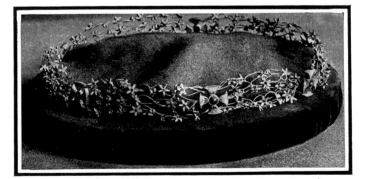

DIADEM OF THE PRINCESS KHNUMIT, FROM DAHSHUR

This exquisite example of the skill of the Egyptian goldsmith of the time of Abraham
(*c.* 2000 B.C.), was found, with the rest of the Treasure of Dahshur, by M. J. de Morgan
(1894–5). The light net-work of gold wire bears florets and berries of semi-precious
stones, while at six points the threads are fastened to golden Maltese crosses, whose
arms are inlaid with blue, inset with a carnelian stud. " The floret crown," says Sir
Flinders Petrie, " is perhaps the most charmingly graceful head-dress ever seen."
(See pp. 107–8.)

reverence than the distant, though formidable, Pharaoh, he quite naturally elected to dwell eternally in the place where he had been known and honoured during his temporal life ; and accordingly the feature of Middle Kingdom funerary practice is that the great baron no longer has his mastaba beside the pyramid of his king, but takes up his eternal habitation among his own people.

This radical change is followed by another, as distinctive, in the type of tomb which is preferred. Pharaoh may still stick to the pyramid type, consecrated by so long a tradition ; but the great lord who rules the Nome of the Oryx or the Hare no longer builds a mastaba, with its tomb-chapel, above the shaft which leads to his eternal abode. His tomb chapel is hewn into the face of the rock which looks down upon the Nile, and the shaft or the sloping pathway, which leads to the actual tomb, far beneath, opens in the middle of the chapel floor. Sometimes the front of the rock, which makes the façade of the tomb, is simply hewn smooth, with a flat terrace in front, on which the door of the tomb-chapel opens ; sometimes the plan is more elaborate, and a pillared portico, its columns hewn out of the living rock, gives access to the actual chapel, whose panelled roof is supported by lofty and well-proportioned columns, whose sixteen sides are slightly fluted, and suggest an early anticipation of the Doric column of the Greeks. The walls of the chapel are covered with painted representations of scenes in which the great man surveys all the activities of his lordship, farming, vine-growing, hunting, fishing, boating, or perhaps receives an embassy of Semites from the desert who come with presents to seek the countenance of the local dignitary. The work which has preserved for us the record of these great Middle Kingdom tombs of the nomarchs can scarcely be called excavation, for the tombs have been well-known from time immemorial. It has been devoted to the endeavour to secure these priceless records from destruction, and to make sure of a complete transcript

H

being made of all that they have to tell us—a transcript which shall survive even when inevitable decay shall have obliterated the originals. This work has been done with the greatest care and patience by various skilled draughtsmen and archæologists, among whom Newberry and Garstang, de Garis Davies, Blackman, Howard Carter, and Blackden deserve to be honourably mentioned ; and its results constitute a living picture of life in ancient Egypt in the days when the great Sesostris ruled the Two Lands, and Abraham was setting out upon his venture of faith.

But if the nomarchs no longer grouped their tombs round the pyramid of their king, they had no objection to seeing the members of their own little courts gathering in death to the side of the baron who had been their local providence in life ; and the desert slope beneath the rock-face whence the pillared portico of the baron's tomb looked out upon the gleaming reaches of the Nile was riddled with the tomb shafts of the great man's dependents—Egyptians of the upper middle class and officials of the local administration. The excavation of these middle-class tombs has been carried on on a very considerable scale at various points ; Garstang, for instance, during his campaigns from 1902 to 1904, investigated 888 tombs of local courtiers and officials in the great Middle Kingdom necropolis which lies beneath the terrace from which the columned tombs of the nomarchs of Beni Hasan, lords of the Oryx Nome, look out over the valley ; while Engelbach, at Riqqeh, in 1912-13, also dealt with a large number of tombs ; and these are only two among many. The results of the excavations have been even more interesting than those of the copyists who have dealt with the pictured work of the nomarch's tombs. For the characteristic feature of these Middle Kingdom inter- ments is the prevalence of an equipment of models—model servants, soldiers, cattle, Nile-boats and boatmen, houses, musicians, and, in short, of everybody and everything which the dead man could be supposed to need or to wish in the spirit world. These models take, in the Middle Kingdom, the place which was filled in the New Empire by the " Ushabtis," or " respondents," and were supposed, like them, to relieve the man who was provided with them of the necessity of doing his own work in the world beyond death. We have seen how a great noble of the late period, like Horuta, might carry a matter of 400 ushabtis with him to his tomb, to secure ample leisure in the next world ; and the Middle Kingdom equipment of the models which were the anticipation of the ushabtis was often quite as elaborate.

Moreover, it was much more interesting. The true ushabti follows almost a standard pattern, and when you have seen one of the little mummy-Osiris figures, with its crook and flail held in the little hands which emerge from the bandages, you have seen what is repeated, with scarcely a variation, in hundreds and thousands of similar figures ; but the Middle Kingdom models, though they also are mainly variations on a few standard themes, are really variations, and deal with their themes with such vivacity and variety that the effect is charming, as well as instructive. Those who have seen such models, for instance, as the XIth Dynasty set which came from the tomb of Mehenkwetre, chancellor of the Pharaoh Mentuhotep, and are since 1920 to be seen partly in the museum at Cairo and partly in the Metropolitan Museum of New York, have seen Egyptian life of 2000 B.C. set before them with infinitely more vivacity than any words could ever picture it with ; and there are many similar sets, scarcely inferior to these charming groups. Mehenkwetre had a whole fleet of boats to serve his needs on the spiritual Nile—boats with sails and canopies to carry him swiftly southwards when the north wind blew, and boats with sails and mast lowered, and rowers straining at the oars, to take him down stream against the wind, boats where an armed champion stood in the bow in place of the leadsman, to guard his master against danger, and boats which towed a seine net between them, to provide him with plenty of fish.

In front of a pillared verandah, the great man sits, and sees his model cattle, " ringstraked, speckled and grisled," driven past him by model herdsmen, while model scribes beside him count the beasts and note their condition. His model villa, with beautifully columned front, opens on a flowery garden, such as the Egyptians always loved ; while models of granaries, bakehouses, breweries, looms, provide for every conceivable physical want, and skilled musicians discourse sweet music to soothe his spirit. No land or period has given us so vivid and attractive pictures of every aspect of its social life as has Egypt of the Middle Kingdom in these delightful models.

From such elaborate equipments as that of Mentuhotep's chancellor, the scale ranges downwards, until the poorer interments may only be provided with one or two models, and those of the roughest execution ; but the amount of material thus acquired is enormous, and its value as first-hand evidence for the details of life in Egypt four thousand years ago is inestimable. What would archæologists not give for corresponding sets of figures of each land and period of the ancient world, strictly contemporary, as are these, and therefore beyond question as to the truth of their details ?

One of the Middle Kingdom tombs excavated by Engelbach at Riqqeh supplied evidence of a different and more gruesome kind, as to the antiquity of the estimable Egyptian custom of tomb-robbery. The tomb in question yielded a fair quantity of Middle Kingdom jewellery, not of the same quality, indeed, as the treasures of Dahshur or Lahun, but still of considerable value ; but it also yielded something which was much more interesting—the evidence of how it came about that the jewellery had not been carried away. When it was opened, the tomb-chamber was found to be blocked by about twelve tons of marl, which had fallen in through the collapse of the roof. When this was removed, two bodies were found locked in one another's arms, and lying across the coffin. The one was that of the legitimate tenant of the tomb—the other, that of a tomb-robber, who had got the dead man out of his coffin, and was beginning to unwrap the body in search of its jewellery, when righteous judgment overtook him, and the collapse of the roof left him with the corpse of his victim in his arms, to wait nearly four thousand years for the stroke of the pick which should let in the light of day upon his evil-doing and its deserved punishment. If a similar judgment were to overtake all the unauthorised tomb-plunderers of modern Egypt, one fears that the fellah population would suffer serious and speedy diminution !

One other most important result of modern excavation with regard to the Middle Kingdom has been the full establishment of the process of democratization which characterises the Egyptian faith of this period as distinguished from that of the Old Kingdom, with regard to the question of immortality. It would perhaps be too much to assert that in the Old Kingdom belief immortality was the exclusive privilege of the Pharaoh ; for the very earliest burials of all ranks, with their universal provision, greater or smaller, for the needs of the dead man in the Under world, testify to a deep-rooted faith in immortality of some kind for all ; but at least we may safely say that the Old Kingdom creed started Pharaoh on his spiritual journey with an equipment which was reserved for him alone, and without which his subjects must have been sorely handicapped. The XIIth Dynasty interments show us that this inequality had been recognised, and was in process of being dealt with on a broader basis. Instead of the religious texts of the period being limited to the utterances which were inscribed on the walls of the tomb-chambers of the pyramids (the Pyramid Texts), we now find that the coffins of the middle-class interments of the Middle Kingdom bear long inscriptions containing all that was held to be necessary to the welfare of their occupants in the world after death.

These texts—the " Coffin Texts," which fill for this period the place that the Pyramid Texts filled in the Old Kingdom, and that the Book of the Dead will fill in the still greater democratization of religion in the New Empire, are of the greatest value for the study of Egyptian religion. They show us the stage when the common man was beginning to assert his claim to a share in the blessings which had formerly been held to be the exclusive property of Pharaoh ; but they also show that the movement had only advanced a single stage. Immortality had descended from the throne to the middle class ; but the undistinguished vulgar had as yet no share in it—or, perhaps we had better say, had no share in the facilities which made its attainment more or less a certainty for their betters. The rich man might be " wafted to the skies on flowery beds of ease " ; the poor man had to get to heaven, if he got there at all, as he best could.

CHAPTER V

THE GLORY OF THE EMPIRE : THEBES OF THE LIVING

WITH the notable exceptions of such finds as those of Dahshur and Lahun, most of the sensational discoveries of excavation in our time have been connected with the great imperial city which was for five hundred years the focus of the empire's life. Thebes rises from the position of a comparatively obscure provincial town to the foremost place in the land about 1600 B.C. From that date to about 1100 B.C. she was supreme ; and these five centuries were the time when Egypt was the cardinal power of the Near East, and the dominant figure of ancient history. Under the great Pharaohs of the XVIIIth Dynasty, who lavished upon her the wealth which flowed in from Syrian conquest and Nubian tribute, Thebes rapidly grew into a splendour which made her the fitting capital for the growing empire, and as she has been called, " the first monumental city of antiquity." One great aspect of her glory was, indeed, essentially evanescent. Her civil architecture, the palaces of the Pharaohs, the buildings of the administration, the mansions of the nobles and high officials, to say nothing of the multitude of houses belonging to the middle and lower classes, and the hovels of the poor, were all composed, according to immemorial Egyptian practice, of nothing more durable than crude brick. Some of them might be of vast extent ; they might be exquisitely decorated with the finest work of the Egyptian artist, and furnished with the costliest and most tasteful furniture ; but they were never designed for endurance. They were only meant to serve their time ; and, even in such a climate as that of

Upper Egypt, that time was short. Consequently, whatever may have been the splendour of the civil architecture of Thebes, it has practically entirely vanished. A few fragments of painted work from the ruined palace of Amenhotep III, on the western bank of the Nile, survive, to suggest to us how pleasant and restful the scheme of decoration must have been ; beyond that we have to try to reconstruct our picture of Thebes from the innumerable pictures of domestic architecture which are given us in the paintings of the Theban tombs.

The case is entirely different, however, with regard to the religious architecture of the city. The Egyptian might, like a sensible man, build his own house to serve his own time ; but the time of the gods was forever, and their houses had to be constructed of " stones of eternity," as he called the noble materials of which he was so great a master. Mud brick might do for Pharaoh's earthly house ; but either for Pharaoh's temple, or for the temples of his brother or father gods nothing would suffice but hard sandstone, and fine grained limestone, with granite of Aswan for purposes of adornment. Consequently, while the palaces and mansions of Thebes have long since gone back to the earth from which they came, the temples of the city have been the wonder and the admiration of the world for more than three thousand years. It is mere nonsense to talk, as a recent writer does, of the Theban temples as though they needed to be discovered by excavation in modern times. Nothing save a convulsion of Nature could ever hide them. In Babylonia or in Mesopotamia, vast temples may be so smothered in the products of their own denudation and the desert sand as to be absolutely unrecognisable beneath their shapeless mounds ; but it was never so with the great Egyptian temples, save in the Delta, where they were first ruined by the ceaseless blasts of war, and then smothered in the Delta alluvium. The great temples of the Upper Valley were, indeed, stripped of much of their splendour,

and sorely defaced. In more than one case, they were
practically carried away stone by stone to be used in new
construction. But the vast columns and courts of Karnak
and Luxor, to say nothing of a dozen temples only less than
these, seemed to defy time and the spoiler alike. " Mariette,"
says a recent book, " who, going up to Thebes, saw a few
columns sticking up out of the sand at Karnak, and began
to excavate the site." It would be difficult to conceive a
more entire misrepresentation of the actual situation. Here
is Belzoni's description of what he saw at Karnak in 1817,
forty years before Mariette laid a hand upon the site. " A
forest of enormous columns, adorned all round with beautiful figures, and various ornaments, from the top to the
bottom ; the graceful shape of the lotus, which forms their
capitals, and is so well proportioned to the columns that it
gives to the view the most pleasing effect ; the gates, the
walls, the pedestals, and the architraves, also adorned in
every part with symbolical figures in basso relievo and
intaglio, representing battles, processions, triumphs, feasts,
offerings, and sacrifices . . . the sanctuary, wholly formed
of red granite, with the various obelisks standing before it,
proclaiming to the distant passenger, ' Here is the seat of
holiness ' ; the high portals, seen at a distance from the
openings to this vast labyrinth of edifices ; the various
groups of ruins of the other temples within sight ; these
altogether had such an effect upon my soul, as to separate
me in imagination from the rest of mortals . . . and cause
me to forget entirely the trifles and follies of life." Pretty
well for " a few columns sticking out of the sand." The
source of so ludicrous a misrepresentation of the state of
Karnak in the middle of the nineteenth century, is, of course,
that the writer has confused Mariette's work at Karnak
with his work at Sakkara, where he did actually see, not a
column, but the head of a sphinx, and part of a libation-tablet
" sticking out of the sand," and was led in consequence to the
discovery of the great underground vaults of the Serapeum.

Karnak never needed to be discovered. Its magnificent ruins asserted themselves in defiance of the assaults of man or time. Much excavating work has indeed had to be done at the temples of Thebes, and has revealed a wealth of priceless material, artistic and historic ; but the main work here is not so much the discovery of what was unknown, as the preservation of what is already well known. Sometimes the excavation which is necessary to the process of securing the stability and security of the buildings has led to very valuable and unexpected results, as when in 1903, M. Legrain, in the course of excavations rendered necessary in connection with his tremendous task of ensuring the stability of Karnak, came upon what has since been known as " The Karnak Cachette," a huge pit filled with pieces of sculpture of all types and periods. " Seven hundred stone monuments have already come out of the water," wrote Maspero, in 1905, " and we are not yet at the end. Statues whole and in fragments, busts, mutilated trunks, headless bodies, bodiless heads, vases on which there were only broken feet, Pharaohs enthroned, queens standing upright, priests of Amon . . . in all the attitudes of their profession or rank, in limestone, in black or pink granite, in yellow or red sandstone, in green breccia, in schist, in alabaster—indeed, a whole population returns to the upper air and demands shelter in the galleries of the Museum."

Such a find is, of course, unusual, though it would be hard to say what wonders may yet lie concealed beneath the ruins of Karnak. How the great temple can help the modern student to reconstruct (literally) the past is seen in the fact that at the present time it is proposed to rebuild the Aten temple at Thebes, which was Akhenaten's declaration of war against Amen, out of the blocks which Horemheb stole from it for the building of his pylon at Karnak. Excavation, moreover, has taught us a great deal about the details of the magnificence of the temples by means of the various building inscriptions which have come to light, and which describe the great buildings as they stood in their pristine glory. We learn from these un-questionable sources to discard our old conception of an Egyptian temple as one of the most sombre and austere of human creations, impressive simply by bulk and mass, and to substitute for it a conception of gorgeousness beyond description, a blaze of brilliant colour under the dazzling Egyptian sunlight, doors of cedar, overlaid with bronze, and inlaid with gold, floors overlaid with silver, steles incrusted with gold and jewels—and, towering above all, the slender red granite obelisks with their gleaming caps of gold-silver alloy, and the vast statues, sometimes in granite, sometimes in gritstone, limestone or sandstone. Karnak and Luxor are almost the most impressive buildings in the world to-day, in their desolate majesty, and it is quite possible that the impression which they make would not be increased but rather diminished if we could see them as they were when Thebes was a living city ; all the same, if we wish to think of them as the Egyptian of the Empire thought of them, we have to think of them in terms of colour, as he did, and to realise that what we see to-day is but the stripped skeleton of the splendour of the past.

The royal palaces, as we have seen, had nothing in their structure to compare with the houses of the gods. Their beauty was not that of imposing mass of superb materials, but of tasteful interior decoration and sumptuous furniture. The palace of the most gorgeous of all the Pharaohs, Amenhotep III, already mentioned, has been excavated twice within recent years. We are to imagine a low, rambling, wide-spreading brick building faced with white stucco, by no means imposing in outward appearance, and not for a moment to be compared with the pretentious splendours of an Assyrian palace, or with the vast Labyrinth which the kings of the House of Minos were rearing in Crete. Sennacherib or Ashur-bani-pal would have thought himself poorly lodged in the mud-brick mansion which the wealthiest monarch of the wealthiest of earthly empires deemed sufficient for his needs. But within the walls, there was abundance of beauty and richness to make up for the lack of external impressiveness. The white walls glowed with soft colour, and the Egyptian's passionate love for nature and the open air found expression on every side in fresco paintings, executed with the best skill of the time, of scenes from the life of woodland, marsh, and river. On the ceilings, birds fluttered across the blue sky, while the floors were gay with representations of pond and marsh life. Recent excavations in the Valley of the Kings have given us many actual specimens of the furniture which Pharaoh used in these beautiful rooms. Its style we knew already from contemporary pictures of it ; now we can see the arm-chairs in which Amenhotep may have sat when he came to visit Prince Iuaa and Princess Tuiu, the father and mother of his much loved wife Queen Tiy, the caskets in which royal and princely jewels were kept, the gilded chariots in which the Pharaoh or a great prince of the empire drove abroad through the city, the state collars which the great man wore, the walking sticks which he used when he took his walks abroad, the very gloves that he wore. Altogether Pharaoh's great house, if less pretentious than that of an Assyrian king, was proportionately more tasteful ; and again one wonders if our modern civilisation can show anything better in the way of housing a man amidst comfort and beauty than this ancient empire had attained 3500 years ago.

The houses of the great nobles and officials repeated on a smaller scale the characteristics of that of their master. The Egyptian noble could be gorgeous enough on occasion ; but he came of too old a stock to riot in tasteless and barbaric gaudiness, and his motto was *simplex munditiis*. All this abundance of comfort and good taste had, of course, a background by no means so admirable, and Thebes, like all other great cities, had its slums, and its poor quarters, where the proletariat huddled together in mud hovels separated from each other by narrow and filthy alleys ; but the great city must have gained unusual beauty from the thoroughly Egyptian proclivity for bringing the beauty of the country into the midst of the town. Each mansion was surrounded by its pleasance, with trees, flower-beds and pergolas, and its sheet of ornamental water, dotted with water-lilies and other aquatic plants.

Altogether, one imagines Thebes as the noblest city of the ancient world. Babylon, no doubt, was as great or greater, and it is scarcely possible to imagine a more gorgeous piece of monumental town-planning than the splendid Procession-street of Nebuchadnezzar's capital, with its endless vista of enamelled bulls and lions, and its towering Ishtar Gate, where the bull and the dragon glittered alternately from the walls in brilliant colour ; but Babylon had nothing to parallel the material of which the vast temples of Thebes were built, or to match the solid magnificence of Karnak and Luxor. Even Etemenanki and Esagila, one imagines, vast as they are, would have looked cheap beside the sumptuousness of Karnak. In this connection, it may be noted that the Egyptian, though he thoroughly appreciated the value of his beautiful granites, used them far less extensively and far more discriminately than is often imagined. Many people seem to imagine that the Egyptian built mainly in granite. Wonderful worker of hard stone as he was, such a thing would have been quite beyond his powers ; nor would he ever have shown such bad taste as is shown in some of our pretentious modern edifices which seem to be plastered with granite facings and columns, without regard to fitness, the one idea, apparently, being to make the building look as costly as possible. The Egyptian architect had more sense, and better taste. For the main of his work he used ordinary workaday stone, such as sand-stone or limestone, of both of which he had abundance in the great quarries of Silsileh and Turah. The pyramids of Gizeh, for instance, are of limestone, and the Hypostyle Hall at Karnak is of sandstone. The nobler stones, granite, red, black, and grey, diorite and basalt, breccia, and porphyry he used much more sparingly, reserving them not for extensive structural work, but for purposes of adornment, where the quality of the material would have its full value— for lintels and door-posts in conspicuous positions, for obelisks, shrines, and colossal statues.

The question of how the Egyptians extracted from the quarry and transported to their ultimate resting-place the great stones which they so frequently used in their buildings, or for the monumental sculpture which adorned them, has always been one of great interest, and has had a considerable amount of light thrown upon it by some of the latest results of excavation. Egyptian building practice, it ought to be noted, was by no means always megalithic. In fact, the common idea with regard to the use of huge blocks in Egyptian buildings is almost as much exaggerated as with regard to the use of granite. The great bulk of building in Egypt is done with stone of quite reasonable size, and the great blocks are reserved for special uses, where they are employed freely and with immense effect. When the Egyptian did use great blocks, however, he did it upon a scale in which he has had no rival. Stones of from forty to one hundred tons weight are used with a frequency which shows that the handling of such weights presented merely a problem of common practice ; the casing-blocks of the Great Pyramid, the architraves of many of the pillared halls of the great temples, and the roofing-blocks which these bear, all evidence the familiarity of the Egyptian builder with the question of moving weights which modern builders, despite their advantages in mechanical means, would be very chary of dealing with. But it is when we come to the finer stones which were used for the purposes of adornment or monumental sculpture already referred to that we begin to realise the Egyptian's almost uncanny faculty for handling weights which seem almost beyond the power of man.

We have seen that the pyramid-chamber of Amenemhat III was one single block of hard yellow quartzite, weighing 110 tons, and it seems sufficiently wonderful that such a mass of hard stone should have been hewn with mathematical accuracy and transported into the position which it now occupies in the heart of a pyramid ; but such weights were of the lesser order of magnitude in Egyptian practice. The next order is that of the granite obelisks which were the standard decoration of the façades of the temples. Of these the most ancient yet extant, the obelisk of the vanished temple of Ra (XIIth Dynasty) at Heliopolis, weighs 121 tons, that of Thothmes I at Karnak 143 tons, Cleopatra's Needle at London 187 tons, and its twin at New York 193 tons, the obelisk of the Place de la Concorde at Paris 227 tons, and its companion before the pylon of Rameses II at Luxor 254 tons, Hatshepsut's splendid shaft at Karnak 323 tons, the Vatican obelisk, Rome, 331 tons, and that of the Lateran, Rome, 455 tons. These weights are sufficiently impressive ; but they are not the greatest which the Egyptian quarrymasters handled. There lies at Aswan a partly wrought obelisk whose extraction from the quarry was never completed because of flaws which were found in the stone as the shaping of it proceeded. The length of this block is 137 feet, or 32·4 feet greater than that of the Lateran obelisk, while it measures 13·8 feet square at the base, against the 9·8 of the Lateran. Its weight is calculated to be 1,168 tons. If it be objected that this stone was not moved, the answer is that the reason of that was not any question of mechanical inability, but the flaws in the block ; and that stones quite comparable with it in weight were moved repeatedly for hundreds of miles, not only to Thebes, but to far-distant Tanis in the eastern Delta. The so-called "Memnon" Colossi of Amenhotep III, on the western plain at Thebes, were of gritstone (conglomerate) from a quarry near Cairo, and are computed to weigh about 700 tons. They are surpassed in weight, however, by the ninety foot granite colossus which Rameses II erected at Tanis, and which must have weighed at least 900 tons ; while the sitting colossus at the Ramesseum, though not so lofty as its standing brother at Tanis, was heavier, and probably touched the thousand tons.

Wonderful theories of lost triumphs of mechanical invention have been often suggested to account for the moving and erection of such monstrous masses of stone ; but modern excavation has made it fairly certain that the means which the Egyptians employed were of a simplicity as remarkable as the feats which they accomplished by the use of them. Of contemporary evidence there is next to none. One picture from El Bersheh gives us the transport of a 60 ton colossal statue of the nomarch Tahuti-hetep, which is being dragged along upon a sledge by a gang of 172 men, and the famous series of sculptures at Der el-Bahri shows us that a similar sledge was used for the land part of the transport of Hatshepsut's great obelisks. Transport down the river was accomplished, according to the same sculptures, by means of a huge barge, on which the two obelisks were placed butt to butt. The barge was towed by three rows of tow-boats, each row consisting of nine rowing-boats, with a pilot boat at the head of the row. It has been calculated by the late Mr. Francis Elgar, Director of Naval Construction, that Hatshepsut's two great obelisks could be carried on a barge about 220 feet long by 69 feet beam, with a draft of water of from 4 feet 6 inches to 5 feet ; and though this may seem a huge vessel for the time, it has to be remembered that the Egyptian boat-builders were quite competent to build such craft at a much earlier stage of their history. Fifteen hundred years before the time of Hatshepsut, Seneferu built vessels of 170 feet in length, while the great barge of Amen, in the reign of Rameses III, measured 224 feet.

During the winter of 1922, Mr. Engelbach, on behalf of
the Service of Antiquities, excavated the great unfinished
obelisk of Aswan to which reference has already been made,
so that the details of the ancient work upon it can now be
seen as the huge stone lies, still attached to its bed, in the
quarry. Mr. Engelbach's results are of the greatest interest.
He has shown that the long prevalent idea that the long
blocks for the obelisks were detached from their beds by
means of a long row of wooden wedges, which were wetted
simultaneously, and split the stone away by their swelling,
must be abandoned. The Aswan obelisk was being detached
from its bed, not by any such picturesque processes, not
even by cutting by means of chisels, but by plain unromantic hammering—" bashing," Mr. Engelbach prosaic-
ally calls it, which was done with dolerite balls attached to
wooden rammers, and gradually wore a trench along the
length of the obelisk. The trenches by which the obelisk
was being cut out can still be seen, with the rough marks
of the rammers perfectly visible, while dolerite balls, whole
and broken, are found in abundance on the site. Mr.
Engelbach suggests that a gang of 130 men worked in each
trench on an obelisk of this size, with two men handling
the rammers above for each man in the bottom of the trench,
and that with a working staff on this scale, and working
continuously in a system of shifts, the work could be done
quite comfortably within the time of seven months which
Queen Hatshepsut affirms to have been the time taken for
the work upon her obelisks. A gang of 1500 men, using
20 feet levers of wood, would be able to raise the obelisk
sufficiently to allow of its being removed from the quarry,
while 6000 men would be sufficient to handle the mass
during its removal down the valley to the barge.

As to the actual erection, we know very little, though
Mr. Engelbach's suggestion of a ramp of sand over the
prepared pedestal, up which ramp the obelisk was hauled
on its sledge, the sand being then gradually withdrawn

I

from beneath the butt of the obelisk until the great shaft
gradually settled upon its base, is in accordance with all the
other existing evidence as to the masterly simplicity of
Egyptian methods.   Nowhere does there exist any evidence
for the existence of ancient mechanical appliances whose
secret has now been lost.   Ancient Egyptian triumphs in
the erection of these vast masses of stone were triumphs,
not of mechanics, but of organisation, in which magnificent
directing intelligence guided the labour of thousands of
perfectly trained men to efforts whose amount and limit had
been anticipated and allowed for, and whose end had been
foreseen.   The idea of brute force and unintelligent slave
labour is as wide of the mark as that of mysterious mechanical
resources ;   slave labour, with its stupid multiplication of
brute force, could only have led to more unmitigated
disaster.   The Egyptian handling of obelisks and colossi
was a business of skilled intellect organising and controlling
skilled labour.

CHAPTER VI

THE GLORY OF THE EMPIRE : THEBES OF THE DEAD

MUCH as we have learned from modern research concerning Thebes of the living, we have learned far more about Thebes of the dead, and we know that it was yet more magnificent than the great city on the eastern bank of the Nile. The modern traveller sees the western plain of Thebes, with its cultivation, and its background of the desert and the Libyan hills, the Memnon Colossi rising out of green crops, or mirrored in the water of the inundation, the ruined splendours of the Ramesseum, and the rest of the long line of funerary temples, stretching from Qurneh to Medinet Habu with its pylons and colonnades. In the background the great cliffs of Der el-Bahri rise in an amphitheatre behind the white terraces of Hatshepsut's temple, with the wrecks of Mentuhotep's earlier building beside them. Everywhere for a background rise the slopes and cliffs of the Libyan hills, honeycombed with gaping black tomb-mouths, and that is all. Excavation has enabled us to reconstruct a huge city of the dead, even more imposing than its rival city of the living on the other side of the river. The Western Thebes has its long row of temples, some of them almost as great as Karnak, and perhaps even more gorgeous, its streets of tombs, not, as now, rifled and gaping wide to show the desolation within, but each duly furnished with its tomb-chapel, gay with white stucco and bright colour, and periodically visited by a crowd of worshipping friends, who bring their offerings and their inevitable bouquets of flowers to rejoice the spirits of the dead within the tomb. Houses for the living are not lacking in this great city of the dead, for the work of the necropolis requires a large resident population of workmen, stonehewers, sculptors for the delicate relief work of the tombs, and painters for the frescoes, carpenters, and metal workers of all sorts for the other furnishings, and in especial scribes, a shifty and unscrupulous lot, who furnish the copies of the various sacred books, the Book of the Dead, the Book of the Gates, the Book of Breathings, the Book of Knowing what is in the Underworld, one or other of which is deemed indispensable for the dead on their long journey. Everywhere the white-robed and shaven priests of the necropolis are coming and going—a set of the greatest rascals who ever betrayed a sacred trust, as the discovered records show. Altogether, the population of the necropolis has a somewhat unsavoury reputation ; and the Mayor of the Western City finds ample employment for the staff of policemen with which he is provided, and who have their work cut out to keep order on the not infrequent occasions when the notoriously turbulent necropolis workmen go on strike, or to handle affairs when thieving among the tombs becomes too flagrant and some show of checking it has to be made. Unfortunately for the reputation of Western Thebes, excavation has made us rather too well acquainted with the actual state of affairs in what ought to have been the most solemn and decorous of cities, and we know, from the Amherst, Abbott, Mayer and other papyri, that the whole administration of the city of the tombs, from the Mayor and the priesthood downwards to the commonest of the necropolis workmen, was absolutely rotten, so that not a single tomb, from that of the proudest of the Pharaohs to that of the humblest of his subjects, was safe from sacrilegious intrusion. The business of tomb-robbery was thoroughly organised, with the men who were most responsible for the security of the tombs most deeply concerned in the ghoulish trade, so that when the Mayor of Eastern Thebes, who fortunately for the interests of decent folk, seems to have had as little love for his rival on the western bank as the mayors of rival towns usually have for one another, tried to secure a genuine investigation into the scandalous state of affairs on the western bank, he had half the bureaucracy of Thebes against him, and made as little of his honest attempt as such reformers generally do. It is curious to realise that we know more about the affairs of the two cities, and their relations with one another, than was known by any of the citizens of either of them, save a handful of the officials of high rank, who were in the heart of the " know," either as investigators or as culprits. Perhaps we know more than even they did ; for we have all the cards on the table at once, whereas they only saw a little at a time, and with long intervals between the instalments.

This western city of Thebes is the area in which excavation has been most persistent in modern times, and in which it has won some of its greatest triumphs. The long row of funerary temples, stretching like the cord of a bow across the great amphitheatre of the Libyan hills, from Qurneh to Medinet Habu, need not detain us long, imposing though it may be. The chief treasure that they have yielded to the excavator has been the famous black granite stele which Merenptah stole from the temple of Amenhotep III, and set up, with a new inscription of his own, in his own temple, where it was found by Petrie, during his excavations in 1896. The stele possesses a double value. Its original inscription tells us the story of the vanished glories of Amenhotep's funerary temple ; the inscription of Merenptah, on the back of the slab, is the song of triumph with which Merenptah celebrated his victories over the Libyans and Syrians, and in which occurs that mention of Israel, which was so long craved by scholars, and which, since its discovery, has made confusion worse confounded in our ideas of the early history of the Chosen People.

These funerary temples, it should be remembered, take

the place, in the New Empire, of the Pyramid Temples of the more ancient Pharaohs ; and when we come to deal with the Valley of the Kings, we shall see the reason for the separation of the temple from the tomb to which it belongs.

Behind the temples lie the innumerable tombs of officials and private persons, beginning at Drah Abu 'l Negga, and stretching by Shekh Abd el-Qurneh, to Qurnet Murrai, while, further west still, lies the group known as the Tombs of the Queens. These tombs have been the scene of wholesale pillage for ages. The fellah of the Theban district is by immemorial tradition a tomb-robber, and thinks no more of " conveying " antiquities from the tombs of his ancestors than we would do of plucking a wild flower by the wayside. At a very early stage of the development of European interest in ancient Egypt, he learned that there was a demand for papyri, as the most convenient and portable form of " antika," and in the early part of the nineteenth century countless tombs were rifled, and countless mummies stripped and destroyed in the search for rolls of the marketable material. To-day an unrifled tomb at Thebes would be something next door to a miracle.

Nevertheless, the tombs themselves still remain, and, though most of them have suffered disastrously at the hands of the Qurnawis, many of them are of surpassing interest, on account of the extremely vivid pictures of Egyptian life under the Empire which they present.

The most important group is that of Shekh Abd el-Qurneh, lying behind the Ramesseum, and between it and Hatshepsut's temple at Der el-Bahri. Here the great court dignitaries and officials of the XVIIIth Dynasty mostly made their tombs, and some of the names with which we meet are those of men who played a great part in the making of imperial Egypt. One of the first tombs we come to is that of Rames (Ramose) who was vizier to Akhenaten, and whose inscriptions here show that he must have been one of the earliest converts to the king's new faith of Atenism. The tomb was never finished, for Rames followed his royal master to Tell el-Amarna, and made himself another tomb there. On the one side of the tomb of Rames lies that of Khaemhat, superintendent of the royal granaries to Akhenaten's father, Amenhotep III. Its exquisite low reliefs are among the very finest products of the Egyptian art of the New Empire. On the other side lies the tomb of Nakht, dating from earlier in the dynasty, and containing paintings as vivacious as the sculptures of Khaemhat. Behind these tombs we come upon what Breasted has called " the most important private monument of the Empire," the tomb of Rekhmara, who was vizier to Thothmes III, and whose pictures of the representatives of all the quarters of the world coming to bring gifts to his master are of the utmost value as historical documents. At the top of the hill lies the tomb of the great man of the preceding reign, Senmut, who was Queen Hatshepsut's factotum, and who built for her the great terraced temple of Der el-Bahri, and set up the two noble obelisks at Karnak. The value of Senmut's much-defaced tomb lies, like that of Rekhmara, in its pictures of the men of various lands offering gifts. Practically all these tombs originally conformed to a single type. They consist of a vestibule, whose roof is often supported by columns, and beyond this a corridor, which terminates in a recess, in which the statues of the dead man were set up. In front of the vestibule, there was an open forecourt, where offerings were made to the dead. The wall pictures, apart from those which, as already mentioned, relate to foreign lands, represent almost every phase of Egyptian life and work in the period of the Empire, and illustrate it as fully as that of the Old Kingdom is illustrated by the mastaba sculptures.

Close to the north-eastern end of the great amphitheatre of the Theban necropolis, and the tombs of Drah Abu 'l Negga, opens the pathway to the Valley which since 1922 has been the most famous bit of ground in Egypt—perhaps in the world—the Valley of the Tombs of the Kings. In this lonely and barren valley there were buried at least thirty of the Pharaohs of Egypt, many of them of that great period when Egypt was easily the foremost power in the Near East, and when the kings of Babylon, Assyria, Mitanni and other great kingdoms were tumbling over one another for a share in the golden stream which flowed from Egypt. Actually the claims of the Valley to fame date only from round about 1500 B.C., that is to say, it is comparatively modern, as things go in Egypt ; but for at least five hundred years from that time the close of each successive reign saw a fresh addition to the store of wealth and artistic treasure which was steadily accumulating in the place, till it may be questioned if there has ever been a spot on earth in which there has been gathered together so much material not only valuable intrinsically, but absolutely priceless historically and artistically. The limelight was, of course, turned upon the Valley of the Kings by the discovery of November, 1922, when Mr. Howard Carter, excavating on behalf of the late Lord Carnarvon, came upon the tomb of the Pharaoh Tutankhamen, one of the less important, and less well-known Pharaohs of the latter end of the XVIIIth Dynasty ; but for many years, as we shall see, the Valley has been the centre of interest in Theban excavation, and the scene of many of the most remarkable finds. We have seen how the practice of the Pharaohs, with regard to tomb-building, varies at different periods of Egyptian history. From the great underground chambers of Abydos, we have passed to the pyramids of the Gizeh group, where security was sought in the protection of vast masses of stone ; and from them to the smaller pyramids of the Middle Kingdom, whose lesser bulk concealed elaborate devices of false passages and chambers all designed to weary out and deceive the tomb-robber. The later Pharaohs of the Middle Kingdom, and the Theban princes of the troubled period

THE TWO TERRACED TEMPLES AT DER EL-BAHRI

This picture shows the two great funerary Temples among the Libyan cliffs at
Der el-Bahri opposite Thebes. The farther and older one is that of the Pharaoh
Mentuhotep, XIth Dynasty. The nearer one was built by the famous Queen Hatshepsut of the XVIIIth Dynasty. The credit for originality of design must be given to
the older temple. (See pp. 131 *sq.*)

(Photo by the kindness of Mr. S. R. K. Glanville, British Museum.)

EXCAVATION IN PROGRESS AT DER EL-BAHRI

Excavation in progress on the approaches to the later Temple. (See pp. 131 *sq.*)

(Photo by kindness of Rev. P. B. Fraser, Hokitika, New Zealand.)

which followed it, still maintained the pyramid tradition, though with variations, and with a general decrease in the scale of the funerary monument, corresponding to the diminished glory and resources of the kings concerned. One and all, however, these great tombs, whatever their type, had entirely failed in the object for which they were designed. Not even the vastest of them succeeded in protecting Pharaoh from the greed of his subjects. The pertinacity of the robber, aided, no doubt, in most cases by the treachery of the priests who should have guarded the dead, broke through all defences ; the mummy was stripped of all its treasures and broken up or burnt, with the most disastrous results, according to the Egyptian belief, on the destiny of the dead king in the Underworld. " At the beginning of the XVIIIth Dynasty," says Mr. Howard Carter, " there was hardly a king's tomb in the whole of Egypt that had not been rifled—a somewhat grisly thought to the monarch who was choosing the site for his own last resting-place." It was quite obvious that the old idea, with its splendid group of tomb and temple together, had completely failed. Something had to be sacrificed ; and if security were to be attained, then splendour would have to go. Whatever might be done with regard to the funerary temple, where the rites were performed, the actual tomb must be hidden away in some obscure place, where the robber was less likely to find it.

No doubt it cost the Pharaoh upon whom this idea first dawned a good deal of thought and worry before he could make up his mind to a step so extreme. He was sacrificing a great deal, not only in the abandonment of the stately monument which had been a sort of public advertisement of greatness, but also in the matter of spiritual convenience. The main object of the close association of tomb and temple was that the spirit of the dead king might be immediately present at the stated ceremonies in his funerary-temple and partake of the offerings which were brought as part of the ritual. It was manifestly a most awkward arrangement for the tomb to be tucked away in some obscure corner and the temple to be in some more conspicuous spot, perhaps a mile or two away from the resting-place of its owner, so that his spirit would have to travel down from tomb to temple every time that an offering was about to be made. Inconvenient or not, however, the separation had to be made, for security was the one matter of supreme importance ; and very reluctantly the Pharaohs of the XVIIIth Dynasty began to face the necessities of the case.

Amenhotep I, the second king of the dynasty, was the first to make a change, and his arrangement was an attempt to compromise between the old and the new. He hid his tomb beneath a rock on the summit of the slope of Drah Abu 'l Negga, some distance away from his temple. His successor, Thothmes I, was more thoroughgoing, and saw that if the thing had to be done, it was as well to do it thoroughly. The spot which Thothmes chose lies in the abrupt face of the western end of the main valley ; and the construction of the tomb was entrusted to the royal architect Anena or Ineni. Ineni has left us a brief autobiography on the walls of his own tomb-chapel, in which he mentions his share in this piece of work. " I superintended the excavation of the cliff-tomb of His Majesty," so he says, " alone, no one hearing, no one seeing." A rather gruesome question arises as to how he secured the silence of the large gang of workmen who must necessarily have been employed on such an excavation. Readers of *Treasure Island* will remember how Captain Flint secured the silence of the seamen who helped him to bury his treasure ; perhaps the measures which Ineni took to close the mouths of his workmen were somewhat similar. Human life, especially the life of a gang of slaves, prisoners of war possibly, was not of much importance in those old days ; of none, indeed, when weighed against the needs of Pharaoh. In point of fact, the new method was no more successful than the old.

When Thothmes's tomb was opened in 1899, there was little left in it save an empty stone sarcophagus. His other sarcophagus had been shifted to the tomb of his daughter, where it was found by the American excavator, Mr. T. M. Davis ; and his mummy was not even allowed to rest in his daughter's tomb, for it was found, along with many others, in the great *câche* at Der el-Bahri in 1881. He had set the fashion, however, and from this time onwards, so long as Thebes remained the capital of Egypt, all the Pharaohs were buried in this stern and desolate Valley, while their funerary temples stood out upon the western plain, between the hills and the river.

The chances are that for some time, at least as long as the XVIIIth Dynasty was at the height of its fame and power, the tombs in the Valley remained comparatively secure. It was not a safe thing to meddle with Pharaoh's ancestors, so long as Pharaoh himself was of the hard-hitting type of the time. But the change wrought by the heresy of Akhenaten loosed the bonds of law and order, not only in the provinces, but within the bounds of Egypt itself, and tomb-robbing became once more one of the regular professions of the rascality of Thebes. We know that the tomb of Tutankhamen was entered and partly plundered within ten, or at most fifteen years of his death ; and a few years later, in the eighth year of the reign of Horemheb, the king had to issue instructions to one of his high officials " to renew the burial of King Thothmes IV, justified, in the Precious Habitation in Western Thebes," which indicates that the robbers had been meddling with even a Pharaoh of the great period, let alone one of the decline. For a time again, under the strong rule of kings like Seti I and Rameses II, there may have been comparative security in the Valley ; but when Rameses III had passed away, and the XXth Dynasty was dribbling to its close in a succession of weaklings who bore the once great name of Rameses, but had neither the spirit nor the power associated with the name, the Golden Age of tomb-robbery began, and the Valley must have witnessed strange and grisly sights.

It was in the reign of Rameses IX that the facts, or at least some of them, began to come to light, owing, in the beginning, to the fortunate quarrel which existed between Paser, the Mayor of Eastern Thebes, and his rival Pewero, Mayor of the City of the Dead. The story of how the Commission which was appointed to investigate the charges which Paser brought against Pewero's administration wriggled and twisted (being no doubt partly composed of men who had a direct interest in the corruption which was going on), and how at last, after years of dodging and trickery, which must have pretty well broken the heart of poor Paser, honest man, the truth did at last begin to leak out—all this would take too long to tell with anything like the fulness of detail which constitutes its interest. One scrap of the evidence produced at the sitting of the Commission may be quoted to show the reverence which the native Egyptian has shown from time immemorial in dealing with his mighty dead. The gentleman involved is one of a gang who had been concerned in the robbery of the pyramid of one of the earlier kings, the Pharaoh Sebek-em-saf, of the XIIIth Dynasty. " We found the august mummy of this god," he says, " with a long chain of golden amulets and ornaments round the neck ; the head was covered with gold. The august mummy of this god was entirely overlaid with gold, and his coffin was covered both within and without with gold, and adorned with every splendid costly stone. We stripped off the gold which we found on the august mummy of this god, as well as the amulets and ornaments from around the neck, and the bandages in which the mummy was wrapped. We found the royal wife equipped in like manner, and we stripped off all that we found upon her. We burnt her bandages, and we also stole the household goods which we found with them, and the gold and silver vessels. We divided all between us ; we divided into eight parts the gold which we found with this god, the mummies, the amulets, the ornaments and the bandages."

By this time even the tombs of the mightiest among the Pharaohs, such as Amenhotep III, Seti I, and Rameses II, were being broken into ; and by the time of the next dynasty the attempt to guard each royal tomb against the ubiquitous robbers had to be given up, and the priests, in frantic terror, were hustling the figures of the greatest kings of Egyptian history from one hiding-place to another, in the vain hope of saving them from the plunderer, and the torch with which he too often completed his ghastly work, and destroyed the dead king's hope of immortality. The priest-kings of the XXIst Dynasty did their best for their predecessors, and most of the royal mummies which were found in the two great finds of 1881 and 1898 bear upon their wrappings a docket stating that they have been reburied in this fashion. Rameses III was reburied no less than three times. Finally, thirteen Pharaohs were all packed together into the tomb of Amenhotep II in the Valley ; while something like forty royalties, Pharaohs and royal princes, were huddled into the unfinished tomb of Queen Astemkheb, outside the Valley altogether, and near the temple of Der el-Bahri. How such a store could escape attention seems a mystery ; but somehow or other the secret was kept until it was forgotten, and these strange collections of royal bodies remained undisturbed for nearly three thousand years.

Meanwhile the tombs themselves remained well known, and objects of considerable interest. Classical tourists, who did not differ from their modern successors in any essential respect, visited them frequently, and inscribed their undistinguished names upon the walls, just as if they had been Brown, Jones, or Robinson, of London or New York—the only difference being that you call the scribble of a classical bounder a " graffito," while you call its modern counterpart an outrage. Strabo tells us that in his time there were in the Valley forty tombs worthy of a visit. From the second to the fourth century A.D. the Valley was largely appropriated by the Christian hermits of the Thebaid, whose amiable habits and characteristics have been pictured by Kingsley in *Hypatia*. They were succeeded by the Qurnawis, who, if we may judge from their reception of travellers like Pococke and Bruce, were just about as amiable as the hermits. Napoleon's expedition had to clear them out with artillery and burning brushwood, in order to secure access to the tombs. Then came the happy days, already described, when Mr. Belzoni made his appearance in the Valley with his battering-ram, and his gentle methods of testing whether a mummy's hair was real or false ; and in 1844 the great German Expedition under Lepsius, which surveyed the whole Valley, and cleared one or two tombs.

The modern work in the Valley which has had such wonderful results may be said to begin with the world-famous find of Pharaohs in 1881. Sometime in the early seventies, one of the fellah families of Qurneh, the Abd-er-Rasuls, came, how no man knows, upon that unfinished tomb of Queen Astemkheb at Der el-Bahri, in which, as we have seen, a matter of forty Egyptian royalties had been hidden. The worthy folks realised, with admirable prudence, that they had got on to a good thing, which was altogether too big to put upon the market right away, and must be handled cautiously, and in small instalments. Accordingly, the tomb became a sort of bank, on which the Abd-er-Rasul family could draw at need. For several years they succeeded in keeping their great secret, and in marketing such portions of their find as could be conveniently disposed of without attracting too much attention. Gradually, however, it became apparent that relics of several notable Pharaohs were being offered so steadily on the tourist market as to make it manifest that some great discovery had been made and was being kept secret.

Suspicion fell at last on the virtuous house of Abd-er-Rasul ; and though no direct proof could be got, and the family sturdily maintained that they had never excavated, and never could, would, or should excavate, the methods of the local Mudir, Daoud Pasha, and "the habitual severity" with which, as Maspero gently puts it, he carried on his investigations, shook the Rasul nerves. One of the family, Mohammed Ahmed Abd-er-Rasul, came in secret to the Mudir, and volunteered to conduct a representative of the Service of Antiquities to the scene of his profitable dealings in departed royalty.

On July 5, 1881, Emil Brugsch Bey, accompanied by Ahmed Effendi Kemal, started out in company with the penitent, or at least communicative sinner, and was led by him to a lonely spot not far from Hatshepsut's temple ; and after a sharp climb the explorers found themselves at the mouth of a black pit, about six feet square, and were informed that the store of Pharaohs was at the foot of the shaft. It must have been with some qualms that Brugsch allowed himself to be lowered into the dark pit by the hands of the very men whose source of wealth he was going to take from them. Armed though he was, his rifle would have been of little use to him if Mohammed had simply let go the rope, and left him to keep eternal company with the Pharaohs. Probably, however, Brugsch felt that he could rely upon the memory of Daoud Pasha's " habitual severity." At the foot of the 40-foot shaft came a long horizontal passage, more or less blocked with funerary furniture, and then, at a turn of the passage, " a cluster of mummy-cases came to light," says the lucky explorer, " in such number as to stagger me. Collecting my senses, I made the best examination of them I could by the light of my torch, and at once saw that they contained the mummies of royal personages of both sexes ; and yet that was not all. Plunging on ahead of my guide, I came to the chamber, and there, standing against the walls, or lying upon the floor, I found even a greater number of mummy-cases of stupendous size and weight. Their gold coverings and their polished surfaces so plainly reflected my excited visage that it seemed as though I was looking into the faces of my own ancestors. The gilt face on the coffin of the amiable Queen Nefertari seemed to smile upon me like an old acquaintance."

Indeed, so far as concerns the royal personalities involved, there has never been a discovery which can for one moment be compared with that of Der el-Bahri. Of famous Pharaohs the find included Seqenen-Ra, the champion who picked up the Hyksos gauntlet, and began the War of Independence, Amenhotep I, and his wife Nefertari, Thothmes II, and Thothmes III, the great soldier of Egyptian history, Seti I, Rameses II, and Rameses III, the greatest Pharaohs of the XIXth and XXth Dynasties, Pinezem I and II of the XXIst Dynasty, together with a host of less distinguished royalties and princes of the blood. The very magnificence of the find caused serious embarrassment. Though the amount of funerary furniture and treasure found was by no means in proportion to the dignity and number of the persons involved, yet the question of removal to a place of safety presented considerable difficulty. The coffin of Queen Nefertari, for instance, measured ten feet in length, and required sixteen men to lift it ; and all this material had to be slung up out of the narrow shaft, and transported over rough and rocky ground to the river bank.

By next morning, Brugsch tells us, he had three hundred Arabs employed on the job—" each one a thief." The work was done with a speed which contrasts, not to its advantage, with the scrupulous care which has been displayed in dealing with the treasures of Tutankhamen's Tomb. Even so, it took Brugsch's three hundred scallywags six days to clear the tomb, and then three more anxious days were spent watching the precious treasures, until the Museum steamboat should arrive to transport this unique cargo of Pharaohs to Cairo. And then there followed that curious scene, which, no doubt, was merely a revelation of the unchanging nature of the Egyptian fellah, when for miles the river banks on both sides were covered with women frantically wailing and tearing their hair, and men shouting and firing rifles, as the dead Pharaohs passed in their uncouth funeral barge to their new resting-place. If Rameses could have wakened he would have found little changed, save the rifle shots and the throb of the engine, from the day when he drifted across the Nile behind the funeral barge of his father Seti I.

The amount of interest aroused by this wonderful haul of Pharaohs was extraordinary ; and, indeed, modern popular interest in Egyptian excavation may be said to begin with Brugsch's find. Shortly after the great event, came the founding of the Egypt Exploration Fund, which has done so much splendid work, and which was the first of the great exploration societies ; while the flood of newspaper and magazine articles which was let loose was almost comparable, considering the time, to that which resulted from the discovery of 1922. The reason for this extraordinary development of interest was not purely an Egyptological one. It was, doubtless, quite sufficiently remarkable that the actual bodies of so many of the mightiest kings of antiquity, dating, most of them from about three millenniums ago, should be discovered ; but the thing which gave an edge to the wonder was the suggestion of Biblical associations for the chief members of this silent assembly of kings. The currently accepted chronology of Egypt and Israel at the time placed the Exodus of the Chosen People somewhere in the reign of the Pharaoh Merenptah, son and successor of the most famous of all Pharaohs, Rameses II, who would thus be himself the Pharaoh of the Oppression. The crowning wonder, therefore, was the thought that it was now possible to look upon the actual face of the man who gave the cruel order which resulted in the rearing in his own court of the man who was to withstand and crush the pride of his successor, and to lead out Israel from bondage. And, if someone grumbled that the mummy of the actual Pharaoh of the Exodus had not been found, was not that

K

the most convincing proof of the reality of the whole thing ; for was not the Pharaoh of the Exodus drowned in the Red Sea ? Scripture, of course, makes no such assertion, and Merenptah, the Pharaoh in question, duly turned up, as we shall see, a few years later ; but meanwhile opinions as to the chronology of events in the joint history of Egypt and Israel had been rudely shaken by Petrie's discovery of the Triumph Stele of Merenptah, and was veering round to wards an XVIIIth Dynasty date for the Exodus, instead ot a XIXth Dynasty one, and Merenptah made little noise in 1898 compared to his father in 1881. Perhaps before very long we shall see a new change, in view of recent discoveries in Palestine, which shall restore poor Merenptah to something of the credit, or at least the fame, which he lost by being found seventeen years too late.

Excavation can scarcely claim the credit of the next great sensation provided by the Valley of the Kings, for M. Loret's discovery of 1898 was not an independent find, but the result of information supplied to the Service of Antiquities by local parties. It had a peculiar interest, however, from the fact that Amenhotep II, whose tomb was in question, was the only Pharaoh who, up to that date, had ever been found resting in his own sarcophagus within his own tomb. With him were found several other Pharaohs, who had been shifted from their own tombs to that of Amenhotep in the vain attempt to escape the attentions of the tomb-robbers. Here were such famous and mighty Pharaohs as Thothmes IV, and Amenhotep III, together with such nonentities as the three Rameses, IV, V, and VI ; while Merenptah also turned up, as we have seen, too late for his own interests.

All regard is due to the sentiment which suggested in 1898, as it has suggested since 1922, that when such a discovery is made as that of a king still lying in the tomb where his mourning nation laid him so many centuries ago, he should be guarded from any further disturbance of his rest, and left, when science has gathered what knowledge is to be derived from his funerary equipment, to sleep his long sleep in peace ; but the story of Amenhotep's tomb shows the difficulties which attend on such a course, right and well-meaning though it may be. Amenhotep was left to rest in his stone coffin under his blue gold-starred roof ; but not, as it proved, in peace. In 1901 the tomb was attacked by armed robbers, the guards driven off, after (so they said) a hot engagement, and the great king ruthlessly tumbled out of his coffin on the floor, while what was left of his funerary furniture was carried off. Nor, though it was fairly well known where the guilt of this sacrilege lay, was it found possible to secure a conviction from the native court, which, no doubt, regarded the attempt to secure such a thing as an indefensible attempt to infringe upon the ancient right of tomb-robbery.

It was in 1902 that Mr. T. M. Davis, an elderly American gentleman of means, began a series of excavations in the Valley, which led to some of the most interesting results which, up to that time, had been attained. It would be more strictly correct to say that Mr. Davis financed the excavations, which were actually directed by skilled servants of the Service of Antiquities, such as Mr. Quibell, Mr. Howard Carter, Mr. Weigall, and the late Mr. Edward Ayrton. In 1903, Mr. Howard Carter, working for Mr. Davis, discovered the tomb of Thothmes IV, in the Valley. The king himself had long vanished from his eternal habitation, and was, as we have seen, one of the Pharaohs found in 1898 in the tomb of Amenhotep II ; and the tomb had been rifled in ancient days ; yet some notable work still remained, the most remarkable piece being the front of the royal war-chariot, a specimen of fine relief work in gesso upon linen, the subjects being battle scenes.

The excavations were continued in 1904 and 1905 under the direction of Mr. Quibell and Mr. Weigall, and it was on February 6, 1905, that Mr. Davis's workmen came upon the first step of a series leading to the mouth of an inconspicuous tomb, which was to yield the richest treasure up to that time found in the Valley.   Mr. Weigall slept close to the new discovery over night, to secure that no unauthorised entry was effected, and on the next day, Mr. Davis and Mr. Weigall proceeded to open the tomb, in the presence of the Director-General of the Service of Antiquities (the late Sir Gaston Maspero), and Professor Sayce.   " At the bottom of the passage," says Mr. Weigall, " there was a second wall, blocking the way ; but when a few layers had been taken off the top we were able to climb, one by one, into the chamber.   Imagine entering a town house which had been closed for the summer : imagine the stuffy room, the stiff, silent appearance of the furniture, the feeling that some ghostly occupants of the vacant chairs have just been disturbed, the desire to throw open the windows to let life into the room once more.   That was perhaps the first sensation as we stood, really dumbfounded, and stared round at the relics of the life of over three thousand years ago, all of which were as new almost as when they graced the palace of Prince Yuaa.   Three arm-chairs were perhaps the first objects to attract the attention : beautiful carved wooden chairs, decorated with gold.   Belonging to one of these was a pillow made of down and covered with linen.   It was so perfectly preserved that one might have sat upon it or tossed it from this chair to that without doing it injury. . . .   There in the far corner stood objects gleaming with gold undulled by a speck of dust, and one looked from one article to another with the feeling that the entire human conception of Time was wrong.   These were the things of yesterday, of a year or two ago. . . .   But though the eyes passed from object to object, they ever returned to the two lidless gilded coffins in which the owners of this room of the dead lay as though peacefully sleeping."

Mr. Weigall's vividly felt description helps one to realise something of the sensations of wonder and awe which accompany such a discovery.   Such sensations, however, have quickly to be subordinated to the urgent necessity of securing the priceless material which has created them, so that the treasure may be available to the whole world. That work is of a delicacy and an anxiety which few realise, and which put a heavy strain upon the fortunate explorers. In these respects, the work at the tomb of Tutankhamen has probably created a record, simply because the treasure involved is of unexampled richness and magnitude ; but it ought not to be imagined that the stores of these earlier discoveries were less carefully handled in their degree. " The hot days when one sweated over the heavy packing-cases, and the bitterly cold nights when one lay at the mouth of the tomb under the stars, dragged on for many a week ; and when at last the long train of boxes was carried down to the Nile *en route* for the Cairo Museum, it was with a sigh of relief that the official returned to his regular work."

The tomb thus brought to light proved to be that in which there had been buried two of the most interesting personalities, apart from the Pharaohs, of Egyptian history, the Prince Yuaa, and his wife Tuiu, father and mother of that Queen Tiy, who, as the idolised wife of Amenhotep III, and the mother of his ill-fated son, Akhenaten, exercised perhaps a greater influence upon the course of events in the ancient world than any other woman who ever lived. It had not escaped the attentions of the inevitable tomb-robber, as the explorers found at once ; but the damage done had not been so great as to destroy the wonderful revelation which the tomb gave of the richness of the funerary equipment of a great grandee of the Empire. The coffers, ushabtis, jewel-boxes, and other furniture of the tomb were of the finest design and workmanship, and the richness of the whole burial reached a standard which had hitherto only been touched by individual pieces of material found here and there. Lest it should be imagined that such a find is typical of the results of the average worker under average conditions, I hasten to add another experience in which Mr. Weigall also was concerned, that it may act as a corrective to any too rash estimate of the joys and triumphs of excavation. " Two years ago," says Mr. Weigall, " I assisted at an excavation upon a site of my own selection, the net result of which, after six weeks' work, was one mummified cat ! To sit over the work day after day, as did the unfortunate promoter of this particular enterprise, with the flies buzzing round his face and the sun blazing down upon him from a relentless sky, was hardly a pleasurable task ; and to watch the clouds of dust go up from the tip-heap, where tons of unprofitable rubbish rolled down the hillside all day long, was an occupation for the damned. Yet that is excavating as it is usually found to be."

The good fortune of Mr. Davis in the Valley lasted for several years, and his most remarkable find, from the point of view of the personalities involved, came in January, 1907, when he and Mr. Ayrton, in the course of clearing the area near the tomb of Rameses IX, came upon the unpretentious entrance to what proved to be not a real tomb, but what Sir G. Maspero has described as " a rough cell in the rock, which had been used as a secret burying-place for a member of the family of the so-called Heretic Kings, when the reaction in favour of Amon triumphed." The entrance was almost blocked by the remains of what appeared to have been a funeral canopy of the type familiar in royal and princely interments, and the excavators had to scramble round and over this to gain access to the chamber. Electric light was at once led into the chamber, " and," says Maspero, " at the first ray that shone forth, reflections of sparkling gold responded in every direction. . . . Gold shone on the ground, gold on the walls, gold in the furthest corner where the coffin leant up against the side, gold bright and polished as if it had just come freshly beaten from the goldsmith's hands, gold half veiled by, and striving to free itself from, the dust of time. It seemed as if all the gold of ancient Egypt glittered and gleamed in that narrow space." The workmen speedily spread the report of what they had seen, and, like all such reports, it gathered as it spread. " The ingots of gold multiplied, the urns overflowed with heavy coins, and the plaques and the vases, the arms, and the massive statues had reached such alarming numbers by nightfall, that it was necessary to give notice to the police to prevent danger of an assault."

In point of fact, it turned out that there was singularly little treasure, in the sense of gold and jewels, in the tomb, and that all the exciting golden glitter came from what was little more than gold foil, with which certain articles of the funerary furniture were overlaid. But the actual personality of the individual buried in the rude cell proved to be such

would have been
n with it. " We
" a splendid coffin,
inlaid in a dazzling
ass." The bier on
he lid of the coffin
e powerful glare of
bare skull, with a
rotruding from the
he sheets of flexible
nd, the whole body
:offin, the letters of
titles of Akhenaten,
irning to the shrine
at King Akhenaten
"

which, in any case,
of some complexity
ib ; and whose was
canopic jars, which
otherwise singularly

devoid of notable objects ? Whether the burial was that of Queen Tiy or that of her unfortunate son, the discovery was at least that of one of the most important personages of one of the most interesting periods of Egyptian history. Examination of the bones by Professor Elliot Smith revealed the fact that they were those of a young man, of certainly not more than thirty years, possibly of only twenty-six or twenty-eight. Greatly, therefore, to the disgust of Mr. Davis, who had set his heart upon the idea that he had discovered the great queen, it seemed impossible to resist the conclusion that he had really done something still more important, and found the remains of the man whose devotion to his new monotheism changed the whole course of the history of the ancient world.

Recently, however, this belief has been assailed on the ground of an inscription as to the celebration of Akhenaten's jubilee which is held to be irreconcilable with his having died at so early an age as that required by the evidence of the bones. It is impossible, here, to enter into the details of the controversy ; and it may suffice to say that the whole weight of positive evidence is on the side of the identity of the mummy with Akhenaten, while on the other side there is the theoretical point of the practice in the case of jubilees, which seems totally inadequate to weigh down actually observed facts. It may quite well be that the inconsistency requires the modification of our ideas as to the strictness of the Egyptian observance of the rule as to jubilees ; scarcely that it requires the rejection of the mass of evidence from the interment. It may be added that the evidence as to the extreme youth of Tutankhamen, Akhenaten's son-in-law, and successor at one remove, corroborates the already existing evidence as to the comparative youthfulness of his father-in-law at the time of his death. Such are the troubles which surround the path of the excavator, even after his good genius has guided him to what seems the most brilliant of successes.

RECONSTRUCTION OF THE THRONE-ROOM OF AN EGYPTIAN PHARAOH

This beautiful reconstitution of an Egyptian state-apartment of the XIXth Dynasty (reign of Merenptah) is an admirable example of the results of excavation.

(Kind permission of the Director of the Museum of the University of Pennsylvania, Philadelphia, U.S.A.)

Mr. Davis's other successes in the Valley included the finding of the tomb of the Pharaoh Si-ptah, and the clearing of that of Queen Hatshepsut, both of which were prior to the great find just described. His last triumph came in February, 1908, when he and Mr. Ayrton lighted upon the already rifled, but finely painted tomb of the Pharaoh Horemheb, the usurping soldier who restored order to Egypt after the shock of the Atenist heresy. The ancient robbers had done their work thoroughly on Horemheb's funerary furniture, and little of any value was left to reward the excavators ; but the great red granite sarcophagus, with its guardian goddesses, was of singularly fine quality, and the wall paintings, though not of the artistic value of those of a tomb such as that of Seti I, were yet of great interest. Not far from this tomb, Mr. Davis had found, the previous season, a small burial-pit (it was scarcely a tomb) containing articles which bore the name of the Pharaoh Tutankhamen and his wife Ankhsenamen, and on this ground he concluded that this pit was the actual tomb of Tutankhamen. In this opinion, fortunately for Egyptology and the world, he proved, however, to have been mistaken ; and the tomb of Tutankhamen was still to remain undisturbed for fourteen years.

When Mr. Davis, in 1912, wrote the preface to his account of the tomb of Horemheb and what he held to be that of Tutankhamen, he closed the record of his wonderfully successful work with the words : " I fear that the Valley of the Tombs is now exhausted." Others, of greater authority in the matter, shared his conviction, and when Lord Carnarvon and Mr. Howard Carter received in June, 1914, the reversion of Mr. Davis's concession to dig in the Valley, Sir Gaston Maspero, as he signed the concession, told them frankly that he did not believe the area would repay further investigation. Lord Carnarvon and Mr. Carter had whetted their appetite for Pharaohs, however, by the discovery of the tomb of Amenhotep I at Drah

Abu 'l Negga ; and they remembered that other and earlier explorers had stated, just as positively as Mr. Davis, their belief that the Valley was exhausted at the close of their researches. " I must say," observed Mr. Belzoni, in 1820, " it is my firm opinion, that in the valley of Beban el-Malook, there are no more tombs than are now known, in consequence of my late discoveries ; for previously to my quitting that place, I exerted all my humble abilities in endeavouring to find another tomb, but could not succeed." One hundred and two years later, this judgment, already badly damaged by the finds of M. Loret and Mr. Davis, was to be finally quashed by the excavators who now succeeded to Mr. Davis, and to his prophecy.

War interrupted all excavation work for a time ; but even in the midst of war time there came to Mr. Carter an experience which seemed to indicate that the possibilities of the royal tombs were by no means exhausted. In 1916, Mr. Carter, then on holiday from war work at Luxor, learned that a tomb had been discovered in a cliff face of the mountain above the Valley of the Kings, and that the original discoverers had been driven off by an armed party of diggers, who were now employed in ransacking the find. Collecting some of his old workmen, he set out over the hills, and arrived by midnight on the scene of this usurpation. What followed gives a vivid idea of the variety of the parts which an excavator may be called upon to play. The tomb was right in the face of the cliff, 130 feet below the top, and with a drop of 220 feet from its mouth to the bed of the Valley. The rope by which the robbers had descended hung over the cliff, and the noise of their operations came up from below. It was known, of course, that they were armed, and their previous conduct rendered it unlikely that they would welcome any intrusion upon their illgotten sphere of operations. " I first severed their rope," says Mr. Carter, " thereby cutting off their means of escape, and then, making secure a good stout rope of my own, I lowered myself down the cliff. Shinning down a rope at midnight, into a nestful of industrious tomb-robbers, is a pastime which at least does not lack excitement. There were eight at work, and when I reached the bottom there was an awkward moment or two. I gave them the alternative of clearing out by means of my rope, or else of staying where they were without a rope at all, and eventually they saw reason and departed. The rest of the night I spent on the spot, and, as soon as it was light enough, climbed down into the tomb again to make a thorough investigation."

The tomb which so dramatically changed hands three times within twenty-four hours proved to have belonged to that masterful lady, Queen Hatshepsut, whose official resting-place in the Valley below had been cleared, thirteen years before, by Mr. Carter himself working for Mr. Davis. It was most cunningly concealed in the face of the cliff, so as to be quite invisible, either from below or above. From its door a passage ran straight into the cliff for about 55 feet, then turned at right angles, and led down a sharp slope into the tomb-chamber, 17 feet square. The robbers, with whom one sincerely sympathises, had burrowed a tunnel through all the rubbish which choked this passage, for a distance of over 90 feet, and Mr. Carter took advantage of the work which they had so obligingly accomplished. It took twenty days, however, to clear the tomb ; and when the work was done, it was discovered that the place had never been finished or occupied, and that the only thing in it was a fine unfinished sarcophagus of crystalline sandstone, whose inscriptions showed that it had been meant for Queen Hatshepsut. That great lady must have changed her mind before the tomb was finished, and given orders for its abandonment, and the hewing out of the much larger, but much less secure tomb in the actual Valley. It is one of the " might have beens " of excavation to speculate on what might have been the find if the great Queen had been

a doorway blocked up, plastered over, and sealed. Up to this point the eager excavator had always been harassed by the dread that his stair might only lead, as in the case of Hatshepsut's cliff-tomb, to an unfinished tomb which had never been used, or, at best, to a tomb which had been completely plundered ; but the discovery of the sealed doorway seemed to promise better things. The seals upon the plaster were impressions of the well-known royal necropolis seal, with the jackal and nine captives, so that the tomb had evidently been that of a person of high rank ; but no clue was as yet forthcoming as to his identity. At this stage the work was stopped for a time, and the stairway filled up once more to ground-level, until Lord Carnarvon, who had been summoned by telegram from England, should arrive, to be present at the actual opening of the tomb. He reached Luxor on November 23, and by the afternoon of the next day the stairway was completely cleared again down to the bottom of its sixteen steps, and the whole doorway laid bare. Now were seen the impressions of other seals, and on these were distinguished the name of the long-sought-for Pharaoh Tutankhamen. Evidence was also found that part of the doorway had been opened at some date later, but probably not more than fifteen years later, than its first closing, and had afterwards been re-sealed by the inspectors of the necropolis. So here, too, the inevitable tomb-robber had been at work ; how much or how little damage he had done remained to be seen.

On the 25th, the sealed doorway was carefully removed, and a passage was disclosed sloping downwards, and filled with chips of stone and rubble. At the end of the passage the work of the 26th revealed a second doorway blocked, plastered, and sealed, precisely as the first had been, and bearing the same marks of disturbance and subsequent re-sealing. Manifestly the excavators were face to face with the crisis of their steadily growing excitement, and triumph or bitter disappointment lay behind that sealed door, to be faced almost at once. One need not wonder that Mr. Carter's hands trembled, as he made a small breach in the upper part of the blocking of the doorway. An iron rod, thrust through the gap, revealed that the chamber beyond, whatever it might be, was not blocked with stone, like the passage. After testing the air as a safeguard against foul gases, the hole was widened a little, and Mr. Carter was able to look into the chamber, by the light of a candle. Lord Carnarvon has described the scene. "A long silence followed, till I said, I fear in somewhat trembling tones, 'Well, what is it?' 'There are some wonderful objects here,' was the welcome reply. Having given up my place to my daughter, I myself went to the hole, and I could with difficulty restrain my excitement. At the first sight with the inadequate light, all that one could see was what appeared to be gold bars. On getting a little more accustomed to the light it became apparent that there were colossal gilt couches with extraordinary heads, boxes here and boxes there. We enlarged the hole, and Mr. Carter managed to scramble in—the chamber is sunk 2 feet below the bottom of the passage—and then, as he moved round with a candle, we knew that we had found something absolutely unique and unprecedented."

"Something absolutely unique and unprecedented" they certainly had found, and one need not wonder that Lord Carnarvon has told us that it was as difficult to get Mr. Carter out of the chamber as to get a ferret out of a burrow full of rabbits. Every one knows now the amazing collection of wonders that the ante-chamber of Tutankhamen's tomb contained—the hideous gilt couches, with their fearsome heads, the two great statues of the Pharaoh, in bituminised wood, with golden head-dresses, kilts and sandals, the gold-plated chariots, the alabaster vessels, the exquisitely painted and inlaid coffers of all sorts and sizes, with their fragile contents, the walking-sticks and bows, carved and decorated with gold and inlay. The place was simply crammed with priceless material such as had never before greeted the eye of any excavator in anything like such profusion ; while another room, opening off the first, was similarly packed with treasures. What was the explanation of such an astonishing collection of funerary furniture ? Was the place really a tomb, or was it merely a store-chamber ?

Closer examination disclosed the fact that between the two black statues of the king there was another sealed door-way. " The explanation gradually dawned upon us. We were but on the threshold of our discovery. What we saw was merely an ante-chamber. Behind the guarded door there were to be other chambers, possibly a succession of them, and in one of them, beyond any shadow of doubt, in all his magnificent panoply of death, we should find the Pharaoh lying."

The temptation must have been almost overwhelming to break down this new obstacle, and to make sure at once of the whole magnitude of the discovery ; but what might have been done without a second thought in the early days of excavation is forbidden to the careful and minute method of the worker of to-day. The ante-chamber and its annexe contained a vast amount of material of the highest delicacy and value, which could scarcely fail to suffer in the necessary confusion of further investigation, and whose fragility demanded immediate attention and treatment with pre-servatives. It was decided, therefore, to secure the contents of these first chambers before proceeding any further with the exploration of the tomb ; and accordingly for weeks the work of clearing the ante-chamber and securing its contents went on, while crowds of tourists sat or lounged around the mouth of the tomb criticising the various articles which emerged, and occasionally startled into something like enthusiasm, as some more than usually beautiful specimen of Egyptian craftsmanship emerged from the depths of the tomb into the blazing sunshine.

THE INNERMOST COFFIN OF TUTANKHAMEN, OF SOLID GOLD

Within his huge sarcophagus, of quartzite sandstone, exquisitely sculptured, the boy Pharaoh lay, enclosed in three successive coffins. Of these two were of wood, overlaid with sheet gold, and beautifully inlaid with colour. The third was of solid gold, chased and inlaid. The bullion value of this coffin has been estimated at £50,000. (See pp. 164 *sq.*)

(By kind permission of Dr. Howard Carter.)

STELE OF RAMESES II, FOUND IN THE EGYPTIAN FORTRESS AT BETH-SHEAN

This stele has been among the chief prizes of the American Expedition at Beth-shean. Great importance was attached to it, owing to a reading now questioned which stated that Rameses employed Semites to build his name city in the Delta (cf. Exodus i. 11). (See p. 335.)

(Kind permission of Director of Museum of University of Pennsylvania, Philadelphia, U.S.A.)

By the middle of February, 1923, the work had advanced sufficiently to allow of a further advance being made with safety ; and on Friday, February 16, the barrier was broken down in presence of a distinguished company of dignitaries and Egyptologists, though the nominally official opening, at which the Queen of the Belgians was present, did not take place for another couple of days. The first glance through the breach in the sealed wall revealed what for the moment seemed to be a solid wall of gold stretching from one end of the inner chamber to the other, and filling up practically all the space. As the opening grew larger, this golden wall revealed itself as something which no human eye had ever seen for more than three thousand years—the complete funeral canopy of an Egyptian king. Fragments and separated members of such canopies were not unfamiliar to archæologists ; but never before had such a sight greeted the eyes of any Egyptologist as that which gladdened Mr. Carter that Friday afternoon.

Soon the wall was removed far enough to allow of entry to the burial-chamber ; and then the full splendour of the canopy was disclosed. It was 17 feet long, 11 feet broad, and 9 feet high, and so completely filled the chamber that there was barely room to sidle round the room between its surface and the painted rock-wall. The whole structure was overlaid with gold, and panelled with blue faience, which formed a background for the familiar Egyptian emblems of strength and protection, the Pillar of Osiris, and the Buckle of Isis. At the eastern end were two folding doors, closed and bolted, but not sealed. These were carefully opened, and a second golden canopy was disclosed, within the first. Over it there was draped a pall of fine linen, decorated with golden rosettes ; and its doors were not only closed and bolted, but the bolts were secured by an intact seal. It was therefore morally certain that whatever the thieves who had broken into the tomb soon after the death of Tutankhamen might have done in the outer

L

chambers, they had not penetrated into the heart of the mystery of the Pharaoh's interment, and that what the explorers had before them was an unrifled royal burial—a thing absolutely without precedent in the annals of Egyptology.

At this stage the progress of the investigation was checked for the first season, for reasons similar to those which had dictated the delay in the opening of the burial-chamber. An immense quantity of additional material of a quality even higher, if possible, than that of the ante-chamber, had been revealed in the burial-chamber and its annexe, which, like the annexe to the ante-chamber, was packed with material of the very finest type—in particular the golden shrine for the Canopic Jars, with its free-standing guardian goddesses ; while the dismantling of the canopies, whose size, of course, rendered it impossible to move them intact, would in itself be a lengthy and difficult process. A week after the official opening, the tomb was once more sealed by filling up its passages with hundreds of tons of rubbish ; and Tutankhamen was left, like King Dunmail's warriors, to sleep a while longer.

The triumph of the most magnificent, if not the most important discovery which has ever rewarded Egyptian excavation was clouded by the lamented death of Lord Carnarvon ; and later, was somewhat tarnished by the unpleasant disagreements which arose between the Egyptian Government and Mr. Carter. The difficulties arising from this source were, however, finally overcome, and Mr. Carter resumed his interrupted work.

On the resumption of the work, the extraordinarily difficult task of dealing with the removal of the sections of the successive canopies, or shrines, of which there proved to be four, one within the other, had to be faced. Some idea of the difficulties may be gained from the fact that the sections of the outer shrine weighed anything from a quarter to three-quarters of a ton each, and that the gold-upon-gesso, with which the wood was overlaid, had separated from its base through the shrinkage of the wood, so that it was extremely liable to be crushed and to fall away. The fourth and innermost shrine, a piece of most brilliant workmanship, its folding doors covered with winged figures of the guardian goddesses in bas-relief, had its roof and cornice all in one piece, instead of in sections. This last shrine was bolted, but not sealed, as the second and third shrines had been ; and the opening of its doors revealed a splendid sarchophagus of hard yellow quartzite, encircled, as in the case of that of Horemheb, with the outspread arms and wings of the guardian goddesses, Isis Nephthys, Neith, and Selk. The lifting off of the roof of the innermost shrine revealed the curious fact that the lid of the sarcophagus was not of the same material as the body. Apparently the original quartzite lid must have broken in transit, and a red granite one was substituted for it, being tinted to make a rough match with the other material. Even this rude substitute had also cracked ; but those in charge of the interment had not deemed it worth while to seek a second substitute ; and so, in the very heart of the golden splendour of the burial-chamber, we have this shabby piece of incongruous patchwork—a curious commentary on the proneness of poor humanity in all ages to scamp work that is not likely to be seen, and a somewhat ironic footnote to the poet's praise of ancient integrity :

> " In the elder days of art,
>   Builders wrought with greatest care
> Each minute and unseen part,
>   For the gods see everywhere."

Egyptian art 3300 years ago had scarcely, to all appearance, reached the lofty standard suggested in Longfellow's verse, and thought no harm of scamping a king's coffin so long as it was not found out. It did not dream of the scientific excavator of the twentieth century and his insatiable curiosity.

This ancient witness against dishonest workmanship being lifted, the first of the inner coffins was disclosed, swathed in a linen shroud ; and when this had been removed some of the actual magnificence of a royal Egyptian burial of the Empire began to reveal itself. The coffin, over seven feet in length, and resting upon a low bier of the usual lion type, was entirely sheathed in gold, and adorned with inlay of rare stones and coloured glazes. It was of the anthropoid type, familiar in Egyptian burial practice, and upon the lid lay the golden effigy of the dead Pharaoh, his hands crossed upon his breast, and bearing the royal emblems of the Crook and Flail in gold, inlaid with coloured glass and semi-precious stones. The eyes of the dead king are wide open, with eyelids edged with lapis lazuli, beneath lapis lazuli eyebrows. On the brow of the head-dress, the royal Vulture and Uræus rear their threatening heads in gold, with inlay of lapis and carnelian, and around their necks still lay a withered wreath, perhaps laid there as a last message of love to her dead husband by his girl-widow Ankhsenamen. The detail of the workmanship was of the most superb quality, so much so that it was hard to believe that there could be anything to surpass it, or even to equal it, in what was yet to be revealed. The removal of the lid of this first coffin showed another shroud, with a necklace of flowers and beads ; and when it was rolled back another splendid gold-sheathed coffin, with a second likeness of the king on its lid, appeared. Again the workmanship was magnificent ; and the coffin was " nested " so closely within the first that a special arrangement of tackle had to be contrived to lower the shell of the outermost coffin, and so separate the two. But this, again, was only the prelude to yet greater splendour ; for the third and innermost coffin, revealed by the opening of the second, proved to be of solid gold ! Mr. Carter has estimated its bullion value at £50,000 ; but bullion value is scarcely to be considered in presence of the artistic quality of this most magnificent of all resting-places for the great dead that mortal eyes have ever seen within the last 3000 years. Description is of little avail in dealing with such a triumph of ancient art and craftsmanship, of which its discoverer has justly said, " This coffin ranks among the world's finest works of art. . . . It measures over six feet in length; it is magnificently engraved, both inside and outside, and is embellished with auxiliary *cloisonné* work of gold and semi-precious stones, such as turquoise, lapis lazuli, and carnelian." Among the incidental finds which were the result of the opening of the coffins, must be included the discovery of about two hundred pieces of jewellery, both articles of personal adornment, and amulets, together with a royal diadem.

The examination of the actual kernel of which all this splendour was but the husk—the mummy of Tutankhamen —was carried out during the winter of 1925. " The mummy," writes Mr. Carter, " unfortunately badly car- bonised by spontaneous combustion, set up by the decom- position of the fatty matters contained in the consecration oils that were poured over it, proved to be that of a youth slightly over eighteen years of age, of highly refined and cultured type, and showing a very perceptible affinity to his father-in-law, Akhenaten." The latter point is not to be wondered at, if, as is quite possible on one interpre- tation of the inscription which Tutankhamen placed on the granite lions of Amenhotep III in the British Museum, he was very closely related by blood to Akhenaten. The head and shoulders of the dead king were covered by another wonder of craftsmanship, a mask of beaten gold, inlaid with rare stones and glazes, and exquisitely modelled into a portrait of the king. In such a piece of work, the richness of the materials employed is apt to distract attention from the artistic quality of the workmanship ; but the mask of Tutankhamen impresses itself at once, quite apart from its rich material, as a genuinely noble piece of work, and in all probability a likeness of high quality. Mr. Carter's description may be quoted : " The whole of the mask is of massive burnished gold, equivalent to £5000 of bullion. The beaten gold is inlaid with lapis lazuli, felspar, carnelian, calcite, obsidian, and polychrome glass. It is a superb example of Egyptian art. Not only is it life-size, but, on comparison with the mummy, a life-like portrait." Comparison of the coloured reproduction of the mask with the painted limestone portrait of Queen Nefertiti, so well known as perhaps the finest example of Amarna art, shows a similarity of the whole style of feature and expression, which can scarcely be explained on any other ground than that of close family relationship—a relationship which, on other accounts, is extremely probable, as Nefertiti seems to have been full sister to her husband Akhenaten.

Such, then, is the story, and such are the results, so far, of the richest and most astonishing discovery which the Valley of the Kings has ever yielded to research. The question remains—What is the actual value of such a discovery, apart altogether from its romantic interest, or the bullion value of its component parts ? With regard to this last aspect of the find, it must be admitted that the tomb of Tutankhamen makes all other such finds, even those of romantic fiction, look shabby and paltry. Schliemann's find of the masked kings at Golden Mycenæ could be estimated in bullion value, at a few poor thousands. Edgar Allan Poe, unhampered by such petty and unnecessary things as facts, and with a larger appreciation of what was due to the legitimate expectations of the reading public, modestly estimated the value of Captain Kidd's treasure, in *The Gold Bug*, at a million and a half of dollars—" greatly under-estimated," as he gratifyingly tells us later. But Tutankhamen's treasure leaves even the Gold Bug far behind, while the Kings of Mycenæ seem mere beggarly impostors. One has heard the value of the treasure of the tomb stated, with nice detail, at three and a half millions of pounds—which is just as much as to say that nobody knows what it is worth. Such things are strictly priceless, and their bullion value is the least part of their worth to the world. Quite apart from it, they have a value historical, a value artistic, a value religious, and a value romantic, to say nothing of other aspects of their worth, each of which is quite independent of the value of the precious metals and the rare stones of which they are composed. These values it will be the work of many years to elucidate ; and the work of their elucidation can scarcely be begun until the whole of the material is published and made accessible to students all over the world.

With regard to historical value, it would seem, though such statements must be made with the necessary qualification that subsequent knowledge may render their withdrawal or modification necessary, that the gain to historical knowledge is comparatively small. The general outline of the facts of Tutankhamen's reign was known before the discovery of his tomb ; we know very little more now. The fact that the king's mummy shows him to have died at not much more than eighteen years of age, however, though it only confirms the belief, already held, that his reign was a very short one, does bear on two points of history. In the first place, it points strongly in the direction of the confirmation of the belief that Akhenaten himself must have died at an early age, probably very much at the age suggested by the examination of the bones supposed to be his. In the second, it confirms the general belief that Tutankhamen's share in the reactionary measures which abolished all the work of his father-in-law was simply that of being a royal cloak for the really efficient agents, the priesthood of Amen.

The time for summing up the artistic value of the find is not yet. All that can be said is that we shall eventually be in possession of a mass of material of the very highest quality for the estimation of the art and craftsmanship of the Egypt of the late XVIIIth Dynasty, such as has never before been available with regard to any period of ancient history whatsoever. It may quite well prove, as has already been suggested by eminent authorities, that the mass includes items of various periods, and that there will have to be an intricate sorting out of styles and periods before the final results are attained. However that may be, the results cannot fail to be of the highest interest and value to all students of Egyptian art and craft.

The romantic value belongs to our subject only as an aspect of excavation, in which sense it has already been dealt with in the account of the discovery. Indeed, from the romance-of-history point of view, there is more romance in the little cuneiform tablet discovered at Boghaz-keui, on which is recorded the vain attempt of Tutankhamen's widow to escape from the toils of the Amen priesthood, which encompassed her after her husband's death, by a marriage with the son of the Hittite king, than in anything actually discovered in the tomb. There is one point, however, about which we may never succeed in gaining any historical evidence, and which may therefore be said, in a sense, to belong rather to the sphere of historical romance than anywhere else. What is the meaning of such a stupendous mass of treasure, stored in the tomb of a little stop-gap Pharaoh, who does not even rank as third-rate, perhaps not even as tenth-rate ? Was it the fact that Tutankhamen was the visible sign and symbol of the triumph of Amenism over the hated heresy of his father-in-law that caused the priests of Amen to heap upon his dead body such lavish equipment ? Or was it quite the other way, as has been suggested, and did his young widow, seeing that in her dead husband the great line which had made Egypt the greatest power of the ancient world was drawing to a close, purposely dedicate in his tomb all the richest treasures of her royal line, resolved that they should not be desecrated by the vulgar hands of a proud priest like the Divine Father Ay, or the usurping soldier Horemheb ? We do not know, and probably never shall.

Or, perhaps most incredible of all, and yet most possible—
Have we missed, in the tombs of really great Pharaohs,
something as much finer than the treasure of Tutankhamen
as that is finer than the treasure of Mycenæ ? It has to be
remembered that Tutankhamen's Tomb is absolutely the
only royal burial which has ever been found even approximately intact. Amenhotep II was found in his sarcophagus,
but his tomb had been most thoroughly rifled before it
was rediscovered in 1898. Not one other of them all,
Thothmes III, Amenhotep III, Seti I, Rameses II,
Rameses III, to say nothing of others, has ever been found
as he was laid to rest " in glory, in his own house." If
Tutankhamen's splendour is not an exception, but only a
type, the imagination staggers at what the glory of the
funeral state of a really great emperor, such as Amenhotep
III, may have been. " In my brother's land," so ran the
stock phrase with which the great kings of the old world,
Babylon, Hatti, Mitanni, Assyria, begged gold from their
wealthy brother Pharaoh of Egypt, " In my brother's land,
gold is as common as dust." If Tutankhamen's tomb is
to be the test, apparently they spoke nothing but the bare
truth.

With this golden climax, the story of excavation in the
Valley closes for the moment. It may be that there are
still royal tombs to be discovered there—the tombs of the
Pharaohs of the XXIst Dynasty, for instance, have never
yet been brought to light. Even so, although it is never
safe to prophesy with regard to Egypt, and above all to the
Valley of the Kings, it scarcely seems likely we can hope for
anything to rival the richness of Mr. Carter's discovery,
for by the time of the XXIst Dynasty Egypt was well on
the downward slope, and her glories were growing dim.

The pathos of the whole story can scarcely fail to touch
the mind, as we part with the tale of splendours which yet
availed so little against death and desecration ; and one
realises and appreciates the thoughts which filled the mind

of the explorer as he left the scene of his labours after the opening of the great sarcophagus. "Our lights were lowered. Once more we mounted those steps, once more in the open we beheld the blue vault of the heavens where 'the Sun is Lord'; but our inner thoughts still lingered over the splendour of that vanished Pharaoh, with his last appeal upon his coffin written upon our minds; 'Oh Mother Nut, spread Thy Wings over me, as the Imperishable Stars!'"

CHAPTER VII

IN the early days of Egyptology, what everybody wanted was to get hold of a papyrus. It was by far the most convenient form of memento to bring home with you from your tour to " Grand Cairo and Carnac." Obelisks were obviously only for Emperors, Kings, or Popes ; even a statue was generally too big and cumbrous ; money was required to shift it, and it was not everybody who had room wherein to stow it. A painted coffin was a little better, but not much ; besides, a coffin generally implied an occupant, and folks were not always sure of having an ancient Egyptian, who might have been in his day a wizard of the most confirmed vindictiveness, in their house. A papyrus, on the other hand, was light, and easily packed ; it was often beautifully illuminated, and almost always it was beautifully written—even if you could not read the writing. So every tourist tried to get his hands upon some papyrus of greater or less importance, and goodness only knows the amount of precious material which was sacrificed in the search for saleable papyri, or how many of the papyri themselves, thus acquired at such a cost, have since vanished, " suddenly, as rare things will," in the inevitable dissolution which waits upon all private collections. One of the most vivacious passages in the *Voyages dans la Basse et la Haute Egypte* of Vivant Denon describes his agitation, and the immediate dissolution of all his principles of morality, when he was brought into touch with his first papyrus. " I was conscious that I grew pale ; I was just going to scold those who, in spite of my urgent requests, had violated the integrity of

You have the stuff of life, not dressed up, combed and brushed into smug respectability by a grave historian, or eviscerated by a dull pedant of a moralist, but raw and unrefined as it actually presented itself in daily practice—an amazing comfort and relief.

Sometimes the interest which is revealed to you may be a serious one, literary or religious. Fragments of lost Gospels, or collections of the Sayings of Our Lord, tell you how widespread was Christian interest in the Gospel story, and how many there must have been who " took in hand," as St. Luke puts it, to tell the story of the Life of Jesus. Fragments of lost poems of Sappho, Pindar, Bacchylides, and a score of other poets, and portions of plays, both known and unknown, of the great Greek dramatists, occur in such numbers as to constitute a salutary check to our modern self-conceit, when we realise that a little provincial town in Egypt has left a far higher percentage of great literature in its rubbish heaps than far more important places in our own land could show in their libraries to-day. It comes as a shock to be told that these out of the way Græco-Egyptian provincials actually loved and read their Homer to such an extent that Homer is a drug in the papyrus market. " The commonest author of all," says Dr. Hunt, "is Homer. The great popularity of the bard is indeed one of the chief trials of the excavator's patience. He sees an extra large literary fragment emerging from the soil, and wonders for a brief moment what new treasure he has found—but ten to one it is only old Homer again." One cannot help wondering what proportion copies of Shakespeare's Plays or Milton's *Paradise Lost* would bear to the rest when our literary remains come to be dug up by some future archæologist, who will have some severe trials awaiting him. Religious persecution in the early days of the Roman Empire becomes a reality to the imagination as one reads the certificates made before some local official of a suspect having sacrificed to the Emperor or to some pagan god to prove that the charge of his being a Christian was untrue. The whole business of local administration is opened out in the private correspondence of innumerable officials, parish clerks, and the like ; and one sees that it had its humours and its seamy side in ancient Egypt as elsewhere.

The lighter side of life is not lacking, to lend variety and verisimilitude to the story. You have family stories of all sorts, pleasant and otherwise—mostly otherwise. The spoiled boy whose father has gone to Alexandria, leaving him at home, and who writes in very bad Greek, " Send for me, then, I beseech you. If you don't send, I won't eat, I won't drink. There now ; " the husband, otherwise a kind and considerate goodman, who writes to his wife Alis to keep the baby if it is a boy, but to throw it out if it is a girl ; the devout Christian woman who complains that her husband is in the habit of locking her out when she goes to church, and that he speaks rudely to her through his nose—this being apparently an unbearable aggravation of the offence ; the certificate of the sad fate of the young slave who broke his neck by falling out of a window as he was trying to get another peep at the two dancing-girls ; and the tale of the two brothers who came after their brother's last illness to the house of the man who had nursed him, took away all the dead man's goods, and departed without even attending to the funeral, leaving the Good Samaritan (who tells the story) justly indignant, and with an unburied corpse on his hands ; the judgment on the priest who *would* wear long hair and woollen garments, instead of going shaven and wrapped in chilly linen—all these things, and a thousand more equally trifling, and equally genuine as windows opened on the life of a past age, you can read to-day in the rapidly growing literature in which the results of the papyrus-hunters are embodied.

The finding of these Græco-Roman papyri is, as I have said, quite a modern business, as compared with that of the larger ancient papyri of the Empire. The first Egyptian papyrus to be published, indeed, the *Charta Borgiana*, was found accidentally in the Fayum as early as A.D. 1778 ; but it was practically a century after this before any additions began to be systematically made to our knowledge of the papyri, though some isolated finds, such as those of the Serapeum Papyri and the Rainer Papyri from Arsinoë, were made in the interval.

Modern papyrus-hunting, by which is meant excavation which is conducted especially with a view to the finding of papyri, other antiquities being regarded merely as a by-product, may be said to date from 1889–90, and to owe its origin, as so many other branches of Egyptological research have done, to Sir Flinders Petrie. In that year he was excavating at Gurob, a town near the mouth of the district— the Fayum—which has since proved richest in this material. The Ptolemaic cemetery on which he was working proved at first most uninteresting, as the coffins unearthed were mostly of the rudest possible workmanship. Gradually, however, a number of coffins came to light of which parts were made of cartonnage, which is the term descriptive of a fabric used by the Egyptians, which in its earlier form consisted of layers of damp linen stuck together and covered with wet gesso. In the later periods, however, papyrus was substituted for linen ; and it was here that Petrie's discovery found its origin. For the local undertakers of Gurob, when they had a coffin to make, instead of using comparatively costly material like linen, or unused papyrus, went round to their neighbours, and bought up the contents of their waste-paper baskets, to be used as the base for the gesso. As the coffins were generally made each from material derived from a single source, the documents com-posing them often formed quite a series ; and from this quaint custom we were presented with sets of documents of all sorts, files of business letters, and records of transac-tions, on a scale previously unknown. The papyri derived

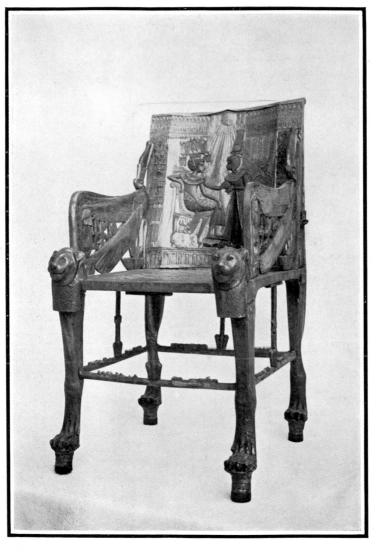

THE GOLDEN THRONE, FROM THE ANTECHAMBER OF TUTANKHAMEN'S
TOMB

This chair of state is one of the most notable examples extant of Egyptian skill in the artistic
crafts. The framework of the chair is of wood, overlaid with sheet gold, the seat is of coloured
inlay, and the panel of the back, in low relief with coloured glazes, represents the Pharaoh
seated and crowned, while his Queen, Ankhsenamen, offers him a vase of ointment.
(See p. 159.)

from the Gurob coffins were entrusted to Sir J. P. Mahaffy and Professor J. G. Smyly and are well-known now as the Flinders Petrie Papyri. They include, among other literary remains, parts of the *Phædo* of Plato, the *Antiope* of Euripides, and a great quantity of official documents of the period round about 300 B.C.

While we are talking about papyri derived from cartonnage coffins, we may notice the curious fate which enriched the world with a number of the Tebtunis Papyri. Messrs. Grenfell and Hunt were working at Tebtunis, when they came across a crocodile cemetery—not an unusual thing in certain parts of Egypt, where the crocodile was regarded as sacred. One of their workmen, in high dudgeon at finding nothing but wretched crocodile burials instead of respectable Egyptians, drove his foot through one of the newly discovered coffins, and brought to light the fact that the creature had been wrapped in cartonnage made of papyri, just as in the case of the Gurob burials. Further, the fact soon came to light that in a number of cases rolls of written papyrus had been stuffed into the animals' mouths or into other cavities in their bodies ; and thus out of the mouth of the crocodile we gained a number of important official papers dealing with the internal administration of Egypt during the later Ptolemaic period.

The discoveries at Gurob stirred the interest of the scientific world with regard to the possibility of Egypt proving as rich in such documents as it had proved to be in respect of other antiquities ; and in 1895 the first excavations specially undertaken with no other object than that of finding papyri were begun in the Fayum by Messrs. Grenfell, Hunt, and Hogarth. Even these first attempts were wonderfully successful ; but their results shrank into comparative insignificance alongside those which were attained when Grenfell and Hunt began in 1897 their memorable series of excavations at Oxyrhynchus. This town is not situated in the Fayum, as are so many of the other papyrus sites, but

M

lies on the edge of the western desert, at a distance of about 120 miles from Cairo. It was in ancient days a place of some local importance, being the capital of the Oxyrhynchite nome or, to put it otherwise, the county town of the county of its own name ; and it was also famous, in early Christian days, for the number of its churches and monasteries. There seemed, therefore, to be an antecedent probability that official papyri might be found here, and also that fragments of the Christian sacred writings might be expected. Everyone who is interested in ancient Egypt knows how these reasonable expectations were fulfilled in such ample measure that the steadily growing mass of the volumes of the Oxyrhynchus Papyri forms almost a library in itself ; while the quantity of the finds has been steadily equalled by their quality, so that we owe to Oxyrhynchus some of the earliest and most precious manuscripts of many of the Greek poets, dramatists, and historians ; while the different series of the Sayings of Jesus Christ, the early manuscripts of the canonical Gospels, and the portions of lost and unknown Gospels have been of vast importance to the students of early Christian literature.

A few words with regard to the nature of a papyrus site, and the methods of papyrus seeking may not be out of place. Generally speaking, the papyrus-hunter does not expect to find his game in the localities where other archæologists carry on their work. The temple-ruins, the house sites, and the cemeteries of an ancient town, which are the likely spots for the general archæologist, are not of commanding interest to him. They may, indeed, contain some papyri to reward exploration, and, as we have seen, the Flinders Petrie papyri came from a cemetery, while other valuable finds have come from temple and house ruins ; but the real treasure ground of the papyrus-seeker lies among the unsightly heaps where the long-dead town dumped its rubbish. It is not every rubbish-mound, however, that will contain papyri, and the hunter has to learn to distinguish between the various types of mounds, so that he may not waste his time on a barren heap. One mound may consist of nothing but builders' refuse, lime, sand, and so forth ; another may be composed mainly of the broken earthenware of the old town ; a third, as in one case at Antinoë, may be made up almost entirely of wool-workers' refuse. Generally speaking, it is useless to look for papyri in mounds of these types. A potsherd mound may contain papyri, for the householder, naturally enough, was not exclusive in his selection of a spot on which to dump the contents of his waste-paper basket, and saw no reason why he should not empty it where his household was dumping its broken crockery, though he would not be likely to wander along to the builder's or the wool-worker's dump to lay down his burden. All the same, it is a pity, from the papyrus-seeker's point of view, that he did not keep his broken crockery and his waste-paper separate ; for a potsherd mound makes a very bad bed for the delicate and fragile papyri, which become excessively dry and brittle in their dry bedding, while their ink is often destroyed.

The ideal mound for the preservation of papyri is one composed of what is locally called *afsh ;* that is to say, earth mixed with vegetable matter, generally twigs and straw. The first rough test for a mound is to walk over it ; when, if it is composed of solid and heavy materials such as lime or sand, it will be hard underfoot, while if its top layers are of *afsh* there will be a certain elasticity and resiliency to the tread. This, of course, is not an infallible test ; but if it gives promise of what is hoped for, the next step is to drive a trial trench into the mound, so as to expose a section of it to a depth sufficient to ensure that no papyrus-bearing strata will be missed. This depth will be indicated, in general, by the presence of damp, which is deadly to papyri. Should the trial trench reveal the presence of papyri, the process of trenching is carried on until the whole mound has been examined by it, either to the damp level,

or to a level where the entire absence of documents indicates
that the lower levels are barren.

Such work, as may be imagined, is often laborious enough ;
for the trenches have, not infrequently, to be carried to a
considerable depth in the mound. One of the largest finds
at Oxyrhynchus was made at a depth of 25 feet below the
surface of the mound. On the other hand, quite a quantity
of material, and much of supreme value, was secured with
very little effort. At Oxyrhynchus in some cases, Dr.
Grenfell tells us, there was little need of trenching. " The
papyri were, as a rule, not very far from the surface ; in
one patch of ground, indeed, merely turning up the soil with
one's boot would frequently disclose a layer of papyri."
Variations such as these give a sporting character to the
work ; you may make a big haul with your very first cast,
or you may " toil all the night," or for many a day, " and
catch nothing."

The very second day of the attack on the rubbish mounds
of Oxyrhynchus, the world-famous fragment of the " Logia "
of Jesus came to light, to be followed next day by a fragment
of the first chapter of St. Matthew's Gospel. Both these
fragments were considerably older than any previously
known manuscripts of the New Testament, so that the
fortunate explorers had, at their very first attempt, drawn
two of the chief prizes in the great papyrus-hunting lottery.
Sometimes, indeed, the richness of the lode was almost
beyond the resources of the workers to deal with it. Such
a day's work as the following must have been almost too
much of a good thing for the leaders of the expedition who
had to deal with its results. " We came upon a mound
which had a thick layer consisting almost entirely of papyrus
rolls. There was room for six pairs of men and boys to be
working simultaneously at this storehouse, and the difficulty
was to find enough baskets in all Behneseh to contain the
papyri. At the end of the day's work no less than thirty-six
good-sized baskets were brought in from this place, several

of them stuffed with fine rolls three to ten feet long, including some of the largest Greek rolls I have ever seen. As the baskets were required for the next day's work, Mr. Hunt and I started at 9 p.m. after dinner to stow away the papyri in some empty packing-cases which we fortunately had at hand. The task was only finished at three in the morning, and on the following night we had a repetition of it, for twenty-five more baskets were filled before the place was exhausted."

This, of course, was an exceptional find ; but it was almost paralleled by another which took place on January 13, 1906, and which even exceeded its predecessor in the value of the texts discovered. " Shortly before sunset we reached, at about six feet from the surface, a place where in the third century (A.D.) a basketful of broken papyrus rolls had been thrown away. In the fading light it was impossible to extricate the whole find that evening ; but a strong guard was posted on the spot during the night, and the remainder was safely removed during the following forenoon." It was the quality of this deposit which made it notable ; for it contained, besides a mass of other material only less interesting, parts of the *Pæans* of Pindar, of the *Hypsipyle* of Euripides, of the *Phædrus*, and the *Symposium* of Plato, and of a new *History of Greece*, the authorship of which has been variously assigned by scholars to Ephorus, Theopompus, or Cratippus. Against such triumphant days there have to be set the long periods of weary waiting, when next to nothing rewards the search, and the excavator has ample opportunity of realising that " hope deferred maketh the heart sick " ; but on the whole the results of papyrus-hunting have proved astonishingly rich. El Hibeh, Tebtunis, Arsinoë, Hermopolis, Antinoë, and other sites have yielded larger or smaller quantities of papyri to excavators of France, Germany, Italy, and America, as well as to our own scholars ; and, indeed, the amount of material collected has become so enormous that it has been suggested that we have already

more than enough of the waste-paper of the last centuries of
the classical and first centuries of the Christian periods.
With this Philistine judgment, however, no one who knows
anything of the amazing interest of the Græco-Roman
papyri will ever agree.

Few things, certainly, are less attractive in appearance
than a fragment of ancient papyrus from an Egyptian
rubbish-heap, tattered, pierced, and defaced, with its ink
faded to such a degree as often to be all but illegible. The
jewellery of Dahshur, Lahun, or the Valley of the Kings
makes an instant appeal to one's sense of beauty, and
scarcely less to one's sense of romance, as one thinks of the
" dear, dead women " who once wore the diadems on their
dark hair and the pectorals and bracelets on their bosoms
and arms. A great papyrus of the Empire may be in itself
a wonderful specimen of ancient Egyptian art, with its
numerous illuminations ; or if it is not that, it may give you
some pages of the romance of a literature, which save for
such things has vanished altogether. The Graeco-Roman
papyrus can claim our attention on no such grounds ; but
it has its own lure, and its charm is of an intimacy to which
hardly anything else which has survived from the past can
lay claim. The golden relics of dead kings and queens
touch only the surface of their life ; the great papyri, while
in a sense they go deeper, giving some insight into the
thoughts and aspirations of a great people, do so only in an
impersonal and official fashion, for they are not a personal
product, but merely a commercial one, some of them,
indeed, the nearest approach to our modern methods of
mass-production that the past has to show to us, written in
batches by the professional funerary scribes, with blanks for
the insertion of the names of the clients who bought them,
and with a cynical disregard of accuracy which shows how
little sentiment or personal feeling was concerned in the
production of them.

But the Graeco-Roman papyri are living documents, bits

of the actual life-stuff of men and women who have here set down their cares and anxieties, their fears and hopes, their loves and hates, their frequent follies, and their infrequent wisdom, without disguise or study. It is human nature as it was, is, and shall be, not even its grammar and spelling corrected : the crude, unrefined product of mind and feeling thrown out before you without reserve. If " The proper study of mankind is man," then the papyri of the Egyptian rubbish-heaps are of far greater value to us than all the glories of the tomb of Tutankhamen, because you get in them the essential man of their period as you can get him nowhere else. From such a point of view, it may justly be claimed for the work of the papyrus-hunter that no results of modern excavation can compare with it in fruitfulness.

BOOK II

ASSYRIA & BABYLONIA

CHAPTER VIII

THE LANDS

Of the two lands with which we are concerned in this section of our story, Babylonia is the older in point of its human history, but the younger in point of existence. Though the one term Mesopotamia is frequently used at the present time to cover the whole area in question, the use is inexact ; for there is a sharp distinction between the upper and lower portions of the area, which having its origin in the very structure of the two countries, was reflected also in the characters of their inhabitants, and continually emphasised by the facts of history. Babylonia is a " made " land, composed of silt brought down by the two great rivers, the Euphrates and the Tigris, which flow through it. Mesopotamia or Assyria is largely upland prairie or steppe land, much less fertile than its southern neighbour, though capable of considerable fertility under a diligent cultivation. Babylonia, being, like Egypt, " the gift of the river," was in ancient days a much smaller land than it is at the present time ; for the rivers, constantly depositing their alluvium, have pushed back the waters of the Persian Gulf more than a hundred miles from the point to which they reached in the time of the greatest prosperity of the country. Thus composed entirely of loam, Babylonia has from time immemorial been a land of a high degree of fertility. Herodotus tells us that the fertility of the country was so great that he is afraid to give precise statements lest he should not be believed, and his declaration is borne out from many other ancient sources. Control of the waters which had formed the land was the first essential of life, as in Egypt ; for both, but particularly the Euphrates, were continually changing their course in consequence of the silting up of their beds ; but control was not an overwhelming task, especially with the Euphrates, " whose lazily moving chocolate-coloured stream may be induced with the greatest ease to spread its fertilising solution of silt over the surrounding fields." Accordingly, we find, as in Egypt, that similar conditions produced similar results, in the shape of an extremely early development of civilisation and all the features of organised state life.

With this advantage, however, went a counterweight. The rich soil, and the enervating climate, very different from that of Egypt, produced in all ages a marked effect upon the character of the inhabitants of the land—an effect which even the introduction of new and virile conquering stocks proved powerless to arrest, save for a short time. " Babylon," says Professor Olmstead, " tends to monotony, to the development of a certain mediocrity of character. As a natural result, its conquerors, no matter how energetic, soon fall under its malign spell. All too soon they become true Babylonians, good business men, devoted to their everyday occupations, highly religious, unenterprising, and the prey of each successive invader." And thus, while civilisation began in Babylonia, the land was continually passing under the yoke of its own more virile descendants. Along with the lack of the " stalk of carle-hemp " in the character of its nationals, went the corresponding lack in the material out of which Babylonia reared the memorials of her culture. The land was practically devoid of building stone—a fact which determined not only the character of its own architecture, but, curiously enough, that of its neighbour, descendant, and rival, Assyria, which suffered from no such poverty of material, yet, probably in reverence to tradition, continued to use in its stony upland the same building materials which its primitive ancestors had used in the alluvial plain of Babylonia.

The natural division between the two lands occurs at a point near the present Samarra on the Tigris. " A line drawn from a point a little below Samarra on the Tigris before its junction with the Adhem to Hit on the Euphrates marks the division between the slightly elevated and un-dulating plain and the dead level of the alluvium, and this may be regarded as representing the true boundary of Akkad on the north. Beyond this line you enter upon a very different type of country. Only along the Tigris and the Euphrates are narrow strips of bottom-land. Back a mile or so from the streams are low bluffs of loose conglomerate resting on sandstone, and back again from these on the low plateau between the rivers stretch the prairies. Although the soil is residual rather than alluvial, it is scarcely inferior to that of Babylonia for fertility. After the spring rains, the country blossoms like the rose. Day by day the colour changes with the flowers—one day red with huge tulips, another blue, another yellow, and the air at times is almost sickeningly odorous. In spite of all this beauty, the general effect is that of desolation, broken only by the solitary Arab camp or the equally solitary flock of sheep."

Apparently the first development of culture in both lands was what is known as Sumerian, deriving its origin from the early Elamite culture whose centre was at Susa. Its long and fruitful prosperity was followed by Semitic conquest, and Western Asia had its first experience of Semitic Empire, under Sargon of Akkad and his successors. The early Semitic Empire was closed by the brief Sumerian renais-sance which has left us so many precious things for the re-construction of ancient history. Finally the stubborn Semite takes once more, and this time keeps, the upper hand ; henceforward, for fifteen hundred years, the dominant spirit of the two lands is the hard and bitter, but amazingly energetic and equally amazingly spiritual, Semitic genius.

Comparatively early in the Semitic story, a branch of the Babylonian Semites went upstream out of the alluvial plain to the prairie land of the Upper Tigris, and there founded the little Assyrian kingdom, eventually to become the Assyrian Empire, under whose upas shadow the nations of the Near East cowered and withered for five hundred years. The colonists may not have been long enough in the softer Babylonian plain to lose the stubborn strength of the original stock ; at all events the conditions of their new home favoured the growth of a hardier race than could long continue to be bred on the enervating flats of Babylonia. The Babylonian Semite had a long start, and had written some of the most brilliant chapters of his history before his descendant makes any show of being anything more than a rather pushful upstart ; but when Assyria did come, it was with a vengeance, in more senses than one. The Babylonian was a trader, a man of science, a lawgiver, a literary man, with a strong inclination to be priest-ridden ; but the Assyrian was a fighter to the backbone. Strife between the mother-country and her pushing children was inevitable. Babylonia, with her consciousness of ancient renown, assumes an attitude of superiority and even suzerainty, which must have been intensely galling to the younger state, which, on its side, was conscious both of its growing strength and of the gradual weakening of its older neighbour. As late as the time of the Amarna Letters you find Burraburiash, the Kassite king of Babylon, writing indignantly to the Egyptian Pharaoh to protest against the ambassadors of " the Assyrians, my vassals," being received as though they represented an independent sovereign state. " Why have they come to thy land ? If thou lovest me, they shall bring about no result ; with empty hands let them go home again." But facts and claims were here in flagrant contradiction with one another ; the claim which Babylon made was one which could only be made good by force ; and between Babylon's efforts to retain her tottering suzerainty, and Assyria's stubborn determination to be not only mistress of her own house, but of her mother's also, the struggle between the two kingdoms became almost chronic.

In the endless strife, Assyria, essentially the fighting people of the ancient East, had almost invariably the upper hand ; but she found again and again that while it was no very difficult task to conquer Babylonia, it was almost an impossibility to hold it. The Babylonian was not " a man of war from his youth," as the Assyrian was. He was a business man, a man of science, a man of religion ; but he had what Carlyle called " a soft invincibility," which was a perpetual disappointment to his impetuous conqueror from the north. One Assyrian conqueror after another swept over Babylonia, " took the hands of Bel " in the great temple at Babylon, and imagined that he had made an end of the age-long quarrel ; only to find, as soon as his back was turned, that Babylonia was up in arms again from one end to the other, and that his work had to start once more from the beginning. Finally, at the very end of the long story, after Assyria had scored perhaps ten victories for every one of Babylon, it was Babylonia, under Nebuchadnezzar, which, with the help of the Medes, wore down at last her exhausted rival, and wiped Assyria off the map. Assyria's failure, of course, was due to the fact that she was too small a state for the task which she set herself, and that with the best will in the world, and with unquestionable ability as a conquering power, she had neither the extent of home territory, of native resources, nor of man-power, to hold down the whole civilised world as she aspired to do.

Her downfall was complete and absolute. Babylonia fell and rose again, time after time, because she corresponded to some of the essential facts of the situation in that ancient world ; but that was not the case with Assyria ; and so, as the Hebrew prophet foretold, " when she ceased to spoil she was spoiled ; and when she made an end to deal treacherously, they dealt treacherously with her." Ere long her great cities passed away from the memory of man, almost as utterly as though they had never been. It was only a matter of two hundred years after the fall of " Nineveh, that great city," that Xenophon led his Ten Thousand Greeks past the desolate spot which had once been the scene of so much glory ; he makes not a single mention of its name. A vague tradition persisted in the neighbourhood of Mosul that the two great mounds of Kouyunjik and Nebi Yunus, on the east side of the Tigris, were associated with Nineveh, and with Jonah's mission to the erring city ; beyond that, men knew next to nothing for two thousand years after the glory of Assyria had passed away. The memory of Babylon kept alive longer ; but after the death of Alexander the Great in the great palace of Nebuchadnezzar, her glory also fades rapidly ; and by the end of the first century (A.D.) she was in ruins and deserted. But the association of the Greeks with her waning splendours had been too close to allow of the oblivion which descended upon her rival alto- gether overshadowing her. The place and name of the city never altogether perished from the earth ; and tradition has always, with perfect clearness, linked the name of Babel with the great mounds which have been induced by the modern excavator to yield up some of the secrets of the capital of Hammurabi and Nebuchadnezzar.

Before we turn to consider the wonderful resurrection of these ancient cities of the conquering Semite from the dust of ages, one word may be said with regard to the reason for the manifest distinction between the excavator's work in Babylonia and Mesopotamia, and his work in Egypt. In Babylonia and Mesopotamia, the work is almost entirely the excavation of a mound or mounds, which cover the site of the ancient city that is being dealt with. Scarcely ever have you a vast complex of ruins clear standing above ground, and maintaining its identity and the admiration of generation after generation right down through the centuries, until in our own days it is completely extricated from its partial

encumberment, and revealed in all its majesty. The Mesopotamian and Babylonian sites are shapeless mounds, where
scarcely a trace of human work is visible above the surface ;
though this was not always the case, and drawings and
reports exist showing that within human memory much
more evidence was in existence of the great buildings which
lay beneath the mantle of earth. The reason for this
complete degradation of the temples and palaces of the
Assyrians and Babylonians, is, of course, the material which
they habitually used in construction. The bulk of their
work was done in crude brick, a good enough material so
long as the fabric is attended to, and kept in careful repair,
water- and weather-tight, but liable to quick and wholesale
disintegration if left to neglect. Even in Egypt, where rain
is the exception, we have seen how little survives of the
crude brick palaces of the Pharaohs. In Babylonia and
Assyria, everything was built of brick, though the chambers
were often faced and lined with alabaster slabs and enamelled
bricks. The natural result has been that in the course of
centuries of unchecked disintegration and denudation the
great buildings of the ancient cities have weathered down
into shapeless and ugly heaps, so different from the stately
ruins of Karnak or Edfu, which mark the sites of vast
temples or palaces.

We have now to trace the process by which these mounds
have—a few of them at all events—been persuaded to tell
us something of the story of their former greatness.

CHAPTER IX

THE RESURRECTION OF ASSYRIA

WE begin our story of excavation in these lands of the childhood of humanity with Assyria, because, though she was the younger nation of the two, it was in Assyria that there began the first awakening out of the dust of the past. Resurrection was later in coming in this quarter of the ancient world than it had been in Egypt. The dawn began for Egypt practically with the close of the eighteenth century ; it was not till nearly the half of the nineteenth had run its course that anything of importance was done in Mesopotamia. Carsten Niebuhr in 1765, and the Abbé de Beauchamp in 1790 had, indeed, visited the mounds of Babylonia, and Claudius James Rich, in 1811, surveyed the ruins of Babylon, and in 1821 extended his researches to the mounds of Assyria, especially Kouyunjik, Nebi Yunus, and Nimrud ; while J. S. Buckingham and Sir R. Ker Porter, with others, followed in the footsteps of these earlier travellers, devoting, on the whole, the most of their attention to the mounds supposed to cover the site of Babylon. In 1835–7 came the surveying expedition of the British Government, commanded by Colonel Chesney, which laid the foundation of our knowledge of the topography of the lands. But all this work was merely superficial, in the literal sense of the word. No real excavation was done, though one or other of the travellers might grub a little in the edge of one of the mounds, and bring away an inscribed brick or two as a sample of what might lie beneath. The reports of all these men, though by no means unimportant, were concerned almost exclusively with what was to be seen on the surface, and were mixed with a considerable amount of theorising whose actual value was in inverse proportion to its bulk.

So far as the western world was concerned, Layard's statement was strictly true, up to the year 1842—" A case scarcely three feet square enclosed all that remained, not only of the great city of Nineveh, but of Babylon itself." Within a very few years, however, all that was to be changed ; and before the half century was out Mesopotamia seemed to have almost surpassed her ancient rival, Egypt, in the wonderful revelations which were being made of her past splendours, and in the hold which she had taken upon the imagination of the civilised world. That she did this, she owed largely to the fact that one of her first explorers was gifted, far above most men, not only with the spirit of the true excavator, but also with something which is perhaps almost rarer, the power of telling the story of his work in such fashion as to make the record of scientific facts read with all the charm of a romance.   Layard's narrative not only revealed to the English-speaking public a whole new world of ancient glory, but did so with the magical touch which makes even the least interested lay aside for the nonce their carelessness, and imagine for a little while that they are really in the grip of a scientific interest.

To the charm of Layard's style was added the same influence which operated so powerfully in the case of Egypt —the connection between the protagonists of the great national story which was being unfolded, and the events recorded in the Old Testament. Sir Henry Rawlinson's discovery of the secret of the cuneiform inscriptions came just in the nick of time to give the new finds their full value ; and people learned, with wonder and admiration, the Assyrian story of great events with which they were familiar in the Books of Kings and Chronicles and the prophets, and saw the pictured representations of the mighty monarchs whose names were sounds of dread and terror in every

Hebrew household of Old Testament days—Sennacherib, Sargon, Tiglath-Pileser, Esarhaddon. Here was a Biblical connection as close and intimate at the end of Israel's national history, as Egypt was to yield in the early 'eighties for its beginning. Probably there has never been a more widespread enthusiasm for the work and the results of Archæology than that which resulted, in the middle of the nineteenth century, from the publication of the work of Botta and Victor Place in France, and that of Layard in England.

Unfortunately, it can scarcely be said that this interest has been maintained to the same extent as it has undoubtedly been in the parallel case of Egypt. For this comparative falling off various reasons are accountable. In comparison with Egypt, the lands concerned have been, at least until recently, inaccessible, unhealthy, and unattractive ; while the government, or rather the lack of government, of them has often added to all the discomforts and vexations of the excavator a very serious element of personal danger from the wild Arab tribes. But perhaps the main reason has lain in the fact that, from the nature of the case, it is not to be expected that excavation in Mesopotamia and Babylonia should yield the rich harvest of intimate *personalia* which has made and continues to make Egyptian exploration so fascinating. The climate and soil of Egypt are about the best preservatives of almost everything that the explorer looks for, and you may expect to find almost anything, no matter how delicate its fabric, preserved there. It is very different in Mesopotamia and Babylonia ; where, with a much more variable climate, and a soil which has often been waterlogged and absolutely sodden, it is next to an impossibility that many materials should be preserved at all. The result is that while stonework, and work in burnt brick may survive to a considerable extent, and while bronze and copper may under favourable conditions be preserved to some extent, it is impossible to look to

N

these lands for all that wealth of illustration of the details
of the personal life of the ages which is so charming a
feature of the Egyptian results. Colossi, winged-bulls and
lions, temple towers and so forth, may be abundant, and
may continue to be so ; but man cannot live by colossi
alone, and winged-bulls are apt to pall after a while ; while
the survival which is really most precious to the student of
the lands—the cuneiform tablet, with its history, its religious
dogma, its tales of ancient heroism, is of a singularly unattractive appearance, and ill-fitted to hold its own, as a
source of general interest, beside the glitter and beauty of
Egyptian diadems, jewellery, or weapons.

Accordingly, Mesopotamian stock, so to speak, has somewhat declined from the high quotations which it touched
during the 'fifties of last century. That is not to say, however,
that work of a highly interesting and useful kind has not
been going on ; but simply that it has occupied a second
place in public favour, compared with the more attractive
results which have been forthcoming in such abundance
from its more favourably situated rival.

It was in 1842 that the chapter of Mesopotamian excavation
was definitely opened by the dispatch of Paul Emil Botta to
Mosul as French Consular Agent there. Botta was a man
admirably qualified for the work which he was destined to
do in Mesopotamia. Long residence in the Near East had
familiarised him with the languages and habits of the people
with whom he was called to deal ; and he was in addition
a trained and practised observer endowed with a considerable
fund of enthusiasm for the great civilisations of the land
into the secrets of whose past he was now determined to
penetrate. In December, 1842, he began his diggings at
the mound of Kouyunjik, and continued them till the
middle of March, 1843. The results were not very en-
couraging. A few inscribed bricks and fragments of reliefs
came to light, but nothing of any great importance, or in
such perfect condition as to suggest that it was worth while

to continue the excavations. Fortune, however, was preparing for the explorer a richer reward in another direction. Among the crowd of Arabs who occasionally gathered round the trenches to jabber and gesticulate over the folly of the Frank, there came one day in December, 1842, a dyer from Khorsabad, a village some distance to the north-east of Kouyunjik. When he was told that the mad foreigner was searching for inscribed stones and bricks, he remarked that if such things were wanted, they were to be had in abundance near his own village, and offered to procure as many as were desired. For a time Botta paid no attention to the suggestion, knowing well that an Arab report is one thing, and the truth generally quite another ; but at last, in March, 1843, disgusted with his comparative ill-success at Kouyunjik, he sent a few workmen to test the mound at Khorsabad. Almost at once they came upon two walls covered with the remains of bas-reliefs and cuneiform inscriptions. When the report of their success reached Botta, he set out at once for Khorsabad, which was then distant about five hours from Mosul. At the time he was only able to spare a single day from his consular duties ; but in that time he saw enough to convince him that his highest hopes had been realised, and that he had opened the book of that ancient civilisation once more to the world. " Though the first sight of these strange sculptures and witnesses of a long-forgotten past, which, out of the depth of a buried civilisation, suddenly rose like the *Fata Morgana* before his astonished eyes, must have filled his soul with great astonishment and delight, yet he could calm himself sufficiently to sit down among his Arab workmen, and sketch the most important reliefs and inscriptions for his friend in Paris."

His letter of April 5, 1843, was read on its arrival to the members of the Societé Asiatique, and was received with tremendous enthusiasm. " I believe myself," he wrote, " to be the first who has discovered sculptures which with some reason can be referred to the period when Nineveh was flourishing." Such words have become almost commonplace to the present generation, which has witnessed similar resurrections of the past repeating themselves in many lands and climes ; but this was the first of such events, and the sensation which it created was extraordinary. The Academy at once requested the French Government to grant the funds necessary for the prosecution of the excavations (up to this point Botta had been financing them himself) ; and with a spirit of enlightened munificence which seems very strange to Britons, accustomed to a very different type of governing mind, the Government at once granted the sum requested, and dispatched a skilled artist, already well known for his work in Persia, to secure accurate representations of all such work as could not be removed to France. Meanwhile Botta had been toiling away in Mesopotamia, and fighting the usual battle which had then to be fought against Turkish misgovernment and stupidity. It was not till May, 1844, that M. E. Flandin, the artist selected, finally brought the firman from Constantinople which secured the expedition from vexatious meddling on the part of the local authorities, and allowed the work to progress unhindered. In November of the same year, Flandin returned to Paris, with a large number of fine sketches, which attracted widespread attention ; and he was followed in 1846 by the sculptures themselves, which were rafted down the Tigris to Basra, and there embarked upon a French warship, the *Cormorant*, which carried them to Havre. The immediate result was a revival and increase of the enthusiasm with which Botta's first letter had been received. " When these gigantic winged-bulls, with their serene expression of dignified strength and intellectual power, and these fine reliefs illustrating the different scenes of peace and war of a bygone race before which the nations of Asia had trembled, stood there again before the eyes of the whole world as a peaceful witness to the beginning of a resurrection of an almost forgotten empire, the enthusiasm among all classes of France knew no bounds."

In 1851, the French Government sent out the architect Victor Place to follow up the work of Botta at Khorsabad; and between that year and 1855, Place completed the excavation of the mound, and made investigations at several of the other mounds of Mesopotamia. The results of his work at Khorsabad gave to the world the fairly complete plan of a great royal city of Assyria of about 700 B.C. Unfortunately the bulk of the original sculptures which he secured never reached their destination. Together with the results of the Fresnel Oppert Expedition, and sixty-eight cases of sculptures from Ashur-bani-pal's palace at Nineveh, which Rawlinson had allowed Place to choose for the Louvre, they were being rafted down the Tigris to Basra, when they were upset and lost for ever.

The royal city which had thus risen out of the dust proved, however, to be, not Nineveh, but Dur-Sharrukin— " Sargon-Burgh ", as we might call it, the city of the great conqueror who destroyed Samaria. It was purely a royal city, built by Sargon for his own residence and glory, and with no history apart from him. The city covered, together with the huge palace, an area of 741 acres, and afforded room for a population of about 80,000. Thus it was by no means a large city, compared with such great places as Nineveh or Babylon. What it lacked in size, it made up for in the magnificence of the royal palace for which alone it existed, and which was its dominating feature. Indeed, this first of Mesopotamian excavations brought us at once face to face with what is the characteristic feature of the Assyrian city. Just as surely as the Temple dominates all Egyptian cities, so does the Palace dominate their Assyrian counterparts. Later excavations have to some extent redressed the Assyrian balance between secular and sacred, and shown us that the Assyrian could be a great temple-builder also ; yet even still the fact remains that the bulk of our knowledge as to Assyrian splendour and culture comes from secular sources, while the case is reversed with regard to Egypt.

Sargon's great palace stood on the north-west side of the city, projecting like a huge bastion from the city wall into the plain. It stood on a lofty platform, raised about forty-five feet above the plain. This platform, a typical piece of Assyrian building practice, was built with crude bricks, and faced with stone. On the western corner of the platform stood a temple, with its accompanying stage-tower ; the rest of the area was occupied by the vast palace. For the first time the world learned with astonishment the magnificence with which a monarch of the ancient East was housed in the days when Assyria ruled the world, and all the nations trembled at the shaking of her spear. The great building was divided into three sections, the public section, containing the great reception halls, and the offices of the administration (for we have to remember that these huge ancient palaces were not only the residences of the monarch, but also the administrative centres of the realms concerned), the harem, or private section of the building reserved for the use of the king and his womenkind, and the domestic quarter, containing all the kitchen and store-rooms with the stables and the bakery.

The public halls were elaborately decorated with great winged-bulls and lions, the guardian genii of the house, and with splendid relief sculptures in alabaster, marred, according to the barbarous Assyrian practice, by bands of inscription running across them, glorifying the king as warrior or huntsman. " We see him hunting wild animals, doing homage to the gods, sitting at the table and listening to the singers and musicians, or attacking strong cities and castles, subduing foreign nations, punishing rebels, and leading back thousands of captives and innumerable spoil of every description." The rooms of the private quarter were much smaller and more simple, but were tastefully decorated.

What time and disaster had destroyed, we were soon to be in a position to appreciate from the glowing words in which the Assyrian kings, never over-burdened with modesty, described their great feats in the building and adornment of their " lordly pleasure-houses." " A palace for my royal dwelling-place," says Ashur-nasir-pal, in inscriptions discovered by Layard, Botta's friendly rival, " for the glorious seat of my royalty, I founded forever, and splendidly planned it. I surrounded it with a cornice of copper. Sculptures of the creatures of land and sea carved in alabaster I made and placed them at the doors. Lofty door-posts of cedar-wood I made, and sheathed them with copper, and set them up in the gates. Thrones of costly woods, dishes of ivory containing silver, gold, copper and iron, the spoil of my hand, taken from conquered lands, I deposited therein." These lordly gentlemen, who housed themselves so magnificently, did not disdain, all the same, to beg, where stealing was not practicable, in order to obtain money sufficient to carry out their grandiose designs. " I am building a new palace," writes Ashur-uballit of Assyria to his " brother " of Egypt, " which I am about to complete. Send me as much gold as is needed for its construction and equipment. At the time when Ashur-nadin-akhi, my father, sent to Egypt, twenty talents of gold were sent to him. Moreover, when the king of Hanigalbat sent to Egypt to your father, he sent to him twenty talents of gold. Surely I am as good as that king of Hanigalbat, and yet you have only sent me a little gold." The kings of Assyria were lodged with a splendour to which Pharaoh of Egypt never aspired ; but, somehow, there is always a suspicion of the vulgarity of the *nouveau riche* about the gorgeousness of the Assyrian, and Pharaoh in his pretty villa, embowered in flowers, manages to create the impression that he is much more of a great gentleman than his pushful brother in the gaudy new palace in Mesopotamia.

Whatever may have been the defects of Assyrian culture,

however, the revelation of it for the first time created a profound impression. "There never has been aroused again," says Hilprecht, "such a deep and general interest in the excavation of distant Oriental sites as towards the middle of last century, when Sargon's palace rose suddenly out of the ground, and furnished the first faithful picture of a great epoch of art which had vanished completely from human sight." But before Botta's results were well before the public they were reinforced by the work of the young English explorer, Austen Henry Layard, who, within two years of excavation, carried on with most inadequate means, had identified the sites of two great Assyrian capitals, Kalah and Nineveh, and revealed the ruins of eight royal palaces !

Layard was already familiar with the Mesopotamian mounds, when in 1842 he met with Botta at Mosul. The French explorer took at once to the young English enthusiast, and from the very first communicated his results to Layard as a matter of course. In those days the international jealousy of explorers, which some slanderous people maintain to be still existent, was a very real and bitter thing, and it is all the pleasanter to see these two pioneers sharing their hopes and enthusiasms with one another without the slightest sign of jealousy. The inspiration of the French explorer doubtless did much to fan the flame that was already kindled in the Englishman's mind ; and though his energies were diverted for a while to the not unduly strenuous work of unpaid assistant to Sir Stratford Canning, afterwards Lord Stratford de Redcliffe, the British Ambassador at Constantinople, yet by October, 1845, he was galloping night and day across Asia Minor on his way to the task which was to make his name famous all over the world. His financial equipment sounds almost comical when it is compared with the work he was facing. Apart from his own personal resources, his excavating fund for the attack on Nineveh amounted to £60 which his chief at

WINGED HUMAN-HEADED BULL FROM
KHORSABAD (LOUVRE)

WINGED HUMAN-HEADED LION FROM NIMRUD
(BRITISH MUSEUM)

The winged human-headed lions and bulls of Assyria were the guardian genii of the Royal Palaces. Of the two here figured, the one on the left, a bull, was set up by Sargon of Assyria in his palace at Dur-Sharrukin (Sargen-burgh). (See pp. 196 *sq.*) The right-hand one a lion, was the work of Ashur-nasir-pal, and was brought to London by Layard. Both are fine examples of Assyrian monimental sculpture. (See pp. 205 *sq.*)

Constantinople had given him to help him in his self-appointed task !

The position when he arrived at Mosul was a delicate one. The Turkish governor on the spot was the kind of man whom one would scarcely believe to be possible except between the covers of a fairy-tale—a regular ogre, who used to charge the villagers of his district for the wear and tear caused to his teeth by the process of consuming the provisions which they were forced to supply to him when he deigned to pass a night among them, and who devised a very happy way of adding to his personal income by pretending to die, and then coming suddenly to life again, and levying a heavy tax on the property of those whose joy at his death had been too plainly manifested. Mohammed Pasha was far too cute to believe that anyone would trouble to dig in the mounds of his province for anything less valuable than gold, and far too patriotic to allow a foreigner to be enriched by discoveries which might have put treasure into his own pocket ; and so Layard had to use the wisdom of the serpent as well as the harmlessness of the dove in making his arrangements. He gave out that he was going upon a hunting expedition, and dropped down the Tigris on November 8, 1845, on a raft well laden with boar-spears and rifles. The explorer had one of the most useful faculties with which such a man can be endowed—a wonderful capacity for making friends out of the wild Arab tribes with whom he had to deal. Before he slept that night, he had become the firm friend of Awad, chief of the tribe whose camp lay nearest to the mound of Nimrud, which he had determined to explore ; and the chief promised to procure workmen for him on the next day.

" Before he tried to sleep," would be nearer to the truth. Layard's imagination had long been wrought to a high pitch by thoughts of what might lie beneath the Mesopotamian mounds. " Those huge mounds of Assyria," he writes, telling of his journey in 1839-40, " made a deeper impression upon me, gave rise to more serious thoughts and more earnest reflection, than the temples of Baalbec and the theatres of Ionia." Now that he was in touch with the task which had been the dream of his life, and that in a few hours he was about to put his fate to the touch, sleep forsook him, and he could only dream of wonders or disappointments. " Visions of palaces underground, of gigantic monsters, of sculptured figures and endless inscriptions floated before me. After forming plan after plan for removing the earth, and extricating these treasures, I fancied myself wandering in a maze of chambers from which I could find no outlet. Then, again, all was reburied, and I was standing on the grass-covered mound. Exhausted, I was at length sinking into sleep, when hearing the voice of Awad, I rose from my carpet, and joined him outside the hovel. The day already dawned ; he had returned with six Arabs, who agreed for a small sum to work under my direction."

It was a small beginning for a colossal undertaking ; but the results were, fortunately, not to be proportionate to the means employed. Almost at once it became evident that the excavation was going to be rewarded with success. The very first attempt at digging revealed a sculptured alabaster slab, and then another and another, until it was plain that the excavators had lighted upon one of the chambers of a palace. At this point, Layard divided his scanty force, leaving some of the workmen to continue the exploration of the chamber they had found, while he led the others to the south-west corner of the mound, where fragments of calcined alabaster gave promise of further treasures lying beneath. Again, almost at once, came the proof of success. Here the palace, to whomsoever it might have belonged, had suffered from the action of fire, and the slabs were in many instances calcined with intense heat ; but everywhere there was evidence of rich material awaiting the explorer.

"Night interrupted our labours," says Layard. "I returned to the village well satisfied with their result." Few men surely have ever had better reason for satisfaction. He had worked for one day, with six men; and he had discovered two Assyrian palaces! Good fortune could scarcely go further. It was not to be all good fortune with Layard, and he was to taste to the full, before he was done with the work, all the bitterness of the opposition that comes from stupidity, ignorance, and, worst of all, jealousy, to see his work misrepresented, to have it stopped by wilful malevolence, and to know that he could not do it as it ought to be done for lack of the funds which were being liberally granted by France to the work at Khorsabad, but which could not be expected from the stolid and unimaginative British Government; but at least none of all this can have marred the sweetness of that first triumphant moment.

The next day the working force at his disposal was almost doubled by the arrival of five Turcomans from the village of Selamiyah, who had heard that regular wages were to be had in consequence of the incomprehensible folly of the Frank who had come among them. Soon there came to light, in the chamber first discovered, a fragment of ivory which had once been gilded, and still bore carving with Egyptian decorative motives. The discovery of the gilding and some fragments of gold leaf greatly intrigued the worthy Awad, who now began to see some method in the madness of the Frank. "O, Bey," said he, "Wallah! your books are right, and the Franks know that which is hidden from the true believer. Here is the gold, sure enough, and, please God, we shall find it all in a few days. Only don't say anything about it to those Arabs, for they are asses, and cannot hold their tongues. The matter will come to the ears of the Pasha." The good man's opinion of Frankish wisdom sadly declined again when he was told that he was welcome to all the gold leaf which he had found, and to any more that he might yet find in the course of the excavations.

By the middle of November, the working staff was again doubled, and with thirty men at work, Layard rapidly laid bare chamber after chamber, each lined with sculptured alabaster slabs, representing the Assyrian king in battle, at the Chase, or besieging cities. Ere long, however, the Captain of Irregulars, who had been appointed, nominally to look after Layard's safety, but actually to spy upon him, and whom the explorer, according to his wont, had speedily converted into a firm friend, reported to him, with many apologies, that the Pasha had ordered him to stop the excavations. Layard at once went to head-quarters, to find the reason for this prohibition, and was informed that the mound contained Mussulman graves, which were being disturbed by the excavations, and that such profanation could not be allowed. As Layard was well aware that there were no modern graves on the mound, he talked the matter over with his friend Daoud Agha, the Captain of Irregulars, and learned without much surprise from that worthy, that, under orders from the Pasha, he and his command had been employed for two nights in bringing gravestones from a distance to make sham graves, so as to provide a case for stopping the excavations. " We have destroyed more real graves of the true Believers in making sham ones, than you could have defiled between the Zab and Selamiyah. We have killed our horses and ourselves in carrying these accursed stones." Such were the methods of Turkish officialdom in 1845 ; and such the joys of excavating under Turkish protection.

Fortunately Mohammed Pasha's time of evil-doing was rapidly drawing to a close, and before Christmas he was superseded, and the virtuous old gentleman was left in a dilapidated room through whose leaks the winter rains penetrated without difficulty, to meditate on the evil fate which awaits those who sacrifice themselves for the good of others. " Thus it is " said he, " with God's creatures. Yesterday all these dogs were kissing my feet, to-day every one and everything falls upon me, even the rain ! "

> " It was roses, all the way,
>
> . . . . . .
>
> A year ago on this very day.
> Now I go in the rain, and more than needs
> A rope cuts both my wrists behind,
> And I think, by the feel, my forehead bleeds ;
> For they fling, whoever has a mind,
> Stones at me for my year's misdeeds."

Thus Mohammed Pasha, anticipating Browning ; but, one may imagine, without the consolation of the Patriot, at least if he was wise. " Now instead, 'tis God shall repay " would probably have meant a poor lookout for the Turkish governor.

With the advent of a new and more, though not too, enlightened Pasha, things began to improve, and by the middle of February there came evidence of the discovery of sculptures of greater size and importance than any which had hitherto come to light, indicating that one of the important halls of the palace had been reached ; and the discovery of some of the strange winged and eagle-headed human figures so frequent in Assyrian sculpture was speedily followed by that of one of those weird colossi, for which Layard had doubtless long been looking and hoping, as the unmistakable confirmation of the fact that he, like Botta, had discovered an unquestionable royal palace.

Layard himself had been spending a few hours in the encampment of one of the Arab tribes on the morning when the discovery took place, and has told us, with inimitable vivacity, the story of his reception on his return. " I was returning to the mound when I saw two Arabs . . . urging their mares to the top of their speed. On approaching me they stopped. ' Hasten, O Bey,' exclaimed one of them—

' hasten to the diggers, for they have found Nimrod himself. Wallah, it is wonderful, but it is true ! We have seen him with our eyes. There is no God but God ' ; and both joining in this pious exclamation, they galloped off, without further words, in the direction of their tents." Here was the realisation of all his dreams, and the reward of all his toils, and one may imagine the feelings with which Layard hastened back to his mound.

"On reaching the ruins, I descended into the new trench, and found the workmen, who had already seen me as I approached, standing near a heap of baskets and cloaks. Whilst Awad advanced, and asked for a present to celebrate the occasion, the Arabs withdrew the screen they had hastily constructed, and disclosed an enormous human head sculptured in full out of the alabaster of the country. . . . I saw at once that the head must belong to a winged-lion or bull, similar to those of Khorsabad or Persepolis. It was in admirable preservation. The expression was calm, yet majestic, and the outline of the features showed a freedom and knowledge of art scarcely to be looked for in the works of so remote a period. The cap had three horns, and unlike that of the human-headed bulls hitherto found in Assyria, was rounded, and without ornament at the top.

" I was not surprised that the Arabs had been amazed and terrified at this apparition. It required no stretch of imagination to conjure up the most strange fancies. This gigantic head, blanched with age, thus rising from the bowels of the earth, might well have belonged to one of those fearful beings which are pictured in the traditions of the country, as appearing to mortals, slowly ascending from the regions below."

I have let Layard tell his own story of this first great success, not because the discovery of one winged-lion more or less among the many was intrinsically a matter of supreme moment ; but because this first winged lion was,

so to speak, the hall-mark of success on the English explorer's work in the eyes of the English-speaking public,
and because the vivid simplicity of the excavator's narrative
helps to explain the astonishing impression which the story
of his exploits produced. In the opinion of the multitude,
Assyrian excavation meant winged lions and bulls and the
like, ever since Botta's work at Khorsabad. If you had
one of them to show, you were genuine ; if not, you were
of no account. Actually Layard was to discover scores of
things of far greater importance, historically and arch-
æologically, than these hybrid monsters ; but it was the
winged-lions and bulls which made him famous. Besides,
the British public cherished a traditional distaste for being
left behind by any other nation in anything ; and since
Botta had discovered winged bulls and lions, Layard had
to make good in that respect also, for the national credit,
if for nothing else.

Meanwhile the local popularity of the find was quite as
great, in its way, as its European celebrity was going to be,
and was much more embarrassing. The excavations had
to be stopped until local piety was satisfied that there was no
disturbance of the pious ancestors of the true Believers.
" The Cadi had no distinct idea whether the bones of the
mighty hunter had been uncovered, or only his image ;
nor did Ismail Pasha very clearly remember whether
Nimrod was a true-believing prophet or an infidel. I
accordingly received a somewhat unintelligible message
from his Excellency, to the effect that the remains should
be treated with respect, and be by no means further disturbed ; that he wished the excavations to be stopped at
once, and desired to confer with me on the subject." Even
when the intelligent, but not too intelligent, Pasha had
been moderately persuaded that no injury to piety was
being done, he had to visit Nimrod in person, accompanied
by a large force of troops and three guns ! whether to do
honour to a pious ancestor, or to secure himself against a

re-emergent devil. The general opinion of the governor's entourage on the sculptures was characteristically summed up by the deputy of the Cadi of Mosul ; " May God curse all infidels and their works ! What comes from their hands is of Satan : it has pleased the Almighty to let them be more powerful and ingenious than the true Believers in this world, that their punishment and the reward of the faithful may be greater in the next."

Soon the first monster, whose appearance had excited such wonder, was matched by a second, and they by successive couples until thirteen pairs were at last discovered ; but long before that, the excavations had been regularised by a firman from Constantinople, authorising " the continuance of the excavations, and the removal of such objects as might be discovered " ; and by August, 1846, the first cases of sculptured bas-reliefs from Nimrud had arrived in England and been safely housed in the British Museum ; and in consequence of the interest thus excited a grant was made through the Museum for the further prosecution of the excavations. In comparison with the liberal manner in which the French Government supported the work of Botta, however, the British grant to Layard was a totally inadequate one, and in consequence the excavator was obliged to carry on his work in the fashion which has already been described in this book as the most unsatisfactory of all methods of working—namely, by tunnelling and digging trenches round the walls of the chambers which he discovered, so as to lay bare their bas-reliefs, while the chambers themselves were left almost entirely unexplored. " As the means at my disposal," he writes himself, " did not warrant any outlay in making more experiments without the promise of the discovery of something to carry away, I felt myself compelled, much against my inclination, to abandon the excavations in this part of the mound, after uncovering portions of two chambers." Indeed, Hilprecht has described the object of

Layard's excavations as being simply " to obtain the largest possible number of well preserved objects of art at the least possible outlay of time and money." This is a pitiful description of work which was done with such splendid enthusiasm and self-denial, and which had as its result the awakening of the whole English-speaking world to an interest in the lands of the Near East which has never since entirely died away ; the shame of the fact that it is, all the same, a true description, lies not for one moment upon Layard, but upon the miserable parsimony and lack of imagination of the home authorities. Even as it is, the magnificent treasures of the Assyrian galleries of the British Museum are a splendid testimony to the skill and energy with which Layard used the paltry resources entrusted to him ; but they might have been so much more, and none knew it better than the man who made them what they are.

With the means at his disposal, such as they were, he continued his task. The first tentative steps towards the decipherment of the cuneiform inscriptions were now being taken, and it began to be possible to discriminate, to some slight extent, between periods, and even between kings, of Assyrian history. One of the palaces which Layard had unearthed at Nimrud proved to have belonged to King Ashur-nasir-pal (885-860 B.C.), and from it a series of very beautiful slabs was recovered, on which the whole business of Assyrian warfare and hunting was depicted with astonishing vivacity. The central palace of the mound had belonged to Ashur-nasir-pal's son and successor, Shalmaneser III, and the work at this point proved somewhat unprofitable for awhile. " The trench," says Layard, " was carried on in the same direction for several days ; but nothing more appeared. It was now above fifty feet in length, and still without any new discovery. . . . Standing on the edge of the hitherto unprofitable trench, I doubted whether I should carry it any further ; but made up my mind at last

o

not to abandon it until my return, which would be on the following day." Actually he was on the very edge of one of his most notable discoveries, for he had scarcely left the mound when his diggers uncovered the corner of a block of black marble, which proved to be a complete and almost uninjured stele, about six and a half feet in height, on which were recorded the exploits and triumphs of an Assyrian king.

The " Black Obelisk " was at once recognised as one of the most important finds yet made, and was carefully guarded until it was dispatched, on Christmas Day, 1846, along with twenty-two other cases of antiquities, to London. There Rawlinson made it the subject of one of his early cuneiform studies, and, greatly to the delight of Biblical students, identified a part of the inscription as referring to the tribute paid by " Jehu, son of Omri," to Shalmaneser.

By the end of April, 1847, Layard, among other less conspicuous finds, had discovered no fewer than thirteen pairs of winged-lions and bulls, to say nothing of fragments of others. The removal of these monsters was not contemplated in London, and he was instructed to cover them with earth again, " until some favourable opportunity of moving them entire might occur " ; a decision which, in fact, meant the relegating of the removal of them to the Greek Kalends. Layard, fortunately, had more faith and pluck than his timorous backers. He chose out one of the smaller lions, and a bull to keep him company, and determined to attempt the removal of the gigantic pair, not by sawing them into pieces, as Botta had done with the bulls from Khorsabad, but entire, merely lightening them by cutting away part of the thickness of the unsculptured backs of the figures. The narrative of how he succeeded in his attempt—the construction of the wonderful cart which all Mosul came out to see, as it passed over the crazy bridge of boats, the breaking of the rubbishy Arab ropes which were used to lower the bull to the cart, and the consequent collapse of the monster uninjured, as if by miracle, exactly in the spot on which Layard had designed to place him, his subsequent transport to the river bank by teams of buffaloes who refused to pull, and gangs of Arabs who pulled like mad creatures, and the voyage of the two colossi to Basra on the raft of a doleful man of Bagdad who was quite convinced that neither he nor his raft would ever survive the voyage—all this, as told by the much-enduring explorer who was the Odysseus of many devices of the piece, is one of the epics of excavation. We may have learned, since 1847, to put a different relative value upon the products of excavation, and to think less of Layard's colossi than of other discoveries which seemed to him of less importance ; but the courage and the skill with which he pursued his object until he had triumphantly attained it can never be regarded with anything but the deepest admiration.

The twin monsters arrived in London, and at the door of the British Museum, just in time to meet Dante Gabriel Rossetti, who had been looking at the Elgin Marbles, and was just going home again when he was confronted by the apparition of the winged-bull being hoisted in. The result was " The Burden of Neneveh," which, however defective its archæology, is yet one of the most remarkable poems of its erratic creator, and as Ruskin said, " a glorious thing." As Layard watched his rafts, with their priceless burdens, disappearing round a bend of the Tigris, he could not help moralising : " I could not forbear musing upon the strange destiny of their burdens. . . . Who can venture to foretell how their strange career will end." He did not foresee their celebration by one of the most curious products of London cosmopolitanism, the Pre-Raphaelite painter and poet. You wonder what old Ashur-nasir-pal would have thought and said of Rossetti and all his works ; and as Samuel Johnson said, " you *may* wonder."

Ashur-nasir-pal's winged-bulls, of course, had nothing to do with the burden, or with anything else, of Nineveh ;

for the mound of Nimrud covered the ruins, not of Nineveh, but of Kalah, one of the earlier capitals of Assyria. Almost immediately, however, Layard turned his attention for a short time to the mound of Kouyunjik, and though he could only spare a month for work there before he returned home, it was enough to identify the ruins as being beyond question those of Nineveh, and the particular palace which he had lighted upon as that of Sennacherib. On June 24, 1847, he left Mosul for England. He had been at work, roughly speaking, for two years, and he had identified two Assyrian capitals and discovered and partially excavated eight royal palaces in that time !

I have told in some detail the story of his first campaign, because it was this venture, and the dramatic account which he gave of it in his *Nineveh and its Remains*, which really marked the epoch of the awakening of the sleeper. It is only possible to summarise briefly the results of his subsequent work. He returned to Mosul in 1849, and after some work at his old hunting-ground at Nimrud, turned his attention to Kouyunjik. Here his remarkable work was the excavation of the great palace of Sennacherib, enlarged and further adorned by that king's grandson, Ashur-bani-pal. His work dealt thus with a period more definitely Scriptural than that covered by the excavations at Nimrud. There, of course, the Black Obelisk gave definite touch with Biblical figures ; but most of the sculptures secured belonged to the much earlier period of Ashur-nasir-pal, a king who does not come into contact with the Scriptural narrative at all. Sennacherib, however, is one of the colossal figures of Scripture, the embodiment of godless power and pride, and the typical instance of their humiliation ; while the British public has early poetic associations with him also from its schooldays, and is still a little hazy on the point of whether " The Assyrian came down like a wolf on the fold " is a quotation from the Bible or from Byron, an uncanonical author. Here, at all events, was Sennacherib's own story of how he came down, and of what he did when he came, not altogether told or pictured in the same perspective as in the Bible, yet with details remarkably accordant, up to a point, with the Scriptural narrative. Hilprecht has observed that we, who " have been under the powerful influence which went forth from the resurrected palaces of Kouyunjik since the earliest days of our childhood," can scarcely comprehend fully " how much the interpretation of the Old Testament books profited from Layard's epoch-making discoveries." Undoubtedly this is true, and one important aspect of the awakening of modern Biblical criticism, and that on the whole a sane and sound one, is due to the impulse given by Layard's work, which gave the student parallel documents, undoubtedly contemporary with the events narrated, to place alongside the accounts of the Hebrew chroniclers and prophets.

The crowning triumph at Kouyunjik came from the additions which King Ashur-bani-pal had made to the palace of his grandfather. The artistic quality of Ashur-bani-pal's reliefs was extraordinarily high, though there is more than a trace of the over-insistence on minute detail which seems to be the outstanding characteristic of decadent art in all lands and ages. Still some of the work is so superb in its dash and vigour, that it is scarcely fair to talk of decadence in connection with it ; and some of the lion-hunting scenes of Ashur-bani-pal must rank among the most wonderful feats of animal sculpture in any land or time ; while some of the battle scenes, though suffering more from over-elaboration, are wonderfully vivid. But the discovery of the Royal Library of Ashur-bani-pal was an event of absolutely first-class importance, far exceeding the mere finding of more sculptured slabs, however fine their artistic quality ; for it introduced us, for the first time on any large scale, to Assyrian literature, and, indirectly, to the kindred literature of Babylonia. The discovery was made in the early summer of 1850, in two comparatively insignificant chambers of the south-west palace at Kouyunjik, one of Ashur-bani-pal's additions to the great palace of his grandfather. " The chambers I am describing," says Layard, " appear to have been a depository in the palace of Nineveh for such documents (cuneiform tablets). To the height of a foot or more from the floor they were entirely filled with them ; some entire, but the greater part broken into many fragments, probably by the falling in of the upper part of the building. They were of different sizes ; the largest tablets were flat, and measured about 9 inches by 6½ inches ; the smaller were slightly convex, and some were not more than an inch long, with but one or two lines of writing. The cuneiform characters on most of them were singularly sharp and well-defined, but so minute in some instances as to be almost illegible without a magnifying glass."

Later, when Layard had retired from the field, Hormuzd Rassam, the assistant who had been trained in his school, completed this great discovery by finding in Ashur-bani-pal's own palace (the north palace of Kouyunjik) the other half of the king's library. The thousands of inscribed tablets thus acquired were rendered available by Rawlinson's discovery of the secret of the cuneiform script. Under his hands, and those of Hincks and others, the work of decipherment rapidly progressed, until in 1857, the experiment carried out by the Royal Asiatic Society, on the suggestion of Talbot, of submitting to several Assyriologists, Rawlinson, Hincks, Oppert and himself, copies of the annals of Tiglath-Pileser I for translation and comparison, resulted in the triumphant vindication of the new learning, the translations of the four being practically identical. It was possible, therefore, even in 1850, to realise something of the value of Layard's crowning discovery. The tablets were found to contain specimens of almost every possible kind of literature. There were

scientific treatises, astronomical, medical, and mathematical, historical records of all kinds, hundreds of hymns,
prayers, dogmatic and mythological texts, books of ritual,
letters and addresses from kings and high officials ; while
by no means the least important part of the collection is the
mass of syllabaries, grammars, and dictionaries, giving
immediate access to the structure and usage of the Assyrian
and Babylonian languages, and more particularly to those
of the ancient Sumerian tongue, the first speech of civilisation in the lands of the rivers.

With this splendid triumph, our record of Layard's
great work may appropriately close.   He relinquished his
excavations in April, 1851, and never returned to the scenes
of his former exploits, though he maintained his interest
in Mesopotamian excavation, and did his utmost to further
it when Ambassador at Constantinople in 1877.   His active
life as an excavator, therefore, lasted almost exactly five
and a half years, and bears a singularly small proportion
to the rest of a distinguished career, in which it may seem
only a trifling interlude.   In point of enduring importance,
however, it may be said, without much risk of exaggeration,
that those five and a half years far outweigh all the rest of
his lifework put together, and that few men have ever
accomplished anything like so much in that period, and
with such inadequate means, as did the first British
excavator in Mesopotamia.

The mantle of Elijah fell, in this case, upon shoulders
not altogether unworthy to wear it, though it must be
admitted that Mr. Hormuzd Rassam wore the robe with
something of a semi-piratical swing quite alien to the
bearing of its first owner.   Rassam's soul soared far above
all the restrictions which could be imposed upon him by
international bargains as to the limits of the spheres of
excavation of England or France, or by the firman of the
Sultan under which he worked.   His great discovery
(December, 1853) of Ashur-bani-pal's palace at Kouyunjik

was accomplished, to put it plainly, simply by the process of "jumping the claim" of the French explorer, Victor Place, to whom the northern half of the mound, in which the palace lay, had been definitely allotted by a bargain made with Sir Henry Rawlinson.   Rassam believed that the palace was there, and was determined that the credit of excavating it should go, not to France, but to England, and perhaps, incidentally, to himself as England's representative.   Accordingly, in the bright moonlight of December, 1853, he began operations with a gang of faithful Arabs, and in three nights' work got definitely down to palace walls.   "For a moment," says the claim-jumper, with the most innocent glee, "I did not know which was the most pleasant feeling that possessed me, the joy of my faithful men, or the finding of the new palace."   It would, of course, be altogether too rude to disturb his guileless self-satisfaction by remarking that what he had really done was not to find, but to steal, a palace.

"If 'twere done when it is done, then 'twere well
    It were done quickly"

is a motto which applied literally in the early days of Mesopotamian excavation.   Once you had definitely got a grip upon the object you wished to thieve, you were secure, and could flaunt your stolen goods under the very noses of the men from whom you had stolen them.   Rassam, therefore, once he had actually, like Nehemiah, surveyed his ruins by moonlight, boldly proceeded with the excavation of them by day.   For "it was an established rule that whenever one discovered a new palace, no one else could meddle with it, and thus, in my position of agent of the British Museum, I had secured it for England."   Quite satisfactory, no doubt, for Mr. Rassam ; but one would have liked to hear the unofficial remarks of M. Victor Place, when he discovered that Ashur-bani-pal's palace had been stolen from under his nose.

LION-HUNT OF KING ASHUR-BANI-PAL

The Assyrian sculptor, inferior to his Egyptian brother artist in the rendering of the human form, was a master of animal sculpture. The Lion Hunts in the British Museum are among the finest examples of later Assyrian work of this type. (See p. 217.)

ONE OF THE BRONZE BULLS FROM THE TEMPLE OF NINKHARSAG, TELL EL OBEID

The goddess to whom this very ancient Babylonian Temple was dedicated was the Sumerian "Lady of the Mountain," a goddess of living creatures and patroness of cattle. These bronze statues date from about 4000 B.C. and stood free among flowers wrought in various coloured stone, and suggested a herd of cattle walking in a flowery meadow. (See pp. 247–8.)

(By the kindness of Directors of Museum of University of Pennsylvania, Philadelphia, U.S.A.)

However it may have been acquired, the north palace of
Ashur-bani-pal was certainly worth acquiring. It was in
one of its halls that the finest series of those animal-sculptures
of Ashur-bani-pal, already alluded to, was discovered.
This was the magnificent set of hunting scenes, where the
king is depicted in chase and in conflict with the lion and the
wild ass. It is scarcely possible to give too high praise to
some of these scenes, whose vivid realism is remarkable.
Hilprecht's comments well sum up the impression made by
these wonders of ancient art—" The furious lion, foiled
in his revenge, burying his teeth in the chariot wheels ;
the wounded lioness, with her outstretched head, suffering
agony, and vainly endeavouring to drag her paralysed lower
limbs after her ; or the king on his spirited horse, with wild
excitement in his face, and in hot pursuit of the swift wild
ass of the desert—all these scenes are so realistic in their
conception, and at the same time so beautifully portrayed,
that from the beginning they have found a most deserved
admiration." It is singularly fortunate that in the British
Museum these masterpieces can be closely compared with
the noble hunting scenes of Ashur-naṣir-pal from Kalah.
The two sets of scenes are separated in time by rather more
than two centuries ; and the changes of outlook and method
wrought by those two hundred years are manifest at once.
In all matters of detail, and in minute knowledge of animal
anatomy, the later sculptor, as was to be expected, is superior
to his predecessor ; but in vigour of conception and largeness of execution, the older artist is even more ahead of his
successor. The course of development is the normal one
of a nation's art, and the higher finish and knowledge of
the later period do not compensate for the loss of breadth
and strength. Both series, however, show one unpleasant
trait in common, though it is more marked in the later reliefs
—the characteristically Assyrian delight in the portrayal
of the painful details of suffering and death. We wonder
at and admire the astonishing realism of the dying lioness,

referred to by Hilprecht, or of the dying lion, shot through the lungs, and vomiting blood in great streams ; we wonder no less at the taste which loved to look habitually on such scenes.

Again, in the case of this new palace, artistic discoveries had to take second place to those of literary importance ; for Ashur-bani-pal's hall of the hunting scenes proved to have been his library also, and here the second half of the great store of books which he gathered came to light in the shape of several thousands of clay tablets, containing writing of the same variety of type as the store previously found by Layard. It was here that there were found the tablets containing the Assyrian account of the Deluge, so interesting alike in its resemblance to, and its variations from, the Biblical story of Noah and the Ark ; and this discovery, in its turn, was responsible for the expeditions of George Smith, and his remarkable contributions to Assyriology.

Rassam's work was now interrupted for awhile, and Loftus continued the excavations, his most interesting find being the famous relief in which Ashur-bani-pal is depicted drinking wine under the trees of his garden, while the head of his vanquished enemy, Te-umman of Elam, hangs from a branch in front of the king, a pleasant spectacle for his eyes to gloat upon. We have been recently told by the latest historian of Assyria that the Assyrian is a shamefully misunderstood benefactor of his kind ; it may be so, but at all events it will be permitted to say that his taste in house decoration was peculiar, and, to our minds, unrefined !

Loftus's work at Kouyunjik, however, was brought to a close owing to lack of funds, and nothing more was done in Assyria till 1873. The work of arranging the tablets from the library of Ashur-bani-pal had been entrusted largely to George Smith, whose extraordinary aptitude for the decipherment of cuneiform texts has seldom been equalled. Among the tablets, he quickly discovered that primitive account of the Deluge already referred to, and proceeding with his work he came upon other fragments of the great Babylonian Epic of Gilgamesh, of which this Deluge story forms a part. The discovery aroused great enthusiasm, and the proprietors of the *Daily Telegraph* offered to advance one thousand guineas for an expedition to Assyria, to be led by Smith, with the object of searching for the remainder of the great epic whose fragments had thus come to light. The offer was accepted, and Smith set out for Mosul in January, 1873. Delayed by the want of the necessary firman for excavation, he employed the waiting time in a survey of the ruins of Babylonia, returning to Mosul in the beginning of April. His early work at Nimrud was comparatively unprofitable ; but he was more successful at Kouyunjik. Here he found that Layard's tunnels had collapsed, rendering the thorough exploration of the mound more difficult than ever ; but though thus obliged to confine his work almost entirely to the library chambers of the two palaces, he had the wonderful good fortune, on May 14, of finding nearly the whole of the missing portion of the account of the Deluge. Overjoyed at his success he telegraphed to London the news of his find, expecting that since he had been so successful he would be instructed to continue his work ; but, to his intense chagrin, the proprietors of the *Daily Telegraph* decided that, as the immediate object of the expedition had been attained, it should return home at once. Accordingly, Smith closed his diggings and returned to London, only to find that the Trustees of the British Museum had meanwhile decided to set aside £1000 for the continuance of the work, and that he was to start for Assyria again at once.

He was back upon the scene of his labours on the first day of 1874. His firman closed at the middle of March, and it is difficult to conceive of a more classical instance of muddling than the process which had resulted in his having to spend the most of his precious time on a fool's errand to London

and back again. The most was made of the two and a half
months left to him, and at one time he had as many as six
hundred workmen employed on the excavations. His
results, of course, were not spectacular, for he was not
looking for great monuments and sculptures, but for inscriptions. Of these he managed to collect more than
three thousand in the short time available, and among these
were many of the most important documents known to
Assyriology ; while the publication of his *Assyrian Discoveries* and his *Chaldean Account of Genesis* once more
aroused public interest to a remarkable extent.

In consequence, he was once more sent out in the spring
of 1876 ; but this time he was destined to find only a prema-
ture death. He found, on his arrival, that cholera was
raging, and that the whole country was in a state of panic
and disorganisation. It seemed almost impossible to organise
excavations ; but the indomitable explorer strove to carry
out his mission, hoping against hope, until at last, worn out
by overwork and exposure, he dragged himself to the house
of the British Consul at Aleppo, and died there. His work
is one of the tragedies of excavation. Limited as he was by
the want of a complete education, and yet so naturally gifted
that he accomplished far more than could have been deemed
possible, the record of his achievement is so remarkable
as to suggest the tragic loss caused, not only by his early
death, but by the misapplication of so much of his brief
opportunity, through no fault of his.

In 1878, Rassam resumed his Assyrian work, which he
carried on, with varying success, for several years. His
methods were still marked by the lightness with which
official restrictions weighed upon his soaring soul. Strictly
speaking, the most remarkable achievement of his new
campaign was one which he had no business to have
achieved, and in the accomplishment of which he took grave
risks, both of offending the Turkish Government, and of
arousing popular indignation against all excavation ; but

Rassam, like Gallio, " cared for none of these things," and he was entirely successful, more so, perhaps, than he deserved to be in the circumstances. His real errand was to continue the work which had been broken off by the death of George Smith, and to search for more of the library of Ashur-bani-pal ; but trifling little tablets seemed scarcely worth considering to Layard's old assistant, who remembered the great days of colossal winged-bulls and lions. He says himself, with perfect simplicity, " Although that (the search for tablets) was the first object of my mission, I was, nevertheless, more eager to discover some new ancient sites than to confine my whole energy on such a tame undertaking. . . . My aim was to discover unknown edifices, and to bring to light some important Assyrian monument."

A year before, a friend of his, dragoman in the French Consulate at Mosul, had sent him some fragments of beaten bronze, inscribed with cuneiform signs, among which the name of Shalmaneser could be made out. Rassam had these definitely in his mind when he resumed work in Mesopotamia, and he quickly found out that they had come from the mound of Balawat, about fifteen miles east of Mosul. The Balawat mound had been genuinely used as a burying-ground by the neighbouring Moslem population and was therefore one of the places from which he was expressly excluded by the terms of his firman. With the same calm disregard of regulations which had marked his jumping of the French claim at Kouyunjik, however, he proceeded to excavate at Balawat, though the excitement among the local Arabs at this violation of the burial-place of their dead was such that on several occasions bloodshed seemed imminent. Finally, he succeeded in his search, and the famous bronze panels from the gates of Imgur-Bel, the palace of Shalmaneser III at Balawat, now adorn the British Museum.

With the close of Rassam's work it may almost be said

that the heroic period of Assyrian excavation also closes. Since his time there have been various other expeditions, of which we may mention those of Messrs. King and Campbell Thompson in 1903-5, and the German excavations, beginning in 1903 at Kalaat Sherghat, the site of Ashur, the most ancient capital of the land. The German excavators, under Dr. Andrae, were successful in tracing many very ancient remains of the city, going back to the days of Ushpia, the first king of the Semitic re-action which blotted out the earliest Sumerian civilisation of the country. A great number of burials of an unusual diversity of types also came to light; but perhaps the greatest contribution to knowledge was the excavation of the remains of the Anu-Adad temple, which was founded in about 1140 by Ashur-resh-ishi. The temple has a double Ziggurat, or temple-tower, a feature corresponding to its double ownership, and has given the opportunity for the most complete study of Assyrian temple architecture yet extant.

It can scarcely be said, however, that so far the results of the continuation of Assyrian excavation have been worthy of its brilliant beginning under Botta and Layard. For this fact many reasons account—chief among them, perhaps, the condition of the country, and its almost complete lack of any government worthy of the name. Yet, whatever the reason, the fact remains that the land of Assyria has hardly been more than touched by the excavator. The words with which Hilprecht closes the Assyrian section of his account of exploration in Bible lands during the nineteenth century still remain true : " Much more remains to be done, before the resurrection of ancient Assyria will be accomplished. Hundreds of ruins scarcely yet known by their names await the explorer." It would be too much, no doubt, to expect from all these results of such magnitude and brilliancy as rewarded the first excavators. Assyria had more royal cities, perhaps, than most ancient lands, but we cannot expect royal palaces to emerge from every

mound of Mesopotamia. Yet though the results of future
excavation may be less imposing than those of the past, it
does not follow that they will add less to our knowledge of
the civilisation which they represent ; and we may hope
that, with more settled government in the land, and, not
less, with an awakening of Western civilisation to the fact
that knowledge of the history of man's past is of prime
importance to his interests in the present, we may see a
new and more adequately financed movement towards the
placing of our knowledge of ancient Assyria on a wider, if
not more solid basis.

CHAPTER X

EXCAVATION of the mounds of Babylonia, though it began
at very much the same time as that of the Assyrian mounds,
and has continued, somewhat intermittently, ever since,
has, on the whole, yielded less imposing results. Nothing
has yet come from any of the Babylonian sites which can
compare, in point of size, or of artistic quality, with the
relics of the great Assyrian palaces. But, on the other hand,
the Babylonian excavations have been extraordinarily
fruitful in relics of the great Sumerian civilisation, which
preceded the Semitic culture, and was eventually obliterated
by it ; and perhaps the most interesting passages of the story
of excavation in Babylonia are those which tell of the work
which has been done on various Babylonian sites, in unearth-
ing the remains which have told us something of the history
of several of the city-states of Sumer and Akkad, the ancient
names for the southern and northern divisions of early
Babylonia. For the fundamental unit of Sumerian civilisation, like that of classical Greece, was not the kingdom,
but the city-state. Each city of Sumer or Akkad was a
unit by itself, ruling its own little circle of territory, and
ruled over by its own priest-governor, or "patesi."
Periodically, of course, one or other of these city-states
would enter upon a brief period of imperialism, in which
it would conquer some of the other city-states round about
it, and add their territories to its own ; in which case its
ruler would probably call himself "King of the Four
Quarters of the World," and consider himself a very big

man indeed, till he was tumbled down from his eminence by another aspirant to wider rule. But essentially Sumerian culture was based upon the city, not the kingdom. Of course, when the Semite came to power in Babylonia, he occupied many of the old Sumerian sites, and made them his own ; and where that has been the case, as in Babylon itself, very little of the more ancient culture has survived ; but, fortunately for us, there have been several instances in which Semitic influence has left the original Sumerian city practically untouched, so that in them we come face to face with the first civilisation of Babylonia, with next to no alien element mixed with it, to render its interpretation difficult. The purpose of this chapter is to describe some of the work on such sites, and its results.

First of all, however, let us try to sketch briefly the outline of the earlier work in Babylonia ; which, indeed, was itself more or less of a sketchy kind. The earliest excavations worthy of the name in Babylonia were made, not upon one of the purely Sumerian sites of which I have spoken, but upon the mounds covering a city which had been occupied and reoccupied many times during its long history. It was first of all in 1850, and then again in 1853-4, that William Kennett Loftus, who has already been mentioned in connection with the work in Assyria, made his attack upon the gigantic mounds of Warka, which represent the ancient city of Uruk or Erech, one of the most famous of old Babylonian cities. The mounds of Warka are colossal, the largest in all Babylonia, covering an area whose circumference is nearly six miles, and Loftus can scarcely be said to have done more than scratch their surface here and there ; yet, even so, he discovered enough to reveal part of the great temple of E-anna, the temple of the goddess Ninni or Ishtar, while his work in another part of the ruins resulted in the discovery of the first example of the characteristic Babylonian decoration of wall surfaces by means of terra-cotta cones of different colours. One of

P

the last pre-war excavations in Babylonia was that of the German Oriental Society at Warka, resulting in the revelation of further details of the great temple which Loftus was the first to discover. But, on the whole, Warka still awaits excavation; and, if Hilprecht's calculation is anything like the truth, and it would require at least fifty years' work, with a fund of not less than $500,000 to make a complete examination of the site, one fears that it is likely to remain unexcavated for some time to come. At Senkereh, fifteen miles south of Warka, Loftus also did some digging, in the course of which he was fortunate enough to strike upon the remains of the ancient temple and stage-tower of Larsa, the Biblical Ellasar, and to find a number of barrel cylinders inscribed with historical data, and clay tablets mostly relating to business.

In 1852, the French Expedition under Fresnel and Oppert, began operations at the great mound known as the " Kasr," covering part of the ruins of Babylon itself. The work was extended to two of the other mounds, " Babil " and " Amran Ibn' Ali "; but, though it was carried on for two years, the results were singularly disappointing; while the ill-luck which seemed to dog the expedition all through culminated in the wreck of the rafts which were carrying down the river the fruits of all its labours. Koldewey's work on the same site has since shown something of the enormous amount of work which must be done before a site like that of Babylon can be said to have been explored; and it is evident that the earlier explorers of Babylonia had no idea of the magnitude of the task which they were facing.

The mounds of Mukayyar, " Covered with Bitumen," which mark the site of that ancient " Ur of the Chaldees," from which Abraham set out on his journey of faith, were visited and partly explored in 1854-5 by J. E. Taylor, then British Vice-Consul at Basra. He succeeded in identifying the great temple of Nannar, the Moon-God of Ur, and traced the line of its walls for some distance, investigating

also part of the stage-tower, of which he could trace two
storeys. At the angles of the tower he found inscribed
cylinders which established the fact that the tower, so far
as Taylor had revealed it, was the work of the early Sumerian
king Ur-Engur, and was repaired by his son Dungi. The
last repair had been the work of the last king of Babylon,
the pious Nabu-na'id, or Nabonidus, to whom the cylinders
owed their origin ; and the conclusion of the inscriptions
was of unusual interest to Biblical students, consisting, as
it did, of a prayer on behalf of the king's son Bel-shar-uṣur,
the Belshazzar of the Book of Daniel. Besides his work at
Mukayyar, Taylor also spent a few days in opening excavations at Abu Shahrain, which was found to be the famous
city of Eridu of ancient days, the abode of Enki, the God of
the Deep. The temple-tower of Enki's temple still rose,
in two stages, to a height of seventy feet ; and the outstanding characteristic of the site was that at Eridu stone
was used as a building material to an extent otherwise
unknown in Babylonia. Taylor's work lasted for a comparatively short time ; but it was remarkably productive, and
it has been said by Jastrow, that until the advent of de
Sarzec, and his work at Tello, " it was to Taylor that we
owed the most valuable part of our knowledge of the mounds
of the south."

For long the work which he had begun at Mukayyar
remained as he had left it, though various explorers cast
envious eyes upon the mounds. " The methodical exploration of Mukayyar and a complete restoration of its
history," wrote Hilprecht in 1903, " belong still to the
desirable things expected from the future." Fortunately
they have now passed from such a category into that of
desirable things which are being gradually realised ; and
we shall see, before the close of this chapter, some of the
results attained by the joint expedition of the British
Museum and the Museum of the University of Pennsylvania,
under Mr. C. L. Woolley.

The preliminary period of Babylonian excavation was
brought to a close very fittingly by Sir Henry Rawlinson's
identification of Birs Nimrud (the conspicuous mound near
Babylon, to be distinguished from Nimrud, the scene of
Layard's early work in Assyria) with the well-known city
of Borsippa. The corner cylinders of the stage-tower (two
of them, and a fragment of a third) were found by
Rawlinson, and proved that the tower in its present form
was the result of a restoration by Nebuchadnezzar II, at
the beginning of the sixth century B.C., and that its name
was "E-ur-iminanki," "House of the seven divisions
of Heaven and Earth."

Thus far the results of the work in Babylonia had been,
on the whole, disappointing as compared with the early
fruits of that in Assyria. Indeed, the absence, already
alluded to, of big and conspicuous pieces of sculpture, such
as the winged-bulls and lions of Khorsabad and Nimrud,
has remained all through the conspicuous feature of
excavation in Sumer and Akkad. Even apart from this,
however, there seemed comparatively little of outstanding
interest in the few inscriptions which had been gleaned
from the southern mounds by the explorers who had visited
them. But it must be remembered that, with the exception
of the work of Taylor and Loftus, it can scarcely be said
that excavation, in the full sense of the word, had been
carried on at all. In most cases, the mounds had been
submitted to little more than a hasty surface scratching,
which could not be expected to reveal more than the very
latest and least interesting of their treasures. This was
now to be remedied to some extent, and the world was to
learn that, while the Sumerian mounds could not yield
anything to match their Assyrian rivals in scale or artistic
quality, they contained treasures of the past whose human
interest was perhaps greater than that of anything which
has come from Nineveh or Kalah.

As in the case of Khorsabad, so now in the revival of

excavation work in Babylonia, or rather, to speak more
strictly, in Sumer, it was France which was the pioneer ;
and again it was in her consular service that she found the
man whose work was to open the new chapter and give the
impetus to the search after buried knowledge. It was in
January, 1877, that M. Ernest de Sarzec, the newly appointed
Vice-Consul of France at Basra, took up his position at the
ancient port of Sindbad the Sailor and at once formed the
plan of penetrating into the district of Southern Babylonia
crossed by the ancient canal known as the Shatt el-Hai.
The district was then occupied by the Muntefik, an Arab
tribe who were practically independent, under their chief
Nasir Pasha, the builder of the modern town of Nasiriyeh,
and de Sarzec wisely sought the friendship of this powerful
local ruler, and by its means acquired a freedom of movement and work which he could have had in no other way.
His local adviser was a well-known native Christian of
Basra, J. Asfar, and under his advice, backed up by the
evidence of sundry inscribed bricks and a fragment of a
fine dolerite statue, the new vice-consul inspected several
sites on the Shatt el-Hai without much result, and had,
he tells us, no very great hopes of what was suggested to
him as the most promising of them all. This was the
mound, or rather the mounds, of Tello, lying in an irregular
oval about $2\frac{1}{2}$ miles long by $1\frac{1}{4}$ broad, about eight miles
from the nearest town.

The district was anything but inviting, " half the year a
desert, and the other half a swamp," says Hilprecht ; but
de Sarzec, almost at the first glance, recognised that he had
fallen upon a site which would amply repay him for all its
discomforts. " Hardly had I approached the *tells* which
I saw before me," he says, " when I recognised, from the
numerous vestiges which strewed the ground, pieces of
pottery, inscribed cones and bricks, fragments of sculpture,
a field of exploration still virgin, where diggings could not
fail to yield happy results. At my very first circuit on

horseback, I fell in with a magnificent fragment of a colossal statue, bearing an inscription on the shoulder, lying on the surface of the ground, at the foot of the principal mound. It had rolled thither from the neighbouring height, which assuredly contained the ruins of an important building. This was, as it were, the starting-point of my discoveries, and the first finger-post which showed me in what direction I ought to carry my researches."

The promise thus offered to the explorer was amply fulfilled. Gathering as many workmen as possible, and setting them to work at the mound whence he believed the statue to have rolled down, he soon determined the fact that the whole mound consisted of a terrace of crude brick crowned by a great edifice of unknown extent. Digging into the debris which filled a ravine marking a recess in the building, he unearthed the lower part of a great statue of dolerite, partly covered with a long cuneiform inscription. He had no means to remove so heavy a block of stone ; but he took a squeeze of the inscription, and re-buried the statue to wait a more favourable occasion. Then he distributed his workmen over the whole area of the mounds, driving trial trenches, which resulted in the disclosure of many fragments of inscribed vases and sculptures, door-sockets in hard stone with inscriptions of the potentates who set them up, a portion of a great carved stele of a king named Eannatum, and, in particular, two great terra-cotta cylinders of another ruler named Gudea, each of them nearly two feet long and nearly a foot in diameter, and inscribed with about 2000 lines of the ancient cuneiform writing now known as Sumerian—the longest inscription in that language then known.

With these results of his preliminary campaign at Tello, de Sarzec returned to Paris on leave in July, 1878. The fruits of his work, so far as it had gone, were by no means imposing in respect of bulk, and compared poorly with Botta's great sculptures from Khorsabad, But he was fortunate in being able to place them in the hands of a man who could recognise their supreme importance, and who was in a position to influence the home authorities in favour of the new excavations. This was M. Leon Heuzey, curator of the Department of Oriental Antiquities, whose sound knowledge of Babylonian antiquities enabled him at once to recognise that in de Sarzec's finds were forthcoming the first remains of that primitive Chaldæan art, which had already been postulated by one or two scholars, and is now known everywhere as Sumerian. Acting on Heuzey's recommendation, the French authorities requested de Sarzec to return to Basra and continue his researches meantime at his own expense and on his own responsibility, but with the understanding that as soon as affairs had been regulated with the Turkish Government he would be recognised as the official agent of his country in the excavations. Accordingly, de Sarzec returned to Tello in 1880, and in that year and 1881 proceeded with the excavation of the Parthian palace which had been reared over the earlier ruins of the ancient Sumerian builders, and with the tracing and identification of these most precious remains. In this campaign he was extraordinarily successful, not only in discriminating between the various builders and periods to whom and to which the ruins before him belonged, but also in accumulating a number of fine specimens of the art of the Sumerians, including nine large statues in dolerite, several fragments of bas-relief, statuettes, and inscriptions. By the spring of 1881 he had completed his second campaign, and in the following year he returned to Paris, with the most wonderful collection of antiquities which had ever entered the Louvre since the epoch-making arrival of the sculptures from Khorsabad.

Already the scientific world was fairly prepared for something remarkable. The announcement of the great discovery had been publicly made before the French Academy, and Oppert, addressing the International Congress of Orientalists at Berlin, had committed himself to the statement that " since the discovery of Nineveh . . . no discovery has been made which compares in importance with the recent excavations in Chaldea." For once in a way, however, expectation was outrun by realisation, and the exhibition of the statues and other works of art which de Sarzec had brought from ancient Sumer created an enthusiasm fairly comparable with that which Botta's achievement had aroused forty years before. The ordinary observer, who sees to-day the two collections of works of art side by side, is for the moment tempted to wonder what all the to-do was about, for there seems to be no comparison between the stately figures from Khorsabad with their air of ineffable serenity and dignity, and the rude and clumsy headless statues and other mutilated fragments which stand as the finest flower of de Sarzec's exploit. But the Tello sculptures are not to be judged thus superficially.

Even in artistic quality, they are by no means despicable. It would not be fair to compare them with the finished and accomplished work which the Egyptian sculptor had been doing for centuries before they were hewn. The diorite Khafra, or the Rahotep and Nefert of the Cairo Museum, for instance, are much too severe tests to apply to such work as that of Gudea's craftsmen. But at least they are worlds above anything else which the Mesopotamian artist ever accomplished again in the realm of portrait sculpture, as a comparison of the Gudea statues with the famous Ashur-naṣir-pal of the British Museum will suffice to show.

But it is not the artistic quality of the finds that constitutes their chief value. It is the fact that you have in them the first-fruits of the revelation of a whole new world of ancient days. For with this Sumerian work you are brought face to face with work which was already ancient and almost forgotten before the Assyrian began to be known as a power in the world at all, work which takes you back to a time before even the Semite in Babylonia had begun to come to his own, or rather to other people's own ; and for the first time you have work which can be fairly equated with the earliest work of civilisation of the Nile Valley. Not that the Gudea statues were anything like so old as that—their equation is with the Middle Kingdom of Egypt ; but that many of the other results of de Sarzec's work go back to a date comparable with that of the rise of Dynastic rule in Egypt.

De Sarzec returned to his field of operations in 1888, and in a series of campaigns carried on between that date and 1900, he accomplished an immense amount of work in revealing the history of the fortunes of the little city-state which had once occupied the site of the mounds of Tello. The work was interrupted by his death in 1901 ; but in 1904 it was resumed again under Captain Gaston Cros, with highly successful results. The most conspicuous result of the work under Captain Cros was the tracing of the massive city wall, 32½ feet thick, which is still standing in some places, to a height of 26 feet. The most humanly interesting result was the finding of the single inscribed clay tablet whose writer, some unknown citizen, and possibly a priest, calls down curses upon the enemy who had sacked and burned his city.

The town thus called up from its age-long burial to tell the story of its past proved to have been the Sumerian city of Lagash. It was an admirable example of that type of city-state which seemed for long to be capable of holding its own against the rival ideal of the great world-empire, and has perhaps counted for more in the intellectual and artistic development of the human race than the great empires ever have—witness Athens. The earliest actual remains found on the site carried the city back to the days of the king Ur-nina, probably round about 3000 B.C. ; but they involved its much earlier existence, as some of them consisted of votive offerings made by Ur-nina in the temple of Ningirsu, the god of the city. The name of one earlier ruler, Lugalshagengur, who may have lived about 3500 B.C., has survived, together with that of another, Enkhegal, who dates from somewhat before Ur-nina ; so that we may imagine Lagash as being in the early and vigorous days of its life as a city, much about the time when the Ist Dynasty of Egypt was starting the Double Kingdom upon its long course. Lagash, however, was destined to a comparatively early fate, for its history closes somewhere about 2000 B.C., when the rise of the Semitic power in Babylon spelled ruin for the city-states of Sumer. We have, in the ill-fortune which caused the destruction of Lagash at so early a date, the great good fortune of being able to deal with a site which has practically lain unoccupied (save for the Parthian relics, which are easily distinguished) since the days of its Sumerian occupiers.

The story of the little state, as revealed by the monuments and tablets gathered by de Sarzec and Cros, is fairly clear, and of considerable interest. We have, of course, no record ; though the older building which was found 12 feet below the pavement of Ur-nina shows that the city must have had its sacred buildings, rising on their platform above the plain, long before his time. A fine limestone mace-head dedicated by the king Mesilim of Kish, was, however, found at Tello, and it enables us to picture the city as already in his time, say about 3500 B.C., so much a settled community as to have a dispute with a similar community in the neighbourhood as to the boundaries of their respective territories, and to have called in Mesilim as arbitrator. Mesilim names Lugalshagengur as *patesi* or priest-ruler of Lagash, and we may suppose that the king claims a kind of suzerainty over the two states whose dispute he settles. Anyhow, communities which adopted arbitration as a means of settling their differences were already fairly highly civilised.

Ur-nina, the first really historical king of the city, has fortunately left us important records and representations of his reign and himself. His reign seems to have been a peaceful one, and his records mainly deal with the building of the temple of Ningirsu, the cutting of canals, and the building of storehouses. Several limestone plaques, carved in low relief, depict him dressed in the heavy scalloped kilt which was evidently the Sumerian male costume, sometimes with a basket on his head, as a labourer bringing material for the building of the temple, sometimes standing before the god, in a posture of adoration, with his sons and his cupbearer behind him. The type is the same in all— entirely un-Semitic, clean-shaven, with almond eyes and prominent, beak-like noses, giving a curious, bird-like appearance to the face. Ur-nina's peaceful reign was evidently looked back to by his descendants as a sort of Golden Age, and he was held in high reverence by them.

The records of his grandson Eannatum tell of more stirring times and doings. One of de Sarzec's most priceless finds was the famous Stele of the Vultures, which was Eannatum's pillar of victory, erected in commemoration of his triumph over the neighbouring city of Umma. The old frontier dispute between the two towns, which Mesilim had settled some centuries before, broke out afresh, and the men of Umma, under their *patesi* Ush, invaded the disputed territory and plundered it. Eannatum gathered his army, and, encouraged by a divine vision which promised him victory, went out to meet his enemy. The battle resulted in a complete triumph for Lagash, in the capture of Umma, and the substitution of a new *patesi*, Enakalli, for the defeated Ush. A new treaty was signed between the two cities, the slain of Lagash were buried under twenty burial mounds, and the slain of Umma were left to have their bones picked by the birds of the air. The Stele of the Vultures derives its name from the scene which pictures this gruesome feast.

Another scene of the great stele pictures Eannatum leading out his heavily armed infantry to battle. The men of Lagash advance in a formidable phalanx behind the wall of their big shields. Their heads are covered with peaked helmets, in which they look extraordinarily like the Norman knights of the Bayeux Tapestry, and their long pikes make a bristling front to the shield-wall, as they tramp forward over the bodies of their fallen foes. Manifestly the Sumerian war-machine of about 3000 B.C. was highly organised, though, so far as the records of Eannatum go, he did not pose as a conqueror, but rather as a vigorous defender of his own land against aggression on the part of other powers. " By Eannatum," he says " was Elam broken in the head, Elam was driven back to his own land ; Kish was broken in the head, and the King of Opis was driven back to his own land." The Vulture Stele, in another of its scenes, pictures Ningirsu, the God of Lagash, as holding in a net a number of prisoners ; and while, with one hand, he grasps the eagle clutching the two lions, which is the cognisance of Lagash, with the other he gently clubs on the head one of the prisoners who is trying to escape from the net. " Who from among the men of Umma," says Eannatum, " will go back upon the word (of the peace-treaty) and will dispute it in the days to come ? If at some future time they shall alter this word, may the great net of Enlil, by whom they have sworn the oath, strike Umma down ! " Victory and peaceful development on every side evidently made Lagash a happy town under Eannatum, for the well-inscription which was another of the finds claims that " In those days did Ningirsu love Eannatum."

More troublous times came with Enannatum I, the brother of the great ruler. The men of Umma under a new *patesi*, Urlumma, risked the wrath of Enlil, broke their oaths, and again invaded the territory of Lagash. Enannatum gave them battle, but no record of victory has survived, and though a later ruler, Urukagina, claims a victory for his ancestor, Enannatum's own son, Entemena, makes no such claims, so that the battle was probably indecisive. It was left for Entemena himself to settle the business. On his accession,

Urlumma again invaded the land ; but on this occasion he was completely overthrown, and the new ruler of Lagash repeated his uncle's triumph, and swept over Umma with fire and sword. The slaughter, however, was not so very alarming, as the loss of the beaten army of Umma was only sixty men.

Entemena's chief memorial is the magnificent silver vase which was found at Tello, and is now one of the treasures of the Louvre. It is adorned with two bands of incised ornament, of which the upper one represents cattle lying down ; while the lower band shows the arms of Lagash, the lion-headed eagle, Imgig, grasping two lions in his talons. The excavations have left us little of the period immediately succeeding Entemena, though we know the names of four of the *patesis* of the city, Enannatum II, Enetarzi, Enlitarzi, and Lugal-anda ; but with Urukagina, who is the first of the rulers of Lagash to take the title of king, we come upon a most interesting record, albeit one of disaster. One of the finds of Captain Cros, in the later excavations, was a small tablet, not belonging to any of the official collections, but evidently written by some priest and lover of Lagash, after the disaster which closed the first chapter of the history of the city. Urukagina, one of the most interesting figures of Sumerian history, seems to have occupied, in the social sphere, a position something akin to that which Akhenaten of Egypt occupied in religion. He was a social reformer, as his successor of Egypt was a religious reformer ; the trouble was that both were born out of due time. The accounts which the king of Lagash has left of his reforms suggest that they were badly needed ; but seemingly they were no more popular than reforms generally are among the governing classes which are being reformed. Disaffection in the state obviously spelled the opportunity of the ancient enemy, Umma, and the *patesi* of Umma, Lugal-zaggisi, grasped his chance, and overwhelmed Urukagina and his city with fire and sword.

What happened is told us in grim detail by the tablet which Captain Cros discovered.

" The men of Umma," writes the unnamed chronicler, " have set fire to the Ekikala ; they have set fire to the Anta-surra ; they have carried away the silver and the precious stones ! They have shed blood in the palace of Tirash ; they have shed blood in the Abzu-banda ; they have shed blood in the shrine of Enlil and in the shrine of the Sun-god ; they have shed blood in the Akhush ; they have carried away the silver and the precious stones." So the story runs on, a litany of slaughter and destruction, becoming impressive at last by its very monotony ; until it closes with a protestation of innocence on the part of the ruler of Lagash, and an imprecation of divine wrath on the heads of the guilty men of Umma and their ruler. " The men of Umma, by the despoiling of Lagash, have committed a sin against the god Ningirsu ! The power that is come upon them, from them shall be taken away ! Of sin on the part of Uruka-gina, King of Girsu, there is none. But as for Lugal-zaggisi, *patesi* of Umma, may his goddess Nidaba bear this sin upon her head ! "

The excavations now reveal a blank in the history of the city for a period of about three centuries and a half, during which we have little more evidence as to the condition of Lagash than the names of some of its *patesis*. The lack of conspicuous material may be traced, not only to the collapse of Urukagina's rule, but to the fact that this is the time in which the first Semitic Empire, under such great rulers as Sargon of Akkad and Naram-sin, was supreme. The fall of the Empire after Shargalisharri's death, however, is succeeded by a temporary renaissance of Sumerian power, and it is from this time of renewed activity that most of the conspicuous results of de Sarzec's work at Lagash were forthcoming. The dolerite statues which were among his first-fruits, and which continued to be discovered throughout the excavations, were chiefly those of a single *patesi*, Gudea, whose reign may provisionally be put about 2500 B.C., and whose great terracotta cylinders have already been alluded to. The richness of the material from Gudea's reign is such as to make de Sarzec's work by far the most valuable source of information as to Sumerian culture as yet extant.

Probably the most interesting feature brought to light is the extent to which the Oriental world of 2500 B.C. was organised for purposes of peaceful intercourse and trade. The fact is gradually becoming generally known that we must give up the old conception of that old world as being divided up into rigidly separated water-tight compartments of nationality within which each people lived and died unto itself, save when conquest altered the arrangement to some extent ; but it was the evidence of Gudea's cylinders which gave us the most ample light upon the falsity of the old idea. For we see in them, at a time at least five centuries before the days of Abraham, how free was the flow of intercourse between the nations of the old world, and how readily the ruler of even a comparatively small state like Lagash could command the transport of weighty and costly materials from great distances.

Gudea was not a man of war, though he has left one solitary record of a victory over the town of Anshan in Elam, whose booty he dedicated to Ningirsu. His great achievement was the rebuilding of the temples of Lagash, and especially of E-ninnu, the great temple of the city-god, Ningirsu. The story which he tells us of how he was inspired to the building by a vision is too long to repeat ; but his list of the sources from which he drew the materials for his task is a revelation of a state of affairs which has seldom existed in the same localities since his day, and which, it may safely be said, does not yet exist over the same area. The pious *patesi* brought costly stone and timber, gold and silver, to adorn the house of his god, from an area which ranges from the Taurus Mountains on the north to Arabia on the south, and from the Mediterranean to the Persian Gulf ; while he made use of skilled craftsmen, not only from his own land of Sumer, but from Elam and Susa as well. Had they produced nothing but Gudea's extraordinarily vivid picture of the range of his search for materials, of the religious customs of his period and land, and of the social conditions prevailing within the circuit of his rule, de Sarzec's excavations would have been amply justified. When we add to this the results for the earlier periods of Ur-nina, Eannatum, Entemena, and Urukagina, the French excavator has secured for us a mass of evidence for the history of one Sumerian city-state for a period of a thousand years, which, though not by any means complete, is at least ampler than exists so far for any other early Mesopotamian community. The very fact that the existence of Lagash came to a sudden and complete close within a comparatively short time after the days of its later prosperity under Gudea, and that it was only revived for a short time under Parthian rule, renders the picture all the clearer and more vivid, since there is little to blur and confuse the impression made by what is practically an unmixed survival of Sumerian culture.

We can only mention in passing Rassam's work in 1880–1882 on several Babylonian sites of which the most important was that of Abu Habba. The mounds here were identified with the ancient city of Sippara, and from the ruins of the great temple of Shamash, the Sun-god, Rassam brought the fine relief of Nabu-aplu-iddina (870 B.C.) together with a huge store, reputed to have numbered originally about sixty thousand, of inscribed clay tablets.

The next series of excavations of importance was that conducted by the American Expedition of the University of Pennsylvania, during the years 1888–1900, at Nippur. Nippur in ancient days occupied a peculiar position with regard to the two lands of Sumer and Akkad, as being a sacred city to both ; while its god Enlil was the chief of the

gods. It was to be presumed, therefore, that excavations
on such a site might yield results of great importance. The
excavations were conducted in four successive campaigns
under different directors. The expedition of 1888–89,
under Dr. Peters, carried out the preliminary survey of the
ground, started excavation on the site of the temple of Enlil,
and discovered what afterwards proved to be a Parthian
fortress which had been superimposed upon the remains
of the ziggurat or stage-tower of the temple. It also discovered over two thousand tablets of various periods, some
of them belonging to the temple library. In 1889–90,
under the late Dr. Haynes, the work on the upper strata
of the Enlil temple was continued, and over eight thousand
tablets were added to the growing store from the library.
In 1893–96, still under Haynes, the excavation of the
ziggurat proved that the main body of the building, as now
left, had been the work of Ur-Engur, king of Ur, though it
had been restored by Ashur-bani-pal of Assyria nearly
eighteen hundred years later. Ur-Engur's tower stood on
an artificial platform, measuring 192 by 127 feet, and was
apparently only of three stages, differing in this respect
from Gudea's tower at Lagash which had seven zones.
But, beneath the Ur-Engur levels, work was discovered
going back to the period of Naram-sin, of the Sargonic
line of Akkad, and beneath that again lay pre-Sargonic
remains forming the innermost core of the tower. More
than 20,000 tablets were also added to the collection of the
expedition. Finally, in 1898–1900, under Haynes and Hilprecht, the temple library was definitely located, and another
23,000 tablets extracted from it, the survey of the temple-
complex was completed, and a large part of the city wall
was traced.

On the whole, the most valuable result of the American
Nippur excavations has been the huge store of tablets thus
accumulated. The larger part of this great store is scientific
and literary in character, dealing with mathematics,

Q

astronomy, geography, history, medicine, grammar, and religion. One of the most interesting portions of the find, however, is the comparatively late group of tablets, known as " The Murashu Tablets." These, numbering about seven hundred, are part of the business records of the firm of Murashu Sons, bankers and brokers at Nippur in the days of the Persian kings Artaxerxes I (464–424 B.C.) and Darius II (423–405 B.C.). The firm of Murashu apparently acted as the official agents and tax-farmers for the Persian kings, and the records of their business offered an interesting parallel to those of the firm of Egibi at Babylon in the days of Nabopolassar and Nebuchadnezzar, found by Rassam. The work of the expedition was unfortunately prejudiced in the public mind by the amount of controversy which accompanied it, and by the bitterness with which the controversy was carried on. Hilprecht's otherwise admirable summary in his *Explorations in Bible Lands*, for instance, is in this respect a classic instance of how summaries ought not to be written, and the tone of bitterness and unfairness with which the self-sacrificing labours of Haynes are described is singularly small-minded and unpleasing. Apart, however, from such petty matters, the work of the expedition was in more respects than one of the utmost value, not least as definitely marking the entry of America on a field in which she had previously done nothing.

Koldewey's great work at Babylon claims a chapter by itself. Before we pass to the latest work in Babylonia, the excavations of the joint expedition of the British Museum and the Museum of the University of Pennsylvania at Ur and Tell el Obeid, mention should be made of the expedition sent out in 1903–4 by the University of Chicago, under Dr. E. J. Banks, with its identification of the mounds of Bismaya, where its work was done, with the ancient city of Adab, its discovery of the temple of the goddess Ninkharsag, with work of Naram-sin and Ur-Engur, and its prize of the fine archaic Sumerian statue of " Lugal-dalu,

King of Adab," a ruler whose figure is one of the very earliest which have come down to us.

It was in 1922 that the joint expedition of the British Museum and the Museum of the University of Pennsylvania began its work at Mukayyar, "Ur of the Chaldees," the ancient city of Abraham. We have already seen that in 1854–55 J. E. Taylor succeeded in tracing part of the line of the temple of Nannar the Moon-god of Ur, and in associating its ziggurat with the names of Ur-Engur and Dungi, the two famous kings of Ur in the Sumerian renaissance (c. 2300–2250 B.C.), while its final repair proved to be due to Nabonidus. The work of the new expedition was under the charge of Mr. C. L. Woolley, the excavator of Carchemish, and his staff throughout the excavations has included both Britons and Americans.

Attention had again been drawn to Ur and its neighbourhood by the work of Dr. H. R. Hall of the British Museum, who did some excavating on a small scale there in 1919. But Dr. Hall's main work in the neighbourhood had been done at a small mound called Tell el Obeid, about four miles W.N.W. of Ur. Here he traced a considerable part of the walls of a very ancient building, on the south east face of which he found a store of objects of beaten copper, heads of lions, stags, and bulls, with portions of a great relief in copper, not only of considerable artistic value, but of the greatest interest as examples of extremely early metal-work. One of the objects of the new expedition, therefore, was to continue the work begun by Dr. Hall at Tell el Obeid, while the main work was to be on the larger site of Ur.

The excavations have been steadily prosecuted ever since 1922, and are still going on. On the whole, they have been remarkably successful. At Ur, the main results have been architectural, and till 1927 the finds in the way of works of art and smaller objects of interest were by no means rich, though there have been one or two finds of supreme quality and importance which will fall to be dealt with in due

course. But the importance of the additions to knowledge
gained by the excavation of the great temple-complex of
the house of Nannar, the Moon-god, with its stage-tower,
its temple of the god, its temple of Ningal, the consort of
the god, its houses for the priestess, and for all the complex
establishment associated with a great Sumerian divinity, and
its Hall of Justice, can scarcely be overrated. No such
complete picture of the elaborate detail of a great Sumerian
religious establishment has ever been presented as has been
gained by these excavations. The expedition is now continuing its work on the city area, beyond the wall of the
sacred enclosure, and has already laid bare the remains of
several houses of private citizens of the Abrahamic period
(c. 2100–1900 B.C.). The results are somewhat surprising.
The buildings are astonishingly well preserved, and suggest
a much higher level of domestic comfort than had been
anticipated from the previous results of house clearing at
Babylon, where the houses dealt with had been of a much
later date. The better-off Sumerian of Abraham's time
was apparently fairly well housed. " The whole plan of
the building anticipates almost exactly that of the richer
houses of modern Baghdad, and a look at one of them gives
a fair picture of the setting in which Terah might have
passed his life at Ur four thousand years ago."

Up to the present, however, the main work of the expedition has been concentrated on the sacred area at Ur, and the
smaller mound at Tell el Obeid ; and it will be best to
survey the work on the latter site, which forms a smaller
unit by itself, before we consider the larger work on the
temple enclosure of Ur.

Dr. Hall's building turned out to have been a temple, or
rather the remains of three different temples which had
succeeded one another upon the site. The original temple,
which, after all the vicissitudes of six millenniums, is still
the best preserved, stood upon the usual platform, faced
with burnt bricks, and mainly composed of sun-dried

bricks. This platform rose upon a little natural hillock. The temple was, or was intended to be, a rectangle, with its corners orientated to the cardinal points of the compass. On its south-east side, a stone staircase led up to the building, and on the south-west side a square platform of crude brick projected from the main building and bore a second stone-built staircase. The stone stairways appear to have been built before the main retaining walls of the platform were laid out, probably that they might serve the double purpose of stairways for the finished building, and ramps for the transport of the materials used during the construction. The intention was good ; but the result was disastrous to the symmetry of the building, for the projecting stairways prevented the builders from sighting accurately along the line of their retaining walls on these sides, with the result that, while the other two sides are fairly parallel, the two interrupted sides are badly out of alignment.

A notable piece of luck was the discovery, about eight metres away from the façade of the temple, where it had been thrown on the destruction of the wall in which it had once been imbedded, of the foundation inscription of the original temple. It was a slab of white marble, shaped like a plano-convex brick, nine centimetres by six. The inscription on it ran as follows : " Ninkhursag : A-an-ni-pad-da, king of Ur, son of Mes-an-ni-pad-da, king of Ur, has built a temple for Nin-khursag." Thus the expedition gained at once one of the very earliest records yet deciphered, and the evidence that the temple with which they were dealing was in all probability the oldest whose authorship and approximate date are known. A-an-ni-pad-da was an unknown monarch ; but his father Mes-an-ni-pad-da is known as the first king of the Ist Dynasty of Ur—a dynasty which, up to the discovery of this tablet, seemed somewhat mythical. The probable date is somewhere round about 4000 B.C., so that we are dealing with a time to be equated with the earliest of Egyptian historic material.

This earlier temple was wrecked, probably by violence, and when it was succeeded by a second building, the new structure was on a more ambitious scale. It has left comparatively little evidence of itself, however, and none of its founders, who may have been the kings of the IInd Dynasty of Ur. Nor has the third temple left much trace of its existence ; but, fortunately, among the poor remains of its foundations which survive are bricks bearing the name of Dungi (Shulgi), the second king of the IIIrd Dynasty of Ur (*c.* 2250 B.C.). He was the last builder at Tell el Obeid, and after his time the temple gradually fell into ruin. There does not seem ever to have been anything of the nature of a considerable town at the place, though the existence of a cemetery close by would seem to indicate a resident population. At all events, the history of el Obeid began and finished before the Abrahamic period, like that of Lagash.

One of the curiosities of the excavation was the discovery on the east side of the temple of a regular kitchen establishment, with its furnaces still containing the remains of burnt wood—a discovery which led Mr. Woolley at the time to speculate on the possibility of the priesthood of Ninkharsag's temple having laid themselves out to attract and provide for the trippers from the neighbouring city of Ur. " The whole thing is the ordinary kitchen range that can be seen in any native cook shop of the Near East ; Tell el Obeid lies sufficiently far out from Ur for a visit to the temple to have been a regular excursion, and I can only suppose that some enterprising caterer set up a restaurant in the temple grounds to supply lunch for the pious excursionists." One tries to picture the pre-Abrahamic " *bona fide* travellers " —just over the legal distance—making the most of their opportunity, and returning refreshed, spiritually and otherwise, to Ur ; but the subsequent discovery at Ur itself of a similar kitchen still more completely equipped, shows us that we must dispense with these pleasing dreams, and realise that each temple, which was a regular town in itself, had to have a regular commissariat department, which was probably fully occupied with its own work, without having to cater for cheap trippers, pious or otherwise.

The astonishing thing about this little temple at Tell el Obeid, however, was the decoration of the earliest building. We have seen that Hall discovered upon the site a mass of copper, wrought into heads of lions and bulls, and other decorative motives. The new excavations revealed the fact that the whole temple had been adorned with a frieze of bulls wrought in copper, and with free-standing figures of bulls in the round, also of copper ; while another feature of the decoration was a second frieze which ran above that of the copper bulls. It was composed of slabs inlaid with figures in mosaic of limestone or shell, laid in bitumen. These figures were of animals and men, and in particular, one part of the frieze represented a byre, with scenes of milking and storing the milk. A further element of decoration was found in the shape of a number of artificial flowers, composed of mosaic of small pieces of coloured stone. These were apparently used in connection with the standing figures of bulls, and suggested that the animals were walking in a meadow spangled with flowers ! The use of this form of mosaic for decorative purposes was also illustrated by the discovery of several wooden columns which had been plastered with bitumen, and then encrusted with tesseræ of red sandstone, black paste, and mother-of-pearl. The resulting column is like nothing so much as a crude anticipation of the Cosmati work of the Italian decorators of the thirteenth century. The form is still favoured in India, and Dr. Hall mentions that when he made the discovery of similar columns, " My Indian mechanics were delighted with this discovery, which confirmed their idea . . . that in days long past their ancestors had conquered Babylonia (an idea very prevalent among the Indian rank-and-file in Mesopotamia)."

The work in copper (heads of bulls and lions, frieze of bulls, and free-standing bulls in the round) is perhaps the most astonishing fruit of the excavation. One instinctively turns to compare it with the copper statues of the Pharaoh Pepy and Prince Mer-en-ra from Hierakonpolis. The work of the Egyptian artist is much in advance of that of his Sumerian brother ; but we have to remember that the Sumerian statues were made possibly about 4000 B.C., in which case they are 1200 years older than the Pepy figure, and that in any case they must be several centuries older than the Egyptian statues. The technique is somewhat similar in both cases. The Pepy statue was made of copper plates (or bronze ?) hammered over a wooden core, and the head was separately cast and afterwards affixed. In the case of the el Obeid bulls, " the bull was carved first in wood, the body, legs, and head in separate pieces which were morticed together, and secured by copper bolts ; then the legs and head, and last the body, were covered with thin plates of copper, whose edges overlapped and were held down by copper nails ; the tail, horns, and ears were attached afterwards." In the case of the frieze of the bulls, however, the method was completely like that of the Pepy statue, for the bodies alone were hammered on the wood in relief, and then the heads, which turn outwards to face the spectator, were cast hollow, and the hollow was filled up with bitumen. Altogether, the figures, as the illustration shows, are a wonderful achievement of the old Sumerian artist of wellnigh six thousand years ago.

Few excavations on a scale so small can have yielded so much information and material of priceless artistic value as these diggings at Tell el Obeid. We carry away from them an impression of the earliest Sumerian temples totally different from the somewhat squalid and unattractive picture which earlier research had suggested. Of the actual structure of Ninkharsag's little shrine, we know comparatively little, save that in its main outline it

(1) RESTORATION OF THE ZIGGURAT (TEMPLE-TOWER) OF UR

(2) EXCAVATION OF THE ZIGGURAT IN PROGRESS. THE HALL OF
JUSTICE TO LEFT

The upper figure presents what is practically a certain reconstitution of the most
complete of the Temple-towers which formed so notable a feature of Babylonian
Temple architecture and gave rise to the legend of the Tower of Babel. The lower
picture shows the actual remains of the tower in process of being revealed.
(See pp. 249 *sq.*)

conformed to the regular Sumerian scheme of sacred building. But instead of thinking of it as a sombre bulk which owes its impressiveness simply to mass and solidity, we have to endeavour to realise a dainty piece of architecture, owing its chief charm to successive zones of sculptured decoration, both in metal and stone, and gay with colour. We are even, in a way, entitled to regard this first of Sumerian temples as a far-off prophecy of the Parthenon, and the great Panathenaic frieze of Phidias—very far-off, no doubt, and very crude, but still in the direct line of the artistic idea which in the fullness of the time produced the immortal work of the Greek master. Apparently the typical decoration of the shrine at el Obeid, the cattle, and the milking scenes, was as characteristic of the Sumerian goddess as the scenes of the Panathenaic Procession are of the worship of Athene. For Ninkharsag, though not, like Athene, a virgin goddess (she is in one aspect Ninlil, the consort of the great god Enlil), is "the Lady of the Mountain," the mother of fecundity, patroness of cattle and other living creatures, a kind of Sumerian counterpart to the Cretan "Lady of the Wild Creatures," and therefore her friezes, with their amazingly realistic and vigorous scenes of animal life under domestication, are singularly appropriate to her divine attributes.

The chief work of the expedition naturally was at Ur, and equally naturally it was the mound covering the ziggurat, the great stage-tower which is characteristic of a Babylonian sacred building, which first attracted attention. The conditions of excavation have considerably changed since the days when Layard drifted down the Tigris towards Nimrud on his first adventure. The same old " keleks " and " gufas " still float upon the rivers ; but the modern pilgrim to the shrine of the Moon-god does not worry over such out-of-date contrivances, which have never changed since the days of Abraham. " Passengers for Ur Junction leave Bagdad by the night train which has good sleepers and a dining car." The shades of Terah, Abraham, and the rest of the clan would find many things to wonder at if they revisited the scene where their great venture started—perhaps not least the existence of " Ur Junction," with all that such a thing implies. The explorer's camp lies two miles south of the Junction. " Our camp is an eighteen-room house built in twenty-one days with old bricks of kings Nabonidus, Nebuchadnezzar, and other worthies of Ur whose stamped bricks are scattered about the whole ruin." . . . " We are lost deep in the desert, in the impressive silence of the immensity around us. . . . The crescent moon and the evening star shine clear in a deep blue sky. The song of the old Sumerian worshipper comes back to our mind : ' O Father Nannar, brilliant, young Bull of Heaven, when thy horn shines over the horizon.' "

It sounds all very fascinating and romantic. To live in quarters built of the handiwork of old kings of two thousand five hundred years ago, while you explore the works of yet other kings who were dead and gone three thousand years before Nebuchadnezzar and Nabonidus were thought of, with the serene Father Nannar shining down upon your nights as he shone upon his worshippers so many ages ago, what could appeal more delightfully to the imagination ? But romance is not everything, and even under modern conditions excavation in the East has its drawbacks. " Everything would be so cosy, except for the white ants, the mice, the mosquitoes, flies and sand flies. The white ants eat the books, the mice eat the cake and jam, the mosquitoes and the sand flies eat us, and the flies are a common nuisance. Wire netting is still an undreamed of luxury, and we eat armed each with a fly killer. There is absolutely no water in the place, no tree, no grass." It may be some consolation, under such conditions, to remember that modern excavators are no worse off than ancient kings, to whom, judging from their reliefs, the fly killer was just as essential as it is to-day to the men who are revealing their ancient glories.

The objects of the first attack were the temple of Nannar, the Moon-god, and its ziggurat. It will be simpler to take each separate unit of the temple-complex by itself, rather than to move from one to another with the progress of the excavations. We take the ziggurat first, as the work there has practically been completed, leaving us with a more satisfactory knowledge of a Babylonian stage-tower than any former expedition had attained. The general idea of a temple-tower was derived partly from the description which Herodotus gives of the tower of the temple of " Belus," at Babylon, and partly from George Smith's translation of the description given of the same tower on an ancient Babylonian tablet. " In the midst of this precinct," says Herodotus, " is built a solid tower of one stade in length and breadth, and on this tower rose another, and another upon that, to the number of eight. And an ascent to these is outside, running spirally round all the towers." According to the Babylonian tablet, the tower measures 300 feet square, and rose in seven stages to a height of 300 feet. But excavations at the various sites in Babylonia and Assyria have shown that there was no uniformity in the size of the towers or in the number of stages of which they might consist ; and we may conclude that the size, and very probably the number of stages also, was chiefly decided by the resources available for building, though there may have been religious reasons which determined in each case the number of stages to be reared.

At all events, the ziggurat of Ur is a structure very different from the traditional conception of " The Tower of Babel," and much more nearly approaching to the idea of an artificial mountain, which was very likely the original conception in the minds of the primitive Sumerian builders who created the form. The tower of Ur was not square on plan, but oblong, measuring 195 feet by 130, and its height was 92 feet. It was orientated with its angles to the cardinal points, and it rose in four stages, of which the lowest was very much the loftiest and most imposing. The stages had a slight inward inclination or batter, and the lowest stage had its faces diversified and strengthened by buttresses of slight projection. On the north-eastern side, three staircases led up to the summit of the first stage, one directly in front of the centre of the side, and at right angles to it, the other two from the angles of the side, and running parallel with the main mass. Each stairway had one hundred steps, and they all converged upon a great doorway in the parapet of the second stage. The angles made between the two side stairs and the central one were filled with solid platform towers, whose tops possibly carried statues. From the top of the first stage, apparently, a double stair led up to the top of the third stage ; while the fourth stage may have been of the nature of a shrine. The whole conception will be more easily understood from the illustration than from description, and on the whole it must have been a very massive and dignified feature of the temple-complex, which it completely dominated, as none of the other buildings was of anything like the same height.

Taylor's excavations in the middle of the last century had already let us know that Nabonidus was responsible for the restoration of the building, which was begun by Ur-Engur, king of Ur and his son Dungi (c. 2300 B.C.) The excavators found none of Dungi's work actually in existence. The lowest stage of the tower was the work of Ur-Engur, and was left unaltered by Nabonidus in his restoration, though he laid down new brick treads on the old stairs. We may suppose that the work of Dungi had been on the upper parts of the ziggurat, and being more exposed and less solid than the massive structure below them, had fallen into disrepair by the time of Nabonidus, eighteen hundred years later. The upper portions of the building which have survived are all the work of Nabonidus. As Nabonidus was a genuine archæologist, however, we may conclude that the tower as he restored it reproduced in its main features the original buildings of Ur-Engur and Dungi, and that in consequence when we look on the building as modern excavation has revealed it we are seeing the architectural features with which Abraham was familiar in the early days of his life. Ur-Engur's great tower would be somewhat more than 200 years old when Abraham saw it for the last time, not impossibly blazing with the fires of the Elamite sack which happened about that time.

The temple of Nannar stood also within the enclosure of which the ziggurat occupied the western corner. It belonged to the same periods and builders, in the main, as its companion. The earliest stamped bricks in its walls belonged to Bur-sin (c. 2250 B.C.) ; but there was earlier construction going back to at least 3000 B.C. About 2150 B.C. there was an Elamite invasion in which the reigning king, Ibi-sin, was carried off into captivity in Elam, and the temple remains show many traces of the violence which accompanied the capture and sack of the place. " Beneath the pavements of some of the rooms were found many evidences of a victorious enemy, such as smashed stone vases and other objects of fine workmanship, often inscribed with royal names." The Elamite king, Kudur-mabug, reconstructed the ruined building, but after his time, possibly about 1900 B.C., there must have been another sack. It is tempting to speculate on the possibility that one or other of these disasters to Ur may have been the voice that spoke to Abraham saying " Get thee out from thy country, and from thy kindred " ; but we must remember that such an idea can only be speculation.

Up to the time of Nebuchadnezzar, the house of Nannar was of the usual type, in which the god dwells in his own private house, attended and worshipped by his priests, whose own houses formed part of the structure on the sacred platform. " There was no room on that platform or in the temple for the public. When the god made a public appearance, he went in procession through the streets of Ur." Nebuchadnezzar, however, as the excavators found, made a radical change in the form of the temple. " The old sanctuary he respected. . . . But the surroundings of the sanctuary he wholly transformed. Two small wings were built out from the front of the sanctuary, and between them stretched a brick-paved courtyard, in the middle of which, in front of the door, was set up a brick altar . . . the brickwork is covered with a heavy coating of bitumen, obviously intended as a bedding for metal plates. . . . The effect of these changes of plan is to substitute for a crowded complex of buildings where only a private ritual was possible, an open temple suitable for, and therefore presumably intended for, public worship. The old rites of feeding the god and goddess and so on were probably continued in the inner chambers of the sanctuary, which as before would be closed to the profane ; but to these there must have been added a new element of congregational service. The upper court, with its altar, can only have been reserved for the priests, the great lower court is as clearly intended for the lay public. These would see the sacrifice performed in front of them ; they would see the gifts upon the altar, the altar itself, the ministrant priest behind it, standing on his footstool, and through the open door behind the priest they would catch glimpses of the god himself half hidden in the gloom of his sanctuary. Irresistibly we are reminded of the Biblical legend of the Three Children. That Nebuchadnezzar should make a golden image was nothing new, every king had done something of the sort ; what brought trouble on the pious Jews who had up to the time of the proclamation lived undisturbed was the order that at the sound of the music everybody should fall down and worship, i.e. that the public was to attend and participate in the service. Such an innovation (and the legend must have had some historical background to give it probability) is precisely what we should deduce from the archæological evidence— that Nebuchadnezzar introduced a new plan of building to accommodate a new form of worship." We need not, of course, run away at once with the idea that this solution of the matter of Nebuchadnezzar's golden image and the defiance of the young Hebrews is certain ; things do not often fit quite so remarkably as that ; but at least it is a suggestion full of interest, and it will be a matter of further interest to see if future excavation on other sites reveals evidence of similar restorations of ancient temples on the part of the great king. Should it be proved that Nebuchadnezzar adopted a similar plan in other cases, the case for this explanation of the Hebrews' difficulty would seem to be fairly proved. But this must wait, and, after all, is not a matter of first-class importance.

One of the most striking and least anticipated results of the excavations came in the campaign of 1924–5. South-east of the ziggurat, and close to the temple of Nannar, lay a pile of rubbish covering a building which Taylor was known to have partially excavated in 1854. Not very much was expected from the clearing of this area ; but almost immediately the work was rewarded. Bit by bit there came to light a great complex of building, consisting of a multitude of chambers, mostly comparatively small, surrounded by large paved courts. The removal of the later and less interesting parts of the structure showed one of the most interesting masses of construction which have come down from the time of the Kassite rulers of Babylonia, its but-tressed and recessed walls standing solid and massive to an average height of eight to ten feet, its doorways opening on the broad courtyards under wonderfully preserved brick arches. The mass of the building as it stands is due to

Kurigalzu the Kassite king of Babylon, about 1600 B.C.
The name of it was " E-dublal-mah " the " House of the
Law " or Justice, and Kurigalzu's work was only the
restoration of a much older building which had occupied
the site, and which goes back at least to the time of Ur-
Engur, 3000 B.C.   By 2000 B.C. it was falling into ruin, and
was restored by King Ishme-dagan of Larsa.   Four hundred
years later came the Babylonian's great reconstruction.
Nearly a thousand years after the Kassite came the Assyrian,
and in 650 B.C. Sin-balatsu-ikbi, the Assyrian governor of
Ur, restored the fabric once more, setting up new doors
made of costly foreign woods adorned with silver and gold.
The Assyrian passed away with his vanishing empire, and
the next ruler to lay his hand on the old Hall of Justice was
the mighty Nebuchadnezzar, who laid out and paved the
great court in front of one of the arched doorways ; while
the pavements of the side-chambers bear the stamp of
Nabonidus, last of the Babylonian kings (550 B.C.).   Here,
then, is a building which covers, in its various strata, the
whole history of the Chosen People, from the first movement
of the Father of the Faithful down to the Restoration.
Abraham knew the old Hall of Justice, getting ruinous in
his day, or perhaps just undergoing the restoration of Ishme-
dagan.   Kurigalzu's messengers may have passed it on their
way down to Egypt, where the children of Abraham were
beginning to find their position doubtful in face of the
flowing tide of Egyptian national sentiment.   When Sin-
balatsu-ikbi set up its doors, the shadow of Assyrian cruelty
was already beginning to pass away from the trembling
lands of the East, though daylight was not yet.   Nabonidus's
pavements were trodden by the feet of the messengers who
brought the news that Babylon the Great was fallen, and
that Cyrus the Restorer of Israel sat upon the throne of the
oppressor.

The campaign of 1925-6 brought another find, not less
interesting.   " From a part of the broken ground where

tombs had replaced the elusive Dungi's palace, the dig was extended over Dungi's shrine, towards the Ziggurat. Out of the soil below three feet of rubbish in what looked like an empty piece of ground, came to light the most complete Sumerian temple of 2400 B.C., with walls, courts, shrines, storerooms, kitchen, wells, altar, statues, stelæ, and over thirty door-sockets, found at every gate, all bearing the same inscription. From these we learn that we have found a temple built by the great Ur-Nammu, King of Ur, and his grandson, Bur-Sin. This was the private house of the Moon-Goddess Ningal, the Mother of the City. It is complete, and so rich in details that we can follow the daily ritual with a vivid sense of life."

The building thus described by Dr. Legrain, the inscriptional expert of the expedition, bore the title of the " Gig-Par-Ku." Actually it goes back much further than he suggests ; for while the door-sockets to which he refers bore the inscriptions of Ur-Nammu (Engur) and Bur-Sin, the excavators discovered also beneath the IIIrd Dynasty walls the remains of walls identical in every respect of construction with the walls of A-an-ni-pad-da's little temple at el Obeid. Ur-Engur's dedication inscription runs thus : " To Nin-Gal, his lady, Ur-Engur the mighty man, the king of Ur, the king of Sumer and Akkad, has built her splendid Gig-Par." His grandson's inscription varies the phraseology a little : " To Nin-Gal, his lady, Bur-Sin the mighty man, the king of Ur, the king of the four quarters of the world, has built the brilliant Gig-Par, her beloved temple, and for his life has presented it." " The old-sounding titles come out of the ground like the voice of the past." Kings who were memories of a great past before Hebrew history began on this spot !

The astonishing thing about the Gig-Par-Ku is the completeness with which its whole plan has been preserved, so that, as Dr. Legrain says, the daily ritual can be reconstructed from the data now available. It is in this direction, of information as to the religious practices of Sumer in pre-Abrahamic times, that this discovery promises to be most valuable. It is impossible to follow out here the details of the temple of Ningal ; but two points may be noticed, out of many. The first is a valuable piece of information as to Sumerian methods of construction. I give it in Mr. Woolley's own words. " The actual procedure was as follows. The site chosen had to be levelled, partly because of the existence of earlier ruins on it, and the best way of doing so was to make of it a low terrace ; therefore a retaining wall was first built round the site, and within it, either by the destruction of the old buildings or by bringing in earth from outside, a fresh level was obtained. The surface of this was beaten hard so as to form a regular floor, and the platform, with its surrounding wall and its hard top, became a unity in itself, a sort of podium. On the floor was traced out the plan of the future building, but with this modification, that the walls were considerably thicker than was allowed for in the building design, and this plan was carried up in mud brick to a height of 1·35 metres. Then fresh earth was brought in and heaped between the standing walls as high as their tops and rammed down ; in other words the foundations, instead of being sunk in the original soil, were built up above it and the soil subsequently brought up to their level. On these mud-brick foundations the walls proper were constructed, this time with the width allowed for in the architect's plans, and the brick pavements were laid over the rammed earth." In this fashion we may conceive of all buildings of any importance being constructed in Babylonia and Assyria.

The other feature, prosaic enough, but perhaps helping us more vividly than anything else to realise the actual daily life of the great religious establishment, we must leave Mr. Woolley again to describe. " The most surprising feature of the temple was its kitchen. It consisted of an open court with two roofed chambers giving on to it. In the court there was a brick-lined well, and by it, against the north-east wall, a bitumen-proofed tank ; on the opposite side of the well, let into the bricks of the pavement, there was a sort of land anchor of bronze with a ring-top to which was made fast the rope of the well-bucket. Against the south-east wall was a fire-place built of bricks and mud ; on one side was a trough-hearth for burning logs, on the other a circular ring-hearth on which must have stood a great cauldron ; this is not really a cooking-place but one for heating water, and that it was well used is shown by the heavy smoke-blackening of the wall above. Between the doors leading to the two roofed chambers was a table of burnt brick covered with bitumen ; the cut and scratched surface of the exposed brick proved, what one might indeed have guessed, that this was the cutting-up bench on which joints were prepared. On the floor in front of it we found the saddle-quern and rubbing-stone left by the cook's assistant. In the annexe in the south corner there was the brick base, partly circular, for the big round bread-oven ; the domed oven itself had disappeared, but the character of the base was unmistakable. In the western annexe next door was the cooking-range proper. Built of mud and brick, it stood ·70 metres high and had two furnaces, vaulted tunnels lined with red fire-clay each running back to a circular flue made round a clay column and communicating presumably with a chimney, though the latter had been destroyed by a wall of later date which had cut through the back of the range. The top of the furnace was flat and was pierced with two rings of small holes going down to the circular flues ; over these would be set the cooking-pots, and as they would be big and be heavy to move, a little flight of brick steps in the corner led up to the top of the range so that one might go up and shift them easily. The preservation of this kitchen, dating from 2000 B.C., was astonishing, and it needed but little imagination to re-people it with the temple servants drawing water and tending the lighted stoves and cutting up and broiling the meat for the sacrifice."

It is one of the unexpected things in life that we can look into an actual kitchen of the days of Abraham, and see the very utensils lying as they were left, and the marks of the chopper on the block, and the smoke of the sacrifices on the walls ; and it is quite evident that we could not teach the Sumerian architect of 2000 B.C. much as to the construction of a kitchen range. Dr. Legrain has pointed out the vividness with which such a discovery illustrates that passage in the Book of Samuel in which the sons of Eli are depicted as making their fraudulent profit out of the offerings which the Hebrews brought up to the Tabernacle kitchen, and the suggestiveness of the illustration is indeed striking ; but you have to remember, in appreciating it, that this kitchen of Ningal is about a thousand years older than the one where Hophni and Phinehas played their sacrilegious tricks, and in all probability a great deal better equipped.

It is thus evident that the main interest of the results of excavation at Ur is architectural, while that of the Obeid work is more definitely artistic. It would be a mistake, however, to imagine that Ur yielded little of an artistic nature, though proportionately its yield was less than that of Obeid. The great artistic find, one of the most important in Sumerian art, ranking with de Sarzec's discovery of the Stele of the Vultures, was made during the campaign of 1924–5. It took place during the clearing up of an unpromising corner of the courtyard near the Hall of Justice, and was the direct reward of the austere virtue which made Mr. Woolley persist in leaving no corner of the place unexamined. " I hesitated," says Mr. Woolley, " to spend money on continuing what had been hitherto the unremunerative task of digging down through seven feet of hard soil to a brick pavement, and it was more obstinacy than anything else that made me go on. Almost the first day produced in one room a door-socket of King Bur-Sin (2200

B.C.) with an inscription in fifty-two lines giving the history of the temple's beginnings, a very welcome record ; but it was in the western wing of the great court that the discovery was made which overshadowed all others. Here the pavement was littered with blocks and lumps and chips of limestone, ranging in size from four feet to an inch or less, some rough, others carved, some pitted and flaked with the action of salt, some as smooth and sharp as when the sculptor finished his work ; and all, or nearly all, belonged to one monument, the most important yet found at Ur.

" This monument was a stela or slab five feet in width and perhaps fifteen feet high, carved on both sides with a series of historical or symbolic scenes arranged in horizontal bands of unequal heights. It bore a long inscription, now fragmentary and with the king's name missing ; but here luck favoured us, for on a mere flake of stone, the drapery of a figure otherwise lost, there is inscribed the name of Ur-Engur, and we can therefore identify the author of the stela with the founder of the IIIrd Dynasty and the builder of the Ziggurat." The artistic value of the reliefs on the stela, particularly those in which the Moon-god Nannar is shown seated on his throne, with a vase in front of him in which a date-palm is growing, and that in the register below this, in which Ur-Engur himself appears, bearing a workman's building tools, with the high-priest following him, while a god in front leads him onwards to the building of the Ziggurat, is very much greater than that of the reliefs on the Vulture Stela, and sets a new standard for our estimate of Sumerian art at this early period (c. 2400 B.C.).

From the Ningal temple came a diorite statue of the goddess Bau, consort of the god Ningirsu of Lagash, " the statue of Mother Goose . . . a squat little person with a large back and a short neck, sitting on the waves of the Euphrates instead of a throne, flanked on either side by two geese, while her feet rest on two ducks." Lagash is only

forty miles north of Ur, and the statue of Ningirsu's wife
reminds one forcibly of the well-known sitting statue of
Gudea, with the plan of Ningirsu's temple on his knee.
Probably the date of this patroness of the poultry farm,
which was one of Bau's functions, is not so very far away
from that of Gudea's statues. The clumsy little piece of
work (extraordinarily clumsy when one thinks of the
accomplished work which was done in Egypt long before
the date ascribed to the statue) is of peculiar interest as
being one of the very few almost complete pieces of female
portraiture of the time and land, and the details of dress
and coiffure are valuable. Of finer workmanship, but more
defaced, is another diorite statue of the goddess Ningal,
bearing a dedicatory inscription by the priest En-an-na-tum
which dates it to about 2080 B.C., or nearly three hundred
years later than the Bau statue ; while a diorite statuette of
King Dungi carries us again to Lagash for its parallel in
style in the larger standing statues of Gudea, which are
headless like this likeness of the king of Ur. The famous
Ur-Nina relief of the king and his family from Lagash is
remarkably paralleled by the limestone plaque from the
Nin-Gal temple which shows in two registers the king,
naked, as performing a priestly function, pouring a libation
before a seated figure of the god Nannar, while in the lower
line a naked priest pours a libation before the door of a
shrine. On the whole the workmanship of the Ur plaque
seems to indicate a somewhat later date than that of the more
primitive relief from Lagash ; but there cannot be much
between the two (c. 3000 B.C.). The only other object
which we need mention is the striking female head which
was found during the excavations of 1926 at the Tomb-
mound. " The head," says Mr. Woolley, " is carved in
fine marble, the eyes are inlaid with shell and lapis lazuli.
It is no exaggeration to say that such a piece of work as this
must modify our whole conception of Sumerian art ; there
is here not only an extraordinary finished delicacy of

technique but an ideal of beauty which we have hitherto had no reason to attribute to the early sculptor of Mesopotamia." It would, no doubt, be trying the Ur goddess head too high to place it alongside the superb Egyptian work of the Middle Kingdom, with which it is possibly contemporary ; but at least it can be said that here, for the first time, the art of Sumer offers us something which in conception, at all events, is not unworthy of being put in the same class as the Egyptian work, however far it may fall below it in execution. The treatment of the eyes is particularly interesting, in view of early Egyptian practice.

After all, however, it is not in individual finds such as these that the value of the Ur excavations lies, but rather in the astonishingly clear picture which is presented to us by them of the religious establishment of one of the great gods of Sumer in the Abrahamic Age and after. Some of the elements which go to make up the picture were already more or less familiar to us from previous excavations on other sites ; but the peculiar merit of the work at Ur is the assembling of all these elements, and their grouping together in their proper mutual relationship, so that the whole establishment of the Moon-god lies before us as a huge unit, amazingly complex, indeed, but still intelligible, as such a thing never was before.

" To understand the real nature of the Moon-god's temple," says Mr. Woolley, " one must rid one's mind of all ideas derived from the self-contained and isolated unity of the temples of Greece, of Rome, or of Egypt ; here there is a different conception of the deity and corresponding to that a different conception of how he should be housed. The Babylonian god was a king, the Lord of his city ; he controlled its destinies much as did the temporal ruler and therefore he must have his ministers and his court ; he was a great landowner, and therefore he needed stewards to manage his estate : there are preserved lists of the functionaries attached to a temple which have a curiously mundane sound ; of course there is a High-Priest and a body of priestly satellites, but we find, too, the Sacristan, the Choir-Master, the Treasurer, Ministers of War and of Justice, of Agriculture and of Housing, a Controller of the Household, a Master of the Harem, and Directors of Live Stock, Dairy Work, Fishing, and Donkey Transport. All these carried on their duties in the Temple precincts, and so the Temple is not a single building but a huge complex which is at once temple and palace, government offices and stores and factories."

One tries to imagine the huge enclosure, surrounded by its mighty wall, with its towers and fortified gateways, and stretching 1200 feet in length by 600 in breadth, an area fairly comparable with that enclosed by the vast temenos-wall of Karnak. " In the west corner of the enclosure was a raised platform also defended by walls, whereon rose the ziggurat tower, and below the ziggurat stood the particular private house of the God. If in some respects we might compare the whole temple to a rambling mediæval monastery, in others we might find the best parallel in a mediæval castle, with the ziggurat and its platform representing the keep, the walled temple enclosure the inner baily, and the walled city beyond the outer baily ; for the God of the Babylonian city was a War-Lord, and his house was a house of defence, the final stronghold of his people."

Within the fortified enclosure there was an extraordinary complication of buildings, houses of many gods, like the saints'-chapels in a great cathedral, monastic and conventual buildings for the accommodation of the priests and priest-esses of the various divinities, factories, where the materials which formed part of the temple revenues were wrought up into finished products, barracks for the workmen and work-women employed in this work, offices where the financial and administrative business of the great god's estate was transacted ; an amazing mingling of the sacred and the secular. The archives of the temple, which have been

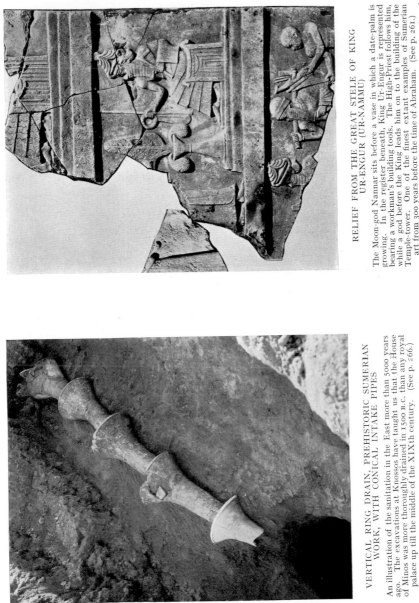

RELIEF FROM THE GREAT STELE OF KING
UR-ENGUR (UR-NAMMU)

The Moon-god Nannar sits before a vase in which a date-palm is
growing. In the register beneath, King Ur-Engur is represented
bearing a workman's building tools. The High-Priest follows him,
while a god before the King leads him on to the building of the
Temple-tower. One of the finest extant examples of Sumerian
art from 300 years before the time of Abraham. (See p. 261.)
(*Permission from the Director of the Museum of the University of
Pennsylvania, Philadelphia, U.S.A.*)

VERTICAL RING DRAIN, PREHISTORIC SUMERIAN
WORK, WITH CONICAL INTAKE PIPES

An illustration of the sanitation in the East more than 5000 years
ago. The excavations at Knossos have taught us that the House
of Minos was more thoroughly drained in 1500 B.C. than any royal
palace up till the middle of the XIXth century. (See p. 266.)
(*By permission of the Society of Antiquaries*)

partly unearthed, and are still in the process of emerging from their hidden hoarding-places, enable the picture to be filled in and shaded with remarkable completeness. " The God as landowner received either rent or a part share in the produce of the soil, and since money was unknown these were all paid in kind ; and since the temple was also a fortress enormous quantities of food-stuffs were stored within it, ready to meet the normal requirements of the temple staff, but also to act as a reserve in case of war. For everything that was brought in a receipt was given, a little clay square carefully dated recording that so-and-so has paid in six pounds of butter of the best quality, so many bushels of barley, so much oil, cattle, sheep, or what not ; and every month a full balance-sheet of all returns was drawn up with parallel columns showing every farmer's contribution under separate headings. Just below the Ziggurat terrace there is a very large building exactly like the modern *khan* of the Near East, with a great courtyard surrounded by storerooms and with living quarters above its main gate ; there is already some evidence for supposing that this was the Ga-nun-makh, the Great Storehouse, and it is easy to picture the countrymen driving in their donkeys laden with sacks of corn and piled baskets of cheese and butter and round-bottomed oil jars, crowding the court-yard, weighing and counting and disputing the tally, and going off at last with the clay receipt of which a duplicate had been duly filed by the clerk in his office over the gate. The Baghdad Customs House to-day must bear a very fair resemblance to the Great Storehouse of Ur four thousand years ago."

Another comparison rises to the mind, and one remembers how our Lord came to Jerusalem and found the courts of the Temple there filled with cattle-dealers, dove-sellers, and money-changers ; and the fanciful suggestion comes up that if the Hebrews of Christ's time made Jehovah's House an house of merchandise, they were only following, at a two thousand years' interval, the precedent which their first ancestors, Terah and Abraham, had seen enacted in the House of Nannar, before the start of the great venture of faith.

Babylonia in Semitic times, we know, was first and last and above all a land of big business ; but the records of the temple of Ur make it manifest that the business instinct was there in the land before the Semite ruled it, and that the Sumerian did not need to be taught anything in this respect by any man. "Numbers of women devotees were attached to the temple, and these were employed in regular factories. . . . The main industry was weaving. In the building E-kar-zida alone 165 women and girls were kept at work, and we have the monthly and yearly accounts of the quantity of woollen thread supplied to each, and of the amount of cloth produced, each sort distinguished by quality and weight, with due allowance for the wastage of thread in weaving. The rations are in proportion to the output, the older women receiving less than the young ones who would have larger appetites and would do better work, no more, in fact, than did the smallest children ; thus if four pints of oil a day was the standard allowance for adults, children of different ages got two pints, one and a half, or one, and the old women one also ; for the sick there were special rates ; if anyone died, her name was kept on the books until the end of the financial year, but the date of death was recorded and an entry made against the name to the effect that henceforward no rations were drawn ! Temple servants sent on a journey were furnished with letters of credit, enabling them to get supplies at the towns through which they passed. The whole system was thoroughly business-like—cold-bloodedly so in fact."

The excavations at Knossos have taught us that in 1500 B.C. the palace of the Kings of the House of Minos was better drained than any European house up till the last quarter of the nineteenth century, and we know that " the queen of Knossos enjoyed conveniences which not all the splendours of Versailles were to offer to the queen of France "; Tell el-Amarna has taught us that 3300 years ago the kings of the Near East were issuing passports and safe-conducts as a regular matter of Foreign Office business ; now the excavations at Ur teach us that in Abraham's time the method of Messrs. Cook's circular notes was already in use for travellers, and that in business practice the Sumerians of four thousand years ago had little to learn from our modern captains of industry. But the main impression, and the priceless gain resulting from these wonderfully fruitful researches, is that another window has been opened upon the magic lands of the past, through which we can begin to see, no longer shrouded with blinding mist, but with a certain clearness of definition, the actual life of the days when Father Nannar, shining in the southern sky, was still a great god to his children of Ur, and when Abraham turned first from the worship of the Host of Heaven, and the gods which his fathers " served on the other side of the flood," to seek the God who is Spirit.

The latest reports from Ur announce further discoveries of considerable importance. Close to Nebuchadnezzar's temenos, there was unearthed a very ancient cemetery, dating from probably 3000 B.C. " The distinguishing feature of the graves was their wealth in precious metals. Diadems and chains, rings and earrings, beads and amulets in gold and silver are quite common, and some of them are wonderful illustrations of the art of the early goldsmith." A new gateway to the temenos has also been discovered, lying in front of the façade of the ziggurat, and as it is the most imposing of all the gates so far discovered, it appears possible that the great temple still remains to be unearthed in line with it. A small building nearly a mile away from the sacred precinct at Ur has yielded a remarkable specimen of the use of the arch in the building of vaulted chambers as early as 2100 B.C. " It is not too much to say that the

history of architecture in the Near East . . . has to be re-
written in view of what Ur has taught us in the last three
years. But this discovery, carrying back to so remote a
date the most advanced features of the building, is more
revolutionary than any other."

CHAPTER XI

OF all the famous sites of the Near East, that of Babylon is the one to which the imagination is most naturally attracted, and from which excavation might naturally have been expected to produce the most wonderful results. The greatest of cities to the mind of the quick-witted Greek travellers, who saw it before the glamour of its ancient fame and splendour had begun to fade, the typical world-capital romantically linked in our fancy with memories of Hebrew exile and heroism, and with the overweening pride and strange humiliation of their conqueror, and later with the early death of the greatest soldier-statesman of the ancient world ; what might not be expected to emerge from the huge mounds which cover the ruins of so much glory and wealth ! Actually, the results of excavation at Babylon have proved comparatively disappointing in many respects, though wonderfully illuminating in others ; and for almost the whole of the early history of the great city, the record of the excavators is practically a blank.

The reason for this is perfectly simple, and lies on the surface of Babylonian history. We owe the poverty of Babylon in remains of the most ancient and interesting periods of its history to those misunderstood benefactors of the human race to whom we owe also so much that is brutal and barbarous in ancient history—the Assyrians. The relations between Babylon and Assyria from the time when the northern kingdom first began to feel its strength to the day when Babylon at last took vengeance for all the humiliations of ages, and wiped Assyria off the map, were almost continually hostile. Assyria triumphed again and again in the field, and one Assyrian king after another entered the great city as conqueror, and " took the hands of Bel " as monarch of the vanquished land ; but the Babylonian, untaught by all the bitter experience of the past, cheerfully rebelled again as soon as his conqueror's back was turned. If the Assyrian king put a viceroy of his own race, even a prince of his own family, on the throne, the chances were ten to one that before long the Assyrian viceroy became more Babylonian than the Babylonians, and had to be removed at the cost of a fresh conquest, or, if he remained true to his allegiance, his turbulent subjects rose against him, called in Elam, or another outside power, to their aid, and massacred their Assyrian rulers. It was an incident of the latter kind which ended in that total destruction of Babylon which has robbed us of so much that we should have prized from earlier days.

Sennacherib, who had done much for the beautifying of Babylon, had set over the city as vassal king his own first-born Ashur-nadin-shum. The usual revolt followed, and in 694 B.C. the Elamites were called in to help the rebels, and the Assyrian Crown-prince was sent into captivity to Elam, where, in all probability, he met the fate which the tender mercies of Eastern warfare usually reserved for notable captives. With a painful effort the Assyrians managed to put down the great revolt ; and then Sennacherib took vengeance. There was a wholesale massacre of the inhabitants of the city until the squares were filled with the dead. All the treasures which ages had gathered were carried off, and the very statues of the gods were impiously smashed, and crushed to fragments. " Every house in the city was destroyed from foundation to roof and fired. The inner and outer walls, the temples, and temple towers were torn down and thrown into the Araḫtu, canals were dug through the site, the city was overwhelmed with water, the brickwork foundations were scattered more than if they had suffered from an inundation, the site was annihilated as if by a swamp ; in future days none might find ground of the city, the temples, or the gods." Sennacherib's son, Esar-haddon, repented him of the evil which his father had done, and did his best to restore the city again ; but the Babylon of ancient glories, of Hammurabi the law-giver, the Babylon that we would have been most fain to recover, was lost beyond recall in Sennacherib's blast of destroying rage. Practically the whole of the remains which were found by the excavations of the German Expedition which began work on the site in 1899 belong to a single period, and that the period subsequent to the great destruction. Only in one locality, which appears to have been the business quarter of the city, was anything discovered more ancient than the time of the Neo-Babylonian Empire of Nabopo-lassar and Nebuchadnezzar. Sennacherib, who, it must be allowed, had reason for being angry, evidently did his work thoroughly.

While this is so, however, it must not be imagined that the results of excavation have been disappointing in any sense save this, and its corollary of the comparative poverty of the site in objects of artistic interest. To have been able to see the remains of Hammurabi's Babylon would, indeed, have been supremely interesting ; but since this is denied us, the next best thing is surely to see those of the Babylon of Nebuchadnezzar. After all, it was Nebuchadnezzar's mighty capital which Herodotus had in his mind's eye when he wrote that wonderful description which reads like the tale of some fairy city ; it was Nebuchadnezzar's capital where Daniel lived and Belshazzar feasted under the shadow of coming doom ; and it was in Nebuchadnezzar's great palace that Alexander's dying lips bequeathed his empire " to the strongest," before he went on his last and greatest venture. Not even Egyptian Thebes has so much about it of the romantic savour of the pride of life as this " great Babylon," whose very name has remained and will remain to all time the type of the vast world-city in its pride, its beauty, its wealth, and its wickedness.

Up till 1899, when the German Expedition started on its long task, excavation at Babylon had been intermittent, superficial, and, on the whole, singularly unproductive, compared with what might have been expected from a site of such importance, and with what had actually been realised from far less important sites. The identity of the site was never lost, as had been the case with Nineveh and other great cities of Mesopotamia. The most northerly of the mounds which mark the site has always been known as Babil, which is just a remnant of the old name " Bab-ilani," " The Gate of the Gods," and another prominent mound bears still more emphatic witness to the accuracy of the local tradition, for it is called " Kasr," " The Castle " or " Palace," and it was from beneath it that the ruins of the great palace of Nebuchadnezzar were unearthed. Benjamin of Tudela, in the twelfth century, and John Eldred in the sixteenth, both testify to the continuity of the tradition ; and Pietro della Valle in 1616, and the Abbé de Beauchamp and Carsten Niebuhr in the eighteenth century carry it on to comparatively modern times.

The nineteenth-century list of visitors to or workers on the site begins in 1811 with the visit of Claudius James Rich. Rich brought back with him an inscription of Nebuchadnezzar and a number of contract tablets. Forty years later Layard came upon the scene ; but his work here was of nothing like the same importance as that which he accomplished in Assyria, though he did succeed in uncovering at the mound Babil remains of building bearing Nebuchadnezzar's imprint. Fresnel and Oppert, during the French Expedition in 1852, were not much more successful, and, as we have seen, all the fruits of their work perished through the wrecking of their rafts. Oppert was misled by the figures of Herodotus into gigantic conceptions of the city's area, including within it both Birs-Nimrud, which covers the site of Borsippa, and El Ohêmir, which is the ancient city of Kish. The work of Hormuzd Rassam, in 1879-82 was more fruitful. He discovered some remarkable wells lined with red granite, which he concluded to be the remains of the famous Hanging Gardens of Nebuchadnezzar, besides finding, in the mound known as Jumjuma, thousands of inscribed tablets, which proved to be the records of the great banking house of Egibi, which flourished in the days of Nabopolassar and Nebuchadnezzar. His most striking find was that of the cylinder on which Cyrus gives his own account of his capture of Babylon, and in doing so, shows us that fiction, as narrated by Herodotus, is sometimes stranger than truth.

On the whole it may be said that, up to the end of the nineteenth century, the mounds of Babylon remained practically untouched ; for the work had scarcely amounted to more than superficial scratching, and our ignorance of the actual condition of the site was scarcely relieved by the few scanty scraps of knowledge which had filtered through a great deal of theorising as to the locality of the Hanging Gardens, and so forth. These world-renowned creations of Nebuchadnezzar, in particular, had a wonderful fascination for the theorisers ; every one who visited Babylon had a theory as to where they had stood, and each theory differed from every other one. The actual scientific solution of the questions and difficulties involved began in 1899, when the German Expedition, under the late Dr. R. Koldewey, began its operations.

The area which had to be dealt with was sufficiently huge. The figures of Herodotus as to the size of the city are not to be accepted as literally representing the truth ; though, on the whole, Herodotus proves himself at Babylon to have been a singularly acute and accurate observer. His vast estimate of the circuit of the Babylonian walls, however, fifty-three miles, is quite out of the question, and it seems not improbable that here, and in some other smaller instances,

s

his figures are to be divided by four, for the reason that he made the simple and pardonable mistake of confusing the complete measure of the circumference for the measure of one of the sides. Thus, if he were told that the walls measured thirteen miles and a fraction, as they may very well have done, he would multiply this by four, thinking that it applied only to one of the four sides of the city, and would arrive at his impossible figure of fifty-three miles. He seems to have made a similar mistake with regard to several other measurements, though in general even his figures seem to be wonderfully near the mark, where this slip was avoided, or was not likely to occur. Even dividing his circuit by four, however, the site remains one of the vastest, and the work of excavation was proportionately great. When Dr. Koldewey, in 1913, published the results of his work up to that date, he computed that after fourteen years' work with from two hundred to two hundred and fifty workmen, about half of his task had been accomplished —a fact which is sufficient in itself to demonstrate the magnitude of the undertaking.

The area which is accepted as falling within the boundaries of the ancient city is now marked by a series of mounds, of which five are of oustanding importance. These are as follows. At the most northerly extremity of the site lies Babil, the mound which retains the traditional name ; in the centre is the most important mound, that known as the Kasr ; on the south is Amran ibn-Ali, so-called from the fact that the tomb of Amran the son of Ali stands upon it ; while to the east lie the two mounds known as Homera and Merkes. North of Amran, and between it and Merkes, lies a little plain called " Sachn," " The Pan," a spot which has proved of great importance. Each of these named points has marked the site of some great building or buildings in Nebuchadnezzar's city.

Perhaps the most stupendous of what seemed to many the romantic fibs of Herodotus is his description of the gigantic fortifications of Babylon. It seemed practically impossible that such walls as the Greek historian describes should ever have been constructed by human hands. Here is a little of the fairy-tale as he tells it. " Such is the size of the city of Babylon," he says, after giving his statement of a circuit of fifty-three miles, which, as we have seen, should probably be divided by four. " It was adorned in a manner surpassing any city we are acquainted with. In the first place, a moat, deep, wide, and full of water, runs entirely round it ; next, there is a wall fifty royal cubits in breadth, and in height two hundred, but the royal cubit is larger than the common one by three fingers' breadth. . . . And on the top of the wall, at the edges, they built buildings of one storey, fronting each other, and they left a space between these dwellings sufficient for turning a chariot with four horses. In the circumference of the wall there were a hundred gates, all of brass, as also are the posts and lintels. In this manner Babylon was encompassed with a wall. And the city consists of two divisions, for a river, called the Euphrates, separates it in the middle. . . . The wall, therefore, on either bank, has an elbow carried down to the river ; from thence along the curvatures of each bank of the river runs a wall of baked bricks. . . . At the end of each street a little gate is formed in the wall along the river front, in number equal to the streets ; and they are all made of brass, and lead down to the edge of the river. This outer wall then is the chief defence ; but another wall runs round within, not much inferior to the other in strength, though narrower."

Strange to say, it is just here, where Herodotus seems to be drawing the most prodigious of long bows, that his credit has been most fully vindicated. Excavation has shown that on every point on which they can be tested, the Greek historian's gigantic figures are simply the statements of actual fact. It is of course impossible to check his statement as to the height of the walls, and 200 royal cubits, over 300 feet, does seem almost an impossible height for a wall otherwise so vast ; but his accuracy in the facts which can be checked is so surprising that one almost hesitates to suggest that even the height which he ascribes to the walls may not be true. The actual wall, as the excavations revealed it, was constructed as follows. The ditch, whose width and depth are not yet ascertained, was faced on its city side by a wall of burnt brick 3·3 metres in thickness, which formed a kind of preliminary defence. Then came the main outer wall. It was of burnt brick, 7·8 metres thick ; then came an interval of 12 metres, filled with brick rubble, and then a wall of crude brick 7 metres thick. Thus the whole wall measures over 26 metres in thickness of solid brickwork ; in other words, it was about 85 feet thick, which agrees remarkably well with Herodotus's measure of " fifty royal cubits." We know of no such stupendous walls as these in the case of any other city of the ancient world. The towers which Herodotus describes as rising one storey above the wall are the cavalier towers which Dr. Koldewey discovered sitting astride the wall at intervals of about 65 feet, and projecting beyond the line of wall on both faces.

Within this gigantic enceinte, which must have made of Babylon one vast fortress, impregnable to any siege-engines of ancient days, and only to be captured by starvation or treachery, the interest of excavation has mainly centred on two points—the work on the mound called Kasr, which covers the ruins of the great southern citadel, including the palace of Nebuchadnezzar, and that on the area where stand the ruins of E-temenanki, the great ziggurat, and E-sagila, the temple of Marduk.

The Euphrates flowed on the west side of the city, following, from a point of its course almost level with the modern village of Kweiresh and the Kasr, a course somewhat more easterly than at present. Through the centre of the great triangular area between the walls and the river ran the most sumptuous artery of Babylon, and probably the most magnificent street of any city, ancient or modern. This was the Procession Street, which ran in a north and south direction past the Kasr, and Nebuchadnezzar's palace, to the great temple of Marduk, E-sagila. The street had existed long before the time of Nebuchadnezzar, and Sennacherib the Assyrian had done a good deal for it before the days of his destroying anger ; but as it stood finally it was practically entirely the work of Nebuchadnezzar, who has told us the story of the making of it. " Aibur-shadu, the roadway of Babylon, I filled up with a high filling for the procession of the great lord Marduk, and with *turminabanda* stone and with *shadu* stone I made Aibur-shadu, from the Illu Gate to the Ishtar-sakipat-tebisha, fit for the procession of his godhead. I connected it with the portions that my father had built, and made the road glorious."

Glorious he certainly did make it, if solidity of construction and sumptuousness of material are to be the criteria. In these days of the construction of great arterial roads it may be of interest to see how the greatest emperor of the last of the despotisms of the ancient East built a road through the centre of his capital, as excavation has revealed the actual details of material and construction to us. It is possible that modern methods of construction may be quite as efficient as those of Nebuchadnezzar ; but our engineers have a long way to travel before they reach the magnificence of the material employed by the Great King. The road was literally built, just as much as the great fortification walls of the city, and of material far more splendid than anything used on the walls. The bed of the road was first laid with a brick pavement ; and this, in turn, was covered with asphalt. Above the asphalt came the flagged causeway which formed the actual surface of the street. The roadway in the centre was laid with mighty flags of limestone, each measuring 1·05 metres in length and breadth ; while the sidewalks on either hand were laid with smaller slabs of red breccia, each 66 centimetres square. The joints of all the slabs were bevelled, and filled in with asphalt. On the edges of each slab, where of course it could not be seen once the slab was in position, ran an inscription. " Nebuchadnezzar, king of Babylon, son of Nabopolassar, King of Babylon, am I. The Babel Street I paved with blocks of *shadu* stone for the procession of the great Lord Marduk. Marduk, Lord, grant eternal life." We have not yet got the length of using such splendid materials as white limestone and red breccia for our pavements ; but there can be no question of the richness of appearance which such a street would present. In laying his pavement blocks, with their concealed inscriptions, Nebuchadnezzar was obviously appealing to posterity ; and though the recognition has come differently from anything that he could have expected, and he has had to wait long for it, it is pleasant to think that it has come at last, and that a great man has got his due.

The Procession Street must have been the central artery along which the life of the great city flowed, as well as a Sacred Way for the God of Babylon ; but we are not to conceive of it as an open street with houses facing upon it, as in a modern town. On the contrary, the great avenue was bordered on either side with high defensive walls, seven metres thick, which linked together the fortifications of the southern citadel with the walls on the north. Thus this artery of traffic was also an element of the city's defence, for an enemy who had forced entrance into it would find himself in a passage closed at the end, and bordered on both sides by massive walls, from the battlements of which the defenders would hail down missiles upon him, rendering the street an absolute death-trap. The splendour and terror of the whole construction were heightened by the long rows of lions executed in low relief in enamelled brick, which adorned the walls on either side, and led up to the sumptuous

decoration of the great gateway which crossed the street
just where it reached the southern citadel.

This was the Ishtar Gate, which Nebuchadnezzar names
in his inscription as the " Ishtar-sakipat-tebisha." It has
been excavated in a wonderful state of preservation, and
is by far the most imposing remnant of the architecture of
ancient Babylon now surviving. It consisted of a double
gateway, flanked at each end with a tower on either side of
the roadway, and with a narrow courtyard or passage-way
running between the two gates with their towers. Here,
again, if an enemy succeeded in forcing one of the gates,
he would only find himself in a narrow yard, closed at its
further end by the remaining gateway, and commanded on
every side by the archery of the defenders. The eastern
towers of the Ishtar Gate are still standing to a height of
about forty feet, and we can see that it was here that the
magnificent but menacing decoration of the Procession
Street reached its climax. The whole surface of the walls
of the towers was adorned with figures of bulls and dragons
(" *sirrush*", a sort of unicorn). These were executed in
brick relief and enamelled in brilliant colours, chiefly white
and yellow upon a bright blue background, and were so
arranged that to anyone approaching the gate they would
appear as though advancing to meet him. The impression
produced upon the mind must have been one of the splendour and strength of the great city whose approaches were
thus decorated with these threatening and sinister genii.

The Procession Street appears to have turned at right
angles when it reached the south of the sacred enclosure of
E-temenanki, the ziggurat of the god Marduk, and to have
run westwards, between the ziggurat and the temple of
Marduk, E-sagila, to the bank of the Euphrates, which,
as we have seen, here followed a more easterly course than
that in which it flows at present. At this point, the work
which has shown us Nebuchadnezzar as a great road-maker
has also shown him as the first bridge-builder of the ancient

world of whom we have any record. Herodotus, who seldom missed seeing much that was worth while, though he sometimes got mixed as to names and traditions, has told us about the wonderful bridge which joined the two halves of Babylon. He ascribes the building of it to his more or less mythical queen Nitocris ; but the bridge was there all right, all the same. " In the next place," he says, " about the middle of the city, she built a bridge with the stones she had prepared, and bound them together with plates of lead and iron. Upon these stones she laid, during the day, square planks of timber, on which the Babylonians might pass over ; but at night these planks were removed, to prevent people from crossing by night and robbing one another." We may doubt if the somewhat clumsy substitute for a drawbridge suggested by the historian actually existed ; but a bridge of a sufficiently solid sort was certainly built by Nebuchadnezzar across the old course of the Euphrates, for seven of its piers have been excavated in the depression west of E-temenanki. The piers are built of burnt brick and asphalt, and are nine metres wide in each case, and placed nine metres apart. They are boat-shaped, the bow of the boat being turned to face the descending current, and suggest a copy in more permanent materials of a temporary bridge of boats. The bridge-head was guarded by a gateway with two massive flanking towers and a walled courtyard similar to that of the Ishtar Gate. Nebuchadnezzar himself states in the India House Inscription that it was his father who was responsible for the inception of this interesting piece of work. " My father, my begetter . . . had erected piers of burnt brick for the crossing over of the Euphrates." Herodotus describes the bridge as built of stone ; but this, no doubt, refers to the upper work of the piers which supported the woodwork of the roadway, and which would be the only part that the historian would actually see.

At the Kasr, the Southern Citadel, a great fortified

enclosure in the heart of the city, the excavations revealed the enormous palace which Nebuchadnezzar reared in place of the comparatively modest building which had contented Nabopolassar. The traveller approaching from the north would see before him a long line of battlemented towers projecting from a massive curtain wall, above which, in the north-eastern angle, close to the Ishtar Gate, waved the palms of the Hanging Gardens. The approach lay through the Ishtar Gate, with its multi-coloured bulls and dragons. After passing through this splendid portal, the wayfarer turned westwards, through the Beltis Gate from the Procession Street into a courtyard surrounded on all sides by the administrative buildings of the Empire, and from this into a second court, also lined with buildings, which led finally into the great courtyard of the palace, a noble enclosure of 55 by 61 metres. In all these three courts it is to be noticed that the larger rooms are placed on the south side of the court, facing the north, so that they would not be exposed to the scorching heat of the direct rays of the southern sun—a very necessary arrangement in a sub-tropical climate like that of Babylon. On the south side of the central court lies the throne-room of the palace, by far the finest chamber found in Babylon. It measured 52 metres in length by 17 in breadth, three wide doorways opened into it from the court, and through the central one the great king could be seen, seated on his throne, by the crowd of courtiers awaiting audience in the courtyard. The decoration of the great hall is striking and tasteful, the surface of the wall facing the courtyard being faced with enamelled bricks which present a scheme of yellow columns with bright blue capitals edged with white, standing out upon a dark blue background.

Here, then, is the very heart of Babylon, the centre of all its splendours, and the almost certain scene of the events recorded in the Book of Daniel. " If any one should desire to localise the scene of Belshazzar's eventful banquet, he can surely place it with complete accuracy in this immense room." On the whole the Throne-room is worthy of its associations, though its decoration, save for the enamelled wall, seems somewhat meagre. The same can hardly be said of the building which has been proposed as the ruin of the world-famous Hanging Gardens. This is a building situated in the north-east corner of the Citadel, and composed, to an extent very unusual in Babylonian practice, of stone. The surviving remains of it consist of fourteen narrow cells, roofed with barrel-vaulting. In one of the cells is a well with a triple shaft adapted to secure a continuous flow of water, and the suggestion is that the Hanging Gardens were a kind of roof-garden raised on the vaulting of these cells and watered by the well. If this be the case, then, in this respect at least, we must revise our views as to the magnificence of Nebuchadnezzar, for the Hanging Gardens, about which so great a to-do has been made, were a very commonplace business after all. Strabo and Diodorus both give the measurement of one side of the structure as four plethra, or about 120 metres ; the actual measurement of the vaulted building is 30 metres, and again division by four is suggested. But it is not impossible that the vaulted building may have been designed for quite other purposes, and that the Hanging Gardens still remain to be found, and to justify their ancient fame.

In one of the walls of the western part of the palace, which belonged mainly to the time of Nabopolassar, the explorers came upon a remarkable burial. The coffin was of pottery, and was of unusual size. The dead man was evidently of high rank, for he had been wrapped in gold-spangled garments, and decked with golden ornaments. Dr. Koldewey has suggested that this burial may be that of Nabopolassar himself, thus laid to rest with fitting reverence by his greater son within the walls of the palace which he had reared for himself. The question cannot be settled, as there are no inscriptions to identify the occupant of the

coffin ; but the contrast between the Babylonian poverty
and the Egyptian richness in the matter of royal burials is
forcibly underlined by this discovery, which, all uncertain
as its attribution may be, is the only approach to a royal
burial found in all the excavations.

What is perhaps the most interesting feature of the work
at Babylon was done in the area lying almost directly south
of the Kasr, between this mound and Amran ibn-Ali, and
known as " Sachn," " The Pan." Here the excavations
revealed a vast enclosure, approximately square, and
measuring no less than 409 metres on the side. It was surrounded by a great temenos-wall of crude brick, which was
double, with ranges of chambers occupying the intervening
space. The eastern gate of this huge courtyard was bordered
with two large buildings with open courts, which may have
been storehouses, and on the south side the enclosure wall
is lined with a series of houses which must have belonged
to the priestly staff of the place. Beyond the enclosure, on
the south side, stands a great temple, a mass of brickwork
measuring 79·3 metres by 85·8, with a central court of 31·3
metres by 37·1, and an annexe larger than itself on its
eastern side. In the south-west angle of the enclosure,
nearest to the temple, stands the core of a stupendous
tower, measuring about 300 feet on a side, and approached
by a stairway at right angles to its southern face—manifestly
the ruin of a ziggurat.

Here we have the famous buildings which Herodotus has
described to us as the " temple of Zeus Belus." " The
precinct of Zeus Belus was still in existence in my time, a
square building of two stades on every side. In the midst
of this precinct is built a solid tower of one stade both in
length and breadth, and on this tower rose another, and
another on that, to the number of eight. And an ascent to
these is outside, running spirally round all the towers.
And in the uppermost tower stands a spacious temple, and
in the temple is placed, handsomely furnished, a large

couch, and by its side a table of gold. . . . There is also another temple below, within the precinct at Babylon ; in it is a large statue of Zeus seated, and near it is placed a large table of gold ; the throne and the step also are of gold."

On the whole, Herodotus comes out triumphantly from the comparison of his account with the actual remains disclosed by excavation. In one or two points he makes mistakes, as can scarcely be wondered at in the case of a tourist writing from memory after such a surfeit of wonders as he had had in Babylon. Thus it appears that the stairway was not a spiral, as he says, but led straight up to the face of the tower ; and the probability is that there were two other stairs at the angles, as at Ur. (This idea is adopted in the late Dr. Koldewey's last restoration of the tower.) Again, the "temple below" is not within the precinct, as he says, but outside it. It is also doubtful whether the tower ever had the eight stages which his statement requires, or the seven which are specified in the cuneiform text translated by George Smith, and recent restorations have proceeded more or less on the idea of two or three stages, as at Ur ; though it is by no means certain that the seven or eight staged building may not turn out right after all. On all other points, however, the description of Herodotus fairly represents the great temple-complex now disclosed by excavation. The great tower is E-temenanki, "The House of the Foundation of Heaven and Earth " ; the "temple below" is E-sagila, "The House of Heaven and Earth," the identifications being assured by bricks of Esarhaddon, Ashur-bani-pal and Nebuchadnezzar, which name the buildings.

In other words, the excavations have revealed to us the great central shrine of the Babylonian faith, the Temple of Marduk, the supreme god of the Babylonian Pantheon, with its ziggurat. E-temenanki itself may fairly claim to be the most famous building in all the world. For this huge

cube of brickwork is all that remains of what the sacred
writer certainly had in mind when he described the building
of the original Tower of Babel. " And they said, Go to,
let us build us a city, and a tower whose top may reach
unto heaven ; and let us make us a name, lest we be
scattered abroad upon the face of the whole earth." The
record of the ziggurat of Ur tells us how often such a tower
needed to be rebuilt, and doubtless there have been many
Towers of Babel since the conception of the ziggurat first
entered the minds of the original mountain-dwellers who
had settled in Babylonia, and longed for something to
remind them, in the dead level of their surroundings, of
their native hills, and to lift them nearer to the stars and
to heaven ; but there is just as little doubt that no matter
how often E-temenanki was rebuilt, the tower has always
stood on the same place. What we see now, is the work of
Nebuchadnezzar ; but he describes his achievement in
terms almost identical with those in which the first builders
of Babel described their plan. " To raise up the top of
E-temenanki that it may rival Heaven, I laid to my hand."

For the rest, the excavations give us much the same
general state of things as was disclosed at Ur—namely, that
the sacred enclosure of a Babylonian temple held a complex
of buildings of which some, perhaps the majority, were
devoted to purposes which, though sacred in the sense of
serving the god, were of an otherwise secular character.
" The priests of E-temenanki must have occupied very
distinguished positions as representatives of the god who
bestowed the kingship of Babylon, and the immense private
houses to the south of our peribolos agree very well with
the supposition in regard to this Vatican of Babylon, that
the principal administrative apparatus would be housed
there. The numerous chambers of the two great buildings
in the east will be recognised by all as storerooms where the
property of the sanctuary and the things needed for processions, etc, could be stored." The phrase, " the Vatican

of Babylon," aptly describes one aspect of the uses of the great mass of buildings ; but for another aspect of it we have to turn to the description already given of the corresponding assemblage of buildings in the temenos of the Moon-god at Ur. " If in some respects we might compare the whole temple to a rambling mediæval monastery, in others we might find the best parallel in a mediæval castle," and also, we might add, in others in a factory quarter of a modern town. As it was at Ur, so, no doubt, it was also at Babylon ; and under the great shadow of the Tower of Babel there lay a large administrative department, a busy manufacturing establishment, the offices of a great landed estate, an extensive monastery and convent, and a fortified citadel, as well as the temple of the supreme God.

South-east from E-sagila, in the mound Ishin-aswad, the excavations revealed the temple of Ninib (Ninurta), named " E-patutila," " The House of the Sceptre of Life." This temple, whose plan is chiefly notable for what seems to have been an arrangement of its gateways specially designed for processional purposes, was built, or rather completed, by Nabopolassar. This king's foundation cylinders were found under the brick flooring, in the doorways leading to the sanctuaries, and are of interest because they give a direct reference to the final triumph of the Babylonian arms over the Assyrians. The inscription runs as follows : " The Assyrian who since many days had ruled the whole of the peoples, and had placed the people of the land under his heavy yoke ;—I, the weak one, the humble one, who reveres the Lord of Lords, through the mighty war power of Nabu and Marduk my lords, kept back their foot from the land of Akkad, and caused their yoke to be thrown off. . . . "

So far as can be judged from the surviving remains, the religious architecture of the great city was characterised by a colouring as sombre as the decoration of the Procession Street, the Ishtar Gate, and the Palace was brilliant.

" While the walls in general were coloured dead white with a thin gypsum wash, certain of the more prominent parts, such as the main entrance, the doorway leading to the shrine, and the niche behind the statue of the goddess (the reference is to the shrine of Ishtar) were washed over with black asphalt in solution, each blackened surface being decorated near its edge with white stripes or line-borders. The contrast in colour presented by this black and white decoration must have been startling in its effect ; no doubt, like the crude brick material of the buildings, it was an inheritance from earlier times, and owed its retention to its traditional religious significance." (*History of Babylon*, L. W. King). Doubtless the religious conservatism of the Babylonian is responsible, as Dr. King suggests, for this extraordinary scheme of mural decoration, which must have made the temples look as if they were built out of mourning note-paper ; but the sombre character of it is thoroughly in keeping also with the grim and joyless type of the Babylonian religion.

Almost due east of E-temenanki lies the mound called Merkes—a name which also preserves a tradition which the excavations proved to be well grounded. " Merkes," according to Dr. Koldewey, means " a city as a trade centre " ; and it was precisely beneath the mound thus named that the business quarter of the town seems to have lain. It was here, too, that the explorers came into touch with the really ancient Babylon, the city of the times of Hammurabi and his successors. The two or three uppermost metres of the mound gave the scanty ruins of the Parthian period. For four metres beneath this, the remains represent " the brilliant time of the city under the Neo-Babylonian kings on into the Persian and Greek periods." The houses at this time were closely crowded together, but were well built, while their equipment as to water supply and drainage bears witness " to the comparatively high level of the requirements demanded by the culture of that time."

At some depth below the Nebuchadnezzar level came houses with tablets bearing the dates of Merodach-baladan, Belnadinshum, and others of the same period. Finally, about 3·4 metres beneath this stratum came the Babylon of the time of Hammurabi, Samsu-iluna, Ammiditana, Samsu-ditana and others. This Babylon of the Ist Dynasty was quite adequately dated also by the tablets found in its houses.

Thus the excavation reached what must always be the most interesting period of the history, though the remains were pitifully scanty. At all events, the condition of the area at the Ist Dynasty level left no doubt as to the correctness of the statement that the Babylon of this period perished in a great disaster. No evidence was forthcoming as to whether the destruction was wrought by a Hittite raid, or, as has been recently suggested, by an Assyrian invasion ; but the existence over the area of a thick bed of undisturbed ashes shows that the ancient city was destroyed by fire. So far as can be judged, the Babylon of Hammurabi's time, though its houses were packed pretty closely together, followed a definite plan of island-blocks, separated by streets which were approximately straight ; and the same appears to have been the case with the Neo-Babylonian city. Herodotus had already told us this, for the later period. " The city itself, which is full of houses three and four storeys high, is cut up into straight streets, as well all the others as the transverse ones that lead to the river." " The main arteries," says Dr. King, " run roughly north and south, parallel to the course of the Sacred Way, while others cross them at right angles. It would appear that, in spite of the absence of open spaces, we have here a deliberate attempt at town-planning on a scientific basis, the original idea of which may be traced back to the Ist Dynasty. . . . It has long been known that Hammurabi did much to codify the laws of his country and render their administration effective. It would now appear that similar system and method were introduced at the same period into the more material side of the national life."

Such are the main results of excavation on the site of the greatest city of the ancient East. It can scarcely be denied that in some respects they are disappointing, and that the Babylon now revealed but poorly takes the place of the gorgeous dream-city which fancy built out of the accounts of Herodotus and the other Greek travellers. Yet we have to realise that the material of which the great city was built was ill adapted to preserve any lasting evidence of its glory, and that the real wonder is, not that so much has perished, but that so much has survived. The surviving relics of the Procession Street and the Ishtar Gate afford us some means of quickening the imagination to an attempt to conceive the splendours of Nebuchadnezzar's great capital in the days when the conqueror went up in state along his Sacred Way to give thanks in the temple of Marduk for the victories which had made him lord of the whole earth ; and if we can see but little of that earlier period when Ḥammurabi ruled and legislated, it is something to be able to feel that, as Ur gave us back the scene of the first beginnings of the national story of Israel, so Babylon has now restored to us something of the glories of the scene in which the national life of the Hebrew race closed.

T

BOOK III

PALESTINE

CHAPTER XII

GENERAL FEATURES OF EXCAVATION IN PALESTINE

OF all the lands of the Near East in which excavation has been carried on, it is safe to say that there is none so interesting to the average educated man or woman as Palestine ; and this, of course, not for any special quality of the land, or any special fascination of its culture, but because of its Scriptural associations, and above all its association with the life and ministry of Jesus Christ. There is nothing in the land itself to account for the attraction which draws the imagination of countless thousands to it with a charm possessed by no other land on earth ; for of all the lands with which we have had to deal it is one of the least attractive intrinsically. It has none of the mysterious beauty in monotony which is characteristic of Egypt, nor any of the reputation for almost miraculous fertility which still hangs about the barren tracts and noisome swamps of Mesopotamia. Scripture speaks of it, indeed, as a land " flowing with milk and honey " ; but we must remember that the words were spoken to people coming in from the arid desert, to whom the slightest approach to fertility would seem wonderful. Judged by normal standards, the country must always have been, on the whole, a grim and forbidding land, though it has its beauty-spots here and there.

Nor has Palestine the charm of having been the home of a race which has proved itself capable of attracting sympathy by its own personal qualities, or by the contribution which it has made to the stock of human culture and art. The native Egyptian, even apart from the wonderful gifts which he has bestowed upon the world in respect of art, architecture, and literature, has revealed himself as one of the most engaging and sympathetic types of antiquity ; the more sombre Semite of Mesopotamia has contributed so much to the growth of human knowledge that it is impossible to ignore his value, even though we may detest his spirit. But of the various races which have successively occupied Palestine the only one which appears to modern ideas to have had anything to contribute to the stock of human culture, or to make any appeal to modern sympathies, is precisely the one which, up till the other day, was regarded as the *pariah* of Palestine—the Philistine. The successive Semitic stocks which held the land for more than two thousand years are among the most unattractive and least profitable of all the stocks of the ancient East in practically all things which make for the advancement of the human race—save one.

That one, however, has proved decisive, and the possession of the spiritual gift which has marked out the otherwise unattractive Hebrew from his more powerful and more attractive neighbours has outweighed all the other gifts which the more gifted races have given to the service of humanity. Palestine is, and will in all probability remain, the most interesting land in the world, simply and solely because of the fact that it is the scene of the lives of the men who have led the human race in the pursuit of spiritual knowledge, and supremely of Him Who is the Chief of all spiritual leaders. Accordingly, one need not wonder at the fact that, for one person who is interested in excavation in Egypt or Mesopotamia, you will find a score who are interested in excavation in Palestine.

Indeed, so much is this the case, that one may safely say that a great deal even of the interest which attaches to research in these other lands arises from the fact that they are more or less directly · Biblical lands, and that their

history is linked with that of the people whose spiritual
gifts to the race have given them such a grip upon our
imaginations. | It is quite certain that if the mummy of
Pharaoh Necho were discovered to-morrow, the point
about him that would interest nine people out of every ten
would be, not that he was one of the most prominent
Pharaohs of the Saite Renaissance in Egypt, but that he
was the king who slew Josiah of Judah at Megiddo, and
that if the tomb of Hammurabi should be discovered in
Babylon, he would appeal to the average reader of the news,
not as the first of the great imperial figures who have given
law to the world, the Justinian of the ancient East, but
rather as being possibly the " Amraphel King of Shinar,"
who defeated the kings of Sodom and Gomorrah, and was
in turn routed by Abraham.

So much has this Biblical interest dominated all others
as a motive in the carrying out of Palestinian excavation,
that it was definitely alleged as the main reason for the
establishment of the Palestine Exploration Fund, which
ever since its inception has been one of the main supports,
as it was the originator, of excavation in the Holy Land.
" No country," so it was said in the original prospectus
of the Fund, " should be of so much interest to us as that
in which the documents of our Faith were written, and the
momentous events they describe enacted," and this
definitely Biblical point of approach, though it has given
place in some respects, in the actual work of excavation,
to the more strictly scientific method, is still in the general
mind the chief matter of interest and value. From the
scientific point of view, an archæological discovery in
Palestine is of no more value and no less than a discovery
in Egypt or Mesopotamia, and must be judged by its intrinsic
importance ; but who can doubt that if the recent excavations on the site of " David's Burgh," at Jerusalem,
had unearthed the harp of the Psalmist King, the splendours
of Tutankhamen's Tomb, and of all the Pharaohs put

together, would have seemed paltry, in the general estimation, compared to such a discovery, while it would at once have been asserted that the discovery of the actual harp to which the Psalms were sung disproved all the theories of the Higher Criticism as to the composition of the Psalter ! Actually, of course, the critical position as to the Psalter, whether it be true or false, remains absolutely unaffected by such a discovery, if it were possible ; and, in spite of rash assertions to the contrary, archæology has had singularly little to say to the criticism of the sacred documents, either in proof or disproof of its results. That is not the business of archæology at all. " It is not unnatural to suppose that the special function of an excavator is to *confirm* written history, sacred or profane. If this were so, he would be the most useless of men." So writes the acknowledged chief of modern Palestinian excavators, Professor Macalister ; yet, though the truth of his words is beyond question, people will still believe that excavation is carried on in Palestine in order to prove that David wrote all the Psalms and Solomon the Proverbs. These positions may be finally justified, or they may not ; but it is safe to say that excavation has done little or nothing either to invalidate or to confirm them.

In point of fact, excavation in Palestine has in some respects been singularly disappointing. It is somewhat pathetic to read the programme of the " few " sites which were named in the original prospectus of the Palestine Exploration Fund as being worthy, among many others, of the work of the new society, and to contrast it with the actual work accomplished, after sixty years, by all the societies of Europe and America put together. The contrast between the much expected, and the little accomplished, shows how grievously the difficulties of the task were underestimated in the days of hopeful beginning. Still more have the results been disappointing in Scriptural quality, so to speak. " When Captain Warren began his work," says

Dr. Macalister, " it was expected by many that a few strokes of the spade would settle the questionings on Biblical subjects that were then being asked with ever-increasing persistence. The dreams of the subscribers centred round records of David's wars and of Solomon's glory ; the Ark of the Covenant and the idols of Manasseh ; some, perhaps, hoped for a letter or two written by one privileged to hear the words of Him who spake as never man spake. Nothing of the kind has come to light, however, with the single exception of the Moabite Stone—and that was not discovered by a professed explorer, but lighted upon by a travelling missionary who had no idea of the value of his find ! "

Dr. Macalister's words do not exaggerate the contrast between hope and realisation. It would hardly have surprised some optimists at the start of excavation, if Captain Warren had found Solomon sitting, " in all his glory," enthroned in his royal tomb, or if the enlarged edition of Jeremiah's prophecies which Baruch wrote after Jehoiachim's destruction of the first copy had come to light as dramatically as did the book of the Law in the days of Josiah. It now seems unlikely that we shall have to add to the Moabite Stone, as referring to known incidents of Hebrew history, that reference to the employment by Rameses II of Semites in the building of his name-city in Egypt which Dr. C. S. Fisher believed that he had found on the stele of Rameses at Beth-Shean ; apart from that no other document, either written or carved, bearing on Scripture history has been revealed, unless the Siloam inscription can be so reckoned. As we shall see later, the results of the recent excavations of the Palestine Exploration Fund at Jerusalem have been of the utmost importance and interest as illustrating the actual site of David's Jerusalem, and the scale of his capital ; but, in objects such as constitute the wealth and interest of the results of excavation in other lands, they have been pitifully barren. One would scarcely be exaggerating if one were to say that hardly ever has any excavation in

Palestine yielded any object which for intrinsic quality—
beauty of design or workmanship or preciousness of material,
would be reckoned even tenth-rate as a specimen, if found on
an Egyptian or even on a Mesopotamian site.

It seems, of course, next door to sacrilege to say such a
thing of results drawn from the sacred soil of the Holy
Land ; but it is the simple truth to which the people who
are always expecting impossible wonders to result from
Palestinian excavation would do well to habituate and
resign themselves. Nor is it difficult to see reasons for the
seemingly extraordinary poverty of the most promising
sites in Palestine. To begin with, the conditions of soil and
climate in Palestine are almost as unfavourable to the preservation of the finer objects of a nation's art or literature
as those of a land like Egypt are favourable. In Egypt,
the dead, from whose tombs nearly all our material has come,
were buried, practically invariably, in the dry sandy soil
of the western desert beyond the margin of the cultivation ;
and the soil, already by its constitution adapted to the
preservation of delicate objects, was only visited at long
intervals by rain, and the consequent dampness which is
so destructive. Accordingly, in Egypt objects of the finest
workmanship and the most delicate materials are preserved
for incredible periods of time, and ivory carvings survive
in amazingly perfect condition from 6000 years ago, and
fragile papyri, with their writing still legible, and their
coloured illuminations still bright, from 3500 years. Mesopotamia can give us nothing to compare with this ; still
less can Palestine, with its variable climate and its heavy
rains. It may have been a relief to the Hebrews, weary of
the monotony of Egypt, to be told that their new home
was " a land of brooks of water, of fountains, and depths
that spring out of valleys and hills . . . a land that drinketh
water of the rain of heaven " ; but it has made all the
difference for the worse to the archæologist.

Further, it ought to be remembered that in dealing with

Palestine we are dealing with what, after all, was never more than a small land and a small power. The romantic interest of the stories of the kings of Israel, and the glowing descriptions of the glory of a king like Solomon are apt to dazzle our eyes, and blind us to the fact that the Hebrew kingdom was in reality merely a pigmy compared with the great and long-enduring empires which bordered it on either hand. One of the great reasons for the paucity of important relics of the country's former greatness is simply that there never was such a thing as greatness, interpreted in the same terms as would be applied to the great empires, in Palestine at all. In Egypt and Mesopotamia we have great and important survivals, because in these countries great and wealthy lines of kings endured for century after century, each generation rivalling or completing the work of the generations before it ; but in Palestine such a tradition of great work never had either the room or the time to grow up. Recent excavation at Jerusalem has taught us how tiny was the scale of the City of David, the first capital of the united Hebrew state. It was a mere swallow's, or perhaps rather hawk's nest clinging to the rock on the tip of the southern spur of what afterwards became the Temple Hill ; and even Solomon's Jerusalem, though it expanded over part of the south-west hill as well as the original east hill, was but a small place. If the space was cramped, the time was still more cramped. The united kingdom lasted only for the latter half of David's reign and the whole of Solomon's, and of that short period, only the forty years of Solomon can really be reckoned as affording an opportunity for great construction. After Solomon's death, the resources of the race were fatally divided, thus reducing still further the likelihood of the production of great architectural work such as the greater kingdoms of the East delighted in ; and the subsequent history of the land, after the brief period of Hebrew domination, was such that even the work which we know to have been done by some of the later kings, such as

Ahab in Israel and Uzziah in Judah, could scarcely be expected to leave much trace of its existence.

For one of the most sufficient reasons against the survival on any large scale of the work of past ages in Palestine is the fact that from time immemorial the land has been the cockpit in which the great empires of the world have fought out their battles. A bridge between the two continents of Asia and Africa, its Maritime Plain the natural war-path by which the armies of Egypt, Babylon, Assyria, Hatti, and Persia swept up and down in their secular strifes, Palestine has kept up the traditions of early history down to yesterday, when Allenby closed the last Crusade at Armageddon, that same Megiddo where Thothmes III won his victory three and a half millenniums ago, and where Josiah of Judah fell before Necho nearly nine hundred years later. No land in the world has been fought over so continuously or for so long a period as Palestine ; while the ferocity of the strife has often matched its duration. The wonder is, not that there is so little to reward excavation, but that anything has survived at all.

One more reason for the poverty of the land in the treasures for which the excavator searches is to be found in the character of the races which were dominant in it during the ages which are of the greatest interest to us historically. The Semitic stock in Palestine, whether it was represented by the " Canaanites " whom the Hebrews partially drove out, or by the Hebrews themselves, has always shown itself, throughout its entire history, and even down to the present day, singularly barren of the creative inspiration which leads to great works of art or architecture, or even to genuinely artistic craftsmanship. \" From first to last," says Dr. Macalister, " there was not a native potter in Palestine who could so much as invent a new design to paint on his water-pots. There was not an armourer who could invent a new pattern of sword or arrowhead. The modern peasants live in houses practically identical in style and construction with those which sheltered the peasants of 2000 B.C.—a community of white ants could not be more unprogressive." The Hebrew had his own sphere, in which his genius was supreme; but he had nothing of that passion for beauty which possessed the ancestors of his great rivals the Philistines, and which flowered again unforgettably in the Greek genius. When even the Wise King wished to create temple and palaces worthy of his God and his own splendour, he had to seek help from the skilful but tasteless craftsmen of Phœnicia, and, no doubt, his temple and his palaces suffered from the usual faults of Phœnician work, and, though rich and gorgeous enough, were also pretentious and vulgar.

Such are some of the reasons which are manifestly sufficient to account for that poverty which has been such a marked characteristic of the results of Palestinian excavation, when compared with the richness of those from some of the other lands of the ancient East. Yet it would be an entire mistake to imagine that because the excavations in Palestine have been singularly barren of work which offers fine museum specimens to the admiration of the lover of art and beauty, they have therefore been unsuccessful. On the contrary, their very poverty has taught us a lesson, not unheeded, as to the environment out of which proceeded the greatest spiritual influences which have ever shaped the destinies of humanity ; and while the noteworthy objects which speak of a great art and culture are lacking, for the good reason that they were never there, there has been no real lack of the humbler evidences which are of the utmost value as aids towards the reconstruction of the actual life of the people of the Holy Land during those ages which will always possess the most profound interest. It is about sixty years since Sir Charles Warren started for the first attempt at real excavation in Palestine. Scarcely one of the items of the programme which those who sent him out fondly imagined that he would carry out almost without difficulty has been actually accomplished, by him and all his successors

put together ; few, indeed, of the brilliant hopes which
dazzled the imaginations of so many have been realised
even in part : but, on the other hand, much that was never
dreamed of has been learned, and, as Professor Macalister
has put it, " our way is illumined by strange lights breaking
through from unexpected quarters. . . . We have obtained,
not a bare confirmation, but what is far better, a wider
comprehension of the familiar history."

A great deal of the work which has been increasing our
knowledge of Palestine, its history, its races, and their
cultures, lies outside of our scope, being topographical,
concerned with the identification of historical sites, and
similar matters, rather than strictly excavational ; while
some of the chief discoveries of individual objects or inscriptions, such as that of the Moabite Stone, and Sir G. A.
Smith's discovery of the Seti I stele at Tell-es-Shihab,
resulted from observation on the surface, not from excavation, and others, such as the finding of the Siloam inscription, were the results of happy accidents. Apart from all
such work and happenings, actual excavation in Palestine
may be said to comprise two great divisions—First, the work
of excavation at Jerusalem which has gone on at intervals
ever since Captain Warren's first campaign (1867–70),
and has only recently been closed down for the time ; and,
second, the work of excavating the mounds or " Tells,"
covering the ruins of various ancient cities, which has been
and is still being conducted by expeditions representing
learned societies and universities of many lands. It will
only be possible to deal in brief outline with the work at
Jerusalem, and with that on one or two typical Tells where
work has been recently carried on.

CHAPTER XIII

RECENT EXCAVATION AT JERUSALEM

THERE are many reasons why the brightest hopes of those who sent out the earliest expedition for the excavation of the chief Palestinian sites should have centred upon Jerusalem. The great antiquity of the site, its historical importance, and above all the immense importance which attaches to it as the scene of the supreme events in the religious history of the world, are quite sufficient to account for the choice of the ancient capital of the Hebrew Kingdom as the first site to be explored by the agent of the newly established Palestine Exploration Fund.

At the same time, there can be no doubt that the selection of Jerusalem for the first experiment in what was, in 1867, practically a new science, was a great mistake. One can only compare it to putting on a boy who has just begun to learn Greek to the translation of one of the Choral Odes of Euripides, instead of allowing him to make his first blundering attempts upon the familiar Anabasis. " A fundamental mistake," says Dr. Macalister. " One of the many minor sites in the country should have been attacked first, and worked out thoroughly, in order to learn the general character and chronology of the antiquities of the country. . . . In 1867 nothing was known about the development of pottery in the country, which is now recognised as being the chief clue to the dating of Palestinian sites and strata. Without potsherds, there is little or nothing to discriminate between a wall of 100 B.C. and a wall of 2000 B.C. ; there is marvellously little difference in the masonry. A site of the first importance, such as Jerusalem, ought therefore to have been left alone, until the excavators had learnt their business on the *corpus vile* of some place less important, the destruction of which would have involved less serious loss."

The early excavators, however, were far from realising the inadequacy of their equipment for the gigantic task which was so lightheartedly undertaken ; nor is it reasonable to expect that they should have done so. They were acting up to the best knowledge of their day, and if that was quite inadequate to the problems before them, they were not to blame for that. Flinders Petrie, and the scientific classification of pottery, with its system of sequence dating, were still below the horizon when Warren's work began, and it was not till 1890 that the new methods which the great excavator had been working out in Egypt for the last ten years were put into operation in Palestine in his rapid but conclusive preliminary survey of Tell-el-Hesy (Lachish). Besides, the chances are that if the actual conditions and probable results of excavation had been laid before the public which supported the initiation of the work as we know them now, it would never have been started. The interested public was, so to speak, expecting David's harp and Solomon's crown to turn up at an early stage of the proceedings, and would have scorned classified pottery. It was doubtless fortunate that they did not know ; for in Cromwell's phrase, " no one goes so far as he who does not know where he is going " ; and the work has gradually drawn its devotees on to a position which they might never have reached had they seen all the difficulties and disappointments of the road from the start.

Further, Jerusalem as a site combines almost all the disadvantages that can beset and hinder the explorer. The ideal site, from an excavator's point of view, would be one where a city, after being occupied for a considerable period by the representatives of a single race and culture, was suddenly overthrown or deserted, never to be interfered with until the excavator appeared upon the scene with his

workmen. In such a case there would be next to none of
the perplexing problems of dating which vex his soul on
ordinary sites, but all would be comparatively plain sailing.
Such sites, however, are hardly to be found in this imperfect
world, though a site like Lagash presents something of an
approximation to the ideal, being Sumerian from start
almost to finish. Next best is a site, which though it may
have been occupied successively by a number of different
races, has not been so knocked about in the reconstructions
as to complicate the questions of stratification unduly, and
which, after its series of changes, has also finally ceased to
be occupied at a definite period, preferably pretty far back.
Such sites are offered by the various Tells which abound in
Palestine—we may instance Gezer, Lachish, and Bethshean
as specimens of the class. Worst and most troublesome of
all, is a city which has not only been occupied by many
races in more or less orderly succession, but has been
subjected to many radical reconstructions, disturbing arti-
ficially the natural arrangement which the strata of ordinary
successive occupation would present to the excavator, and
which, in addition, continues to be in active occupation at
the time when excavation has to be carried on.

Such a site presents every imaginable difficulty which can
distress the explorer. Its stratification is naturally complex,
to begin with, because of the very long period during which
it has been occupied. It has been additionally complicated
by the drastic destructions and reconstructions involved in
sieges and sacks, with their subsequent renewals. To crown
all, most of the area is either built upon, or is in occupation
or cultivation as garden-ground or field, so that when access
to the surface can be had, it is only after infinite trouble,
and with weary negotiation with greedy and troublesome
proprietors, and when access cannot be had, recourse must
be had to the least satisfactory and most expensive method
of excavation—by tunnelling. Jerusalem combines all these
disadvantages, and offers them, raised to the nth power, to

the excavator. The site has been occupied for at least four thousand years (probably far longer), by samples of almost all the races of the Near East, and it has been subjected to almost every kind of disturbance that the mind can imagine. " Besides the earthquakes which have periodically rocked her foundations, the City has endured nearly twenty sieges and assaults of the utmost severity, some involving a considerable, others a total, destruction of her walls and buildings ; almost twenty more blockades or military occupations with the wreck or dilapidation of prominent edifices ; the frequent alteration of levels by the razing of rocky knolls and the filling of valleys ; about eighteen reconstructions, embellishments, and large extensions . . . the addition of suburbs and the abandonment of parts of the inhabited area ; while over all there has gathered the dust and the waste of ordinary manufacture and commerce." Such a site would seem to be offered to the unhappy explorer as a nightmare of excavation ; and when you add to all this the difficulties arising from the fact that almost all the most interesting points of the area are occupied by the sacred buildings of the most touchy and fanatical of religious sects, the cup of the excavator's troubles overflows.

Such was the site upon whose excavation Sir Charles Warren, then a young captain of Engineers in his twenty-seventh year, embarked in 1867. He lived to see the publication of the results of the last excavation by his old Society, conducted almost on the very spot where he made his most notable discovery—that of " Warren's Shaft," the great shaft and tunnel by means of which the Jebusites brought the water of the Virgin's Fountain within the walls of their fortress, and by which David's captain Joab captured the old stronghold for his master. The programme drawn up for the young excavator is interesting, though such a programme was, according to modern conceptions of the duty of an excavator, a fundamental mistake. He was expected to settle the following questions : 1, The Site of the Temple,

within the Haram esh Sherif ; 2, The true Site of the Holy
Sepulchre ; 3, The course of the First, Second, and Third
Walls of the City, involving the sites of the towers Hippicus,
Phasael, Mariamme, and Psephinus, and also bearing upon
2 above ; 4, The positions of the Gates of the City ; 5, The
date of the erection of the Dome of the Rock ; 6, The
positions of the Tower of Antonia, the Beautiful Gate of
the Temple, the course of the Tyropœon Valley, Millo,
Acra, the Pool of Bethesda, the Gate Gennath, " *and many
other places* " *!* Courage and hope were certainly not lacking
to those who suggested such a programme, though there
was a woeful lack of comprehension of the actual conditions
with which the excavator would have to deal. " It was
expected that the projected excavations would settle, once
for all, the controversies regarding the Holy Places. A
programme sufficient for several lifetimes was laid before
the man who was to work for three years. It is almost
pathetic to look back to those early days, and to read of the
eager hopes that problems of this nature would be settled
by the expenditure of a few hundred pounds, and the turning
over of some spadefuls of earth." Nearly all the items of
the programme still remain unsettled ; and even if some of
them were settled to-morrow, there is little likelihood,
looking to the vested interests involved, that the settlement
would be generally accepted. The path of the Jerusalem
excavator, for the last sixty years, has always been a Via
Dolorosa.

All the same, though Warren did not clear up all the
vexed questions about the Holy City, he did accomplish a
vast amount of useful and interesting work. The great
shaft and gallery which he sank to lay bare the foundations
of the retaining wall of the Temple enclosure gave the first
true conception of the stupendous magnitude of this structure ; for he proved that, huge as the walls seem to be at
present, their bases are masked by rubbish which has
accumulated to a depth of from 80 to 120 feet. He proved

the former existence of another arch, prior to that known as Robinson's Arch, and spanning, like it, the Tyropœon Valley from the Temple area to the south-west hill; he traced the old watercourse which once ran along the bed of the Tyropoeon, and determined the rock-levels here and in other parts of the city. Further, he examined the great reservoir north of the Temple area, known as the *Birket Israin* or " Pool of Israel," and started the investigation of the course of the ancient walls of the city. But his most remarkable achievement was the discovery of the great Jebusite shaft which was devised and executed in pre-Davidic times, to secure for the garrison of the little fortress on Ophel access to the Virgin's Fountain without the necessity of going outside their walls. This remarkable piece of work begins at a point about fifty feet north of east in the tunnel which leads out from the back of the cave of the fountain. It runs straight up through the rock to a height of forty-four feet, and then a sloping passage, terminating in a flight of stairs, leads out from it to the surface of the hill, within the original Jebusite fortress. It is easy to see what an advantage such a shaft must have been to the garrison, so long as its existence was not known by their enemy; but also how it might become a source of danger once its existence was known, if the besiegers had a man bold enough to attempt the hazardous task of climbing up it. This was precisely what happened when David besieged the fortress. Somehow the secret of the shaft did become known to him; " it is difficult to keep a secret in the East, if it is worth anyone's while to divulge it." " Smite me these blind and lame ones," ordered David, in answer to the Jebusite taunts, " *Go up by the gutter and do it !* And he that doeth it, will I make my general." Joab led the daring attack, and the Jebusite stronghold was captured.

In 1873, Warren was followed by Lieutenant Conder, who, among other things, re-mapped the course of Hezekiah's tunnel from the Virgin's Fountain to the Pool of

U

Siloam ; and in 1875 Mr. Henry Maudslay discovered the
great rock scarp which still goes by his name, on the edge
of the Wady er-Rababi, west of the Cœnaculum. In 1880–81,
Mr. C. Shick and Dr. H. Guthe excavated round the outflow
of Hezekiah's tunnel, and on the southern slopes of Ophel.
But the most important work of the latter years of the
nineteenth century was that of Messrs. Bliss and Dickie,
who succeeded, in the face of most exasperating difficulties,
in tracing the course of the southern walls of the city from
Maudslay's scarp down the northern side of the Valley of
Hinnom, and across the mouth of the Tyropœon to the
Pool of Siloam. "The foundations of gates and towers
were traced and mapped, and thus the whole of the southern
limit of the city, at the time of its greatest extension, was
finally determined." During the course of these investigations a number of other finds came to light. Of these the
chief were the foundations of the Church built over the site
of the Pool of Siloam by the Empress Eudoxia, several
sections of paved streets, and mosaic floors of dwelling-
houses, and especially one beautiful fifth-century mosaic of
Armenian workmanship.

In 1909–11 some excavations were conducted on Ophel
by the Parker Mission, "with the intention, so gossip avers,
of seeking King Solomon's treasure." No success was, of
course, attained in this highly problematical search, and the
excavations were brought to a sudden close by the angry
suspicions of the Jerusalem mob, who believed that the
excavators were tunnelling under the Dome of the Rock
with a view to its destruction or desecration. In the course
of the work, however, a remarkable ancient gateway formed
of three great stones was discovered. This had evidently
been the Water-gate of the earliest of all the ramparts of
Jerusalem, dating perhaps even from before the shaft to
the Virgin's Fountain. The clearing of the Siloam Tunnel
of silt, and the diversion of its water during the excavations,
allowed Père Hugues Vincent to make a fresh survey of the

tunnel and its related workings, and to discover several pre-historic burial caves. The last of the series of excavations prior to the recent expedition under Dr. Macalister and Mr. Garrow Duncan was the work carried out by M. Raymond Weill on behalf of Baron E. de Rothschild in 1913–14, and again in 1923–4. The earlier work resulted in the discovery of the great Round Tower, a Hebrew structure, and of certain graves, known as the Passage-Graves ; the later in the discovery of the Great Tower, at the south end of the old Jebusite fortress, and the southern wall of the fortress, looking down upon the Pool of Siloam and the Birket el-Hamra.

Our brief summary brings us at last to the excavations whose results have newly been published by the Palestine Exploration Fund. The history of their inception is in itself interesting, linking up the latest effort of the excavator with the far-back expedition of George Smith, half a century ago, with its sudden success, and its sad close. In August, 1922, the Department of Antiquities of the Government of Palestine intimated to the Palestine Exploration Fund that it was invited to co-operate with the French, American, and Jewish Archæological societies in the excavation of Mount Ophel, a preliminary condition being that each society taking part in the work should vote the sum of £5000 as its share before work could begin. Early in 1923, the first £1000 towards the share of Britain in the work was offered by Lord Burnham and the proprietors of the *Daily Telegraph*, who thus continued that traditional connection of the paper with exploration which had begun with the financing of George Smith's expedition of 1874. Another thousand was voted from the Fund's own resources, a third was granted by the British Academy from the funds of the Schweich Bequest, and the remaining £2000 was raised by the efforts of Sir Charles Marston. By such painful efforts has the stupendous sum of £5000 to be raised in a nominally enlightened land like our own for work of the highest importance in the most interesting spot in the world !

The work began in September, 1923. The site of the excavations was to be on the southern spur of the east hill of Jerusalem, south of the Haram esh Sherif. It was impossible to choose a site near to the enclosing wall of the Haram, owing to the prejudices of the Jerusalem mob, who would have imagined, as they did in the case of the Parker Expedition, that the Dome of the Rock was to be undermined and destroyed. On the other hand, M. Raymond Weill, whose excavations on behalf of Baron de Rothschild have just been mentioned, had a prior claim to the southern extremity of the spur, and it was necessary to avoid anything like an infringement of his rights. Accordingly, a field was chosen at a distance of 200 metres from the wall of the Haram, and negotiations were entered upon with the owner or owners for its purchase, with the not unreasonable hope that, as the crops on the field were " quite conspicuously poor," the price might be moderate. In this hope, however, the excavators reckoned without the predatory instincts of the folk whom Dr. Macalister elsewhere calls " the ubiquitous and iniquitous inhabitants of Silwan," the squalid village of Siloam on the eastern side of the Kedron valley (which has no connection with the Siloam of the Gospels, though it bears the name). The field was owned by a little syndicate of three, of whom two were Silwanis, and it had been recently bought by them simply with a view to obtaining a fancy price from excavators. Accordingly, this poverty-stricken Naboth's vineyard immediately became as valuable as a gold mine in the eyes of its owners when they were asked to part with it. The original owner of the field afterwards stated to one of the excavators that he had sold it for £E200, and that he never got more than £E6 a year profit from it ; but finally the expedition had to pay £E200 compensation for the vegetables on the spot, and £E50 rent for four months' occupation. Quite obviously the spirit of Jacob has not died out of the land of his inheritance yet, and the neighbourhood of " cool Siloam's shady rill," though it has been opprobriously described as " a noisome-smelling mud hole," is still dear, very dear, to the hearts of its owners, however little they may have to do either with the Law or the Gospel. The troubles of the expedition with their Silwan syndicate of rascals, sometimes amusing, but always irritating, are specimens of what every similar piece of work has to expect in the way of difficulty from the cosmopolitan avarice and rascality of Jerusalem and its neighbourhood.

The field selected had the advantage of lying almost above the famous solitary spring of Jerusalem, the Virgin's Fountain, and therefore, presumably, in a position which the original inhabitants of Jerusalem would be likely to choose for the site of their stronghold ; and the expectations of the excavators in this respect were not long in being realised. The first discovery was made on the northern side of the area, where a cave came to light from which, in times prior to human occupation, a stream had once flowed down the hillside into the Tyropœon Valley, then, of course, much deeper. This stream had cut a small valley through the ridge from its point of origin, and, so far as it went, it formed a natural boundary on the north side to the southern spur of the hill above the Virgin's Fountain. The trouble was that it did not go far enough, so that something more was wanted to carry the boundary line across the ridge to where the levels began to fall on the eastern side towards the Kedron Valley. This also was soon forthcoming, in the shape of an artificial trench, some ten feet wide and eight feet deep, which the first occupants of the site had cut in the rock. Thus almost the first result of the excavations was the long-desired establishment of the probable northern limit of the early city which had existed on the southern spur of Ophel. The newly discovered valley was appropriately named the Zedek Valley, the name linking the place with that early city-god whose name survives in the names Melchi-zedek and Adoni-zedek.

Close to the trench lies a rock-surface, which has been carefully isolated by cuttings from the surrounding rock, and which has several cup-markings associated with it in the rock immediately at hand ; and the excavators suggest that here we have the oldest cult-site of ancient Jerusalem, and link their suggestion with the remark that " it is not irrelevant to recall that Abraham paid tithes on his visit to the priest-king of Salem." It is surely an amazingly interesting thing to think that the rude rock which excavation has laid bare after so many centuries of oblivion may be the very altar on which Abraham laid the spoil of his victory over Hammurabi and his allies ; but it is also well to realise that, after all, the matter is quite incapable of proof. In any case, the facts, as they are now coming to light, bear in upon us, with the force of a strange disappointment, the tiny scale of the stage on which these early dramas of religion were played, and the humble character of the players. From the trench on the north to the Jebusite walls which M. Raymond Weill has discovered at the most southerly point of the spur, the city of Melchizedek measured about 1290 feet in length ; its breadth at the widest point from east to west was a little more than 300 feet. In other words, if you could rearrange the old city a little so as to make it compact, it would all go comfortably into Trafalgar Square, and leave about a matter of 75,000 square feet available for a " lung " to the little place, which it would badly need, unless it was unlike all other towns of its land and time. We are apt to think of the meeting of Melchizedek and Abraham as that of two stately potentates of the great days of old, as we see them, mitred priest and mailed soldier, on the porch of Rheims ; the reality is the priest-headman of a little hill stronghold blessing the nomad sheikh, who had turned away a pressing danger from his little bird's nest on the rock, and the sheikh doing homage to the priest of " El-Elyon," the God of the hills, who had given him victory among the hills over his enemy. Melchizedek's material importance you may judge by the size of his town—A King of Brentford would have been a mighty monarch compared with him ; and as " without contradiction the less is blessed of the greater," the importance of Abraham must have been less still than that of the man to whom he did homage ! Fortunately, the spiritual importance of the cardinal figures of sacred history does not fall to be measured by their material greatness or insignificance.

The earliest northern boundary of the ancient Jerusalem remained the limit of the city in that direction until roughly about 1600 B.C., as is evidenced by the fact that the potsherds which abound in the debris which fills the valley largely date from about that period. We may therefore imagine that, much about the time when Egypt was beginning to shake off the yoke of the Hyksos, the little city of Melchizedek was beginning to find its narrow limits, in the contracted space between the Zedek, the Tyropœon, and the Kedron Valley, too strait for it, and was expanding on the north side, the only side on which expansion was possible. Here excavation revealed, beyond the trench which continues and supplements the Zedek Valley, a flimsy wall, not more than three feet thick, which was evidently the first protection for the new northward extension of the town. Later, perhaps about 1200 B.C., a much more substantial wall was built, of good masonry, and about twenty feet in thickness, and this was the northern defence of the Jebusite stronghold, when David, about two hundred years later, sat down before the fortress which was splitting his kingdom into halves, and was taunted from its battlements by the over-confident defenders. But before we go on to see what befell this northern wall in David's time, as excavation has taught it to us, we turn for a moment to the eastern face of the hill, where meanwhile the most imposing relics of the old defences have been coming to light. Here, just at right angles to the eastern end of the rock-cut trench which continues the Zedek Valley, the excavators unveiled what is not an exaggeration to call a great and massive bastion of Jebusite workmanship extending in a roughly north and south line along the face of the slope of the Kedron Valley for some distance on either side of the end of the trench. This massive wall is built in the form of a steeply sloping ramp of large stones, and is still twenty-three feet in height, and seventy feet in length along its bottom line. At a short distance south from the end of the trench, it is interrupted by the intrusion of a great tower, whose perpendicular walls of hewn masonry are obviously of later date than the ruder ramp which they supplement ; and this tower is ascribed to the early Hebrew period. It would not be rash to call it Solomonic. Below the south face of the Solomonic tower, the Jebusite ramp appears again for a short distance, and south of that again a wall of the Maccabæan period, with a gateway leading down to the Virgin's Fountain in the valley below, takes up the line of defence, with Jebusite and early Hebrew remains behind it. Lower down towards the valley, on the line of the gate of the Maccabæan wall, lies the still more ancient water-gate of the very earliest Jebusite stronghold, the earliest specimen of Jebusite fortification which has yet come to light, apparently, in the Jerusalem area. This, as we have seen, we owe to the unlucky Parker Expedition of 1909-11. Altogether, the result of excavation has been to leave us here with a most impressive example of the strength of the ancient Jebusite city which David captured and made his capital. The frowning walls which still look down upon and command the city's solitary spring may not be, all of them, those of the Jebusite fortress, but enough of the Jebusite work is left to witness to its massive strength, and to enable us to fill in imagination the places now occupied by the Solomonic tower and the Maccabæan wall with the lines of the original curtain and towers. As one looks at the picture of the Jebusite bastion, and imagines the defenders looking down from the vanished battlements,

(1) GENERAL VIEW OF OPHEL, SHOWING THE EXCAVATIONS OF THE PALESTINE EXPLORATION FUND IN PROGRESS, AND THE JEBUSITE RAMP

(2) CLOSER VIEW OF THE JEBUSITE RAMP, SHOWING ITS INTERRUPTION BY THE SOLOMONIC TOWER

The upper view, the steep slope which Mt. Ophel presents on the East, above the Kedron Valley. In the background are the Moslem walls of Jerusalem. In the lower view, the foreground is the rough sloping stonework of the Jebusite fortifications, captured by David. The tower of squared masonry was probably erected by Solomon.
(See pp. 312 *sq.*)

(1) (*By the kindness of Rev. P. B. Fraser, Hokitika, New Zealand*)
(2) (*By the kindness of the Authorities of the Palestine Exploration Fund*)

perhaps a hundred and fifty feet above the heads of David
and his men in the valley below, it does not surprise us that
they fancied it safe to taunt the Hebrew captain with his
helplessness in face of their great defences. " Thou come
in hither! The blind and the lame would be enough to
keep thee out ! "

When we turn again to the northern end of the site,
however, we discover, or rather Dr. Macalister and
Mr. Duncan discover for us, how unsafe it may be to presume
upon even the strongest defences, in face of a daring and
stubborn foe. For here the Jebusite wall, strong though it
may have been, has been violently breached in a manner
which, as the excavators observe, " afforded a most graphic
picture of the grim destruction of ancient warfare." We
remember how Jerusalem was actually captured, how
David said that whosoever went up " the gutter," and
smote the blind and lame with whom the Jebusites had
been taunting him, should be chief captain in the host.
Warren's Shaft has made plain that question of what the
Gutter could be, which was once a puzzle ; and now we can
picture Joab and his forlorn hope scrambling up the
unguarded water-shaft, and bursting in upon the rear of
the defenders on the north wall, while David was thundering
against the wall in front. The ruin of the breach in the
north wall, as laid bare by the excavations, tells us the result.

It does not, however, tell us the whole story, for which the
excavations have also suggested a conclusion. It is obvious
that David, when he sat down in his newly acquired stronghold (" So David dwelt in the Fort, and called it ' David's
Burgh ' "), could not leave the gaping breach in the north
wall unstopped. Accordingly, we read in the continuation
of the passage just quoted (2 Samuel v. 9), " and David
built round about, from Millo and inward." What Millo
may have been we shall see directly, for here the excavations
have suggested a solution for what has been a standing
problem for generations ; we have meantime to see what is

meant by his building " round about . . . and inward."
Pretty manifestly it suggests what a man would do when he
wanted to close speedily a gap which was a standing danger,
yet did not want to commit himself to a great scheme of
reconstruction—that is, build a temporary wall covering
the gap, and masking it till such time as he could undertake
more thorough reconstruction of the ruined fortifications.
Such a temporary wall might run either outside the breach,
or inside it ; but outside would made a weak salient, and so
David built his masking wall inside the breach—" round
about and inward." Just on this spot, then, the excavators
found a wall running in a straight line for about eighty feet
east and west, with a square tower, suggesting a gate, at
one end—the companion tower had apparently been
destroyed to make place for a Herodian house which had
occupied the site later. This wall just masks the breach
in the old Jebusite wall, running " inward," i.e. on the
southern side of it, and joining up with the older wall on
the east side, the west being still unexcavated. It is built of
alternate courses of fairly large stones and small ones.
The walls of the Jebusite fort were mainly of huge blocks
which took three or four men to move ; it is pretty obvious
that David, being in a hurry, smashed down the big blocks
to sizes more easily handled, and built his wall with courses
of the medium-sized stones which he thus obtained, alter-
nating with courses of the smaller fragments which also
resulted from his hasty method. We may therefore take it
that his action, as described in 2 Samuel, is accounted for,
and that we have now the actual repair which he carried
out on the ancient wall which he had breached.

There remains the question of " Millo "—what it was,
and where it was. Plainly it was a building of later date
than David's temporary repair of the breach, though the
writer of the passage in 2 Samuel uses the name as that of
a building familiar in his day to his readers ; for it was
built by Solomon after he had completed the great complex

of buildings on the Temple Hill, and established Pharaoh's daughter in her new palace (1 Kings IX. 24). It was also near to the Davidic work already mentioned, as the passage in 2 Samuel shows. Further, the root of the word Millo is connected with the idea of " filling." Now, right upon the breach in the Jebusite wall, the excavation revealed the scanty remains of what had once been a strong tower, of more solid construction than the rough wall behind it, using still the old stones from the breach, but squaring and fitting them more carefully. Here, then, is a tower which superseded David's temporary wall in its function of closing the breach ; which fills the gap in the Jebusite wall, and so answers to the meaning of Millo. Surely it would seem that we are justified, *provisionally*, at all events, in assuming that the long-sought Millo has been found, and that it is neither more nor less than the tower with which Solomon finally closed David's breach in the northern wall of the old fortress, when he felt that David's hasty patch was too shabby to be kept up in connection with his gorgeous new buildings to the north of it, especially now that he had taken a step up in social status by his marriage with so great a lady as the daughter of Pharaoh. " Provisionally " is underlined, because one remembers the various other identifications of Millo, down to that of M. Raymond Weill ; at least it can be said that no other candidate for the position seems to fill it (quite an appropriate term in the circumstances) so well as this discovery of the Palestine Exploration Fund's expedition. One of the curiosities of the work on this interesting tower was the discovery of the faint traces of a grotesque painting of what, when closely examined, seemed to have been intended for the Goddess Ashtoreth. The painting is extremely faint, so that only the eye of faith could have suggested enough encouragement to warrant the eye of sense in its patient tracing out of the crude detail of the figure ; but faint and crude as it is, the figure is there, and one is reminded how, " when Solomon was old, his wives turned away his heart after other gods. For Solomon went after Ashtoreth the goddess of the Zidonians." Did some devotee of the Zidonian goddess scrawl her figure on the great tower ; or was it (more likely) some ribald citizen who thus derided the uxorious king's devotion to foreign abominations ? Anyhow, it is one of the most curious survivals of those long-past days—one of those humblest of things which help to make the past human and real to us.

Such are the main results of the recent expedition of the Palestine Exploration Fund ; indeed, one may say the only results which are of much interest to the general reader. For here again we have emphasised for us the extraordinary poverty of Palestinian excavation in work of artistic or cultural value, and the miscellaneous finds are of singularly small importance, and next to no attractiveness ; while the remains of other construction, such as the "Eusebius" house, are extremely scanty. But as Dr. H. R. Hall has said in his preface to the "Annual" of the Fund in which the work of the expedition is recorded, the discovery of the Jebusite and Solomonic walls alone "would be a sufficient return for the money expended on the excavation." "It is not often given to an archæological society to lay bare such fine and such extraordinarily interesting examples of ancient city fortifications—walls, too, that have seen so much history enacted on and near them. It was not expected that at Ophel treasures of gold would be discovered, nor in Palestine are Tutankhamen tombs likely to reward the spade of the digger. What we have discovered is new light on the building and topography of the most ancient Jerusalem, the little city on the steep hill of Ophel that already existed there in the third millennium B.C. . . Ophel saw the invasion of the Khabiri and retained its Jebusite independence after Joshua's confederated tribes had overrun Canaan, until the fateful day when David stormed 'Millo' and set up his kingship in Zion. These walls saw that event ; they saw the labours of Hiram's workmen on the rising ground above them, when Solomon built his palace and temple on the spot where the Haram now is, the palace now covered by the mosque of al-Aksa, the temple by the Dome of the Rock. They saw the Assyrian siege under Hezekiah and the final captivity of Judah by Nebuchadnezzar." No city on earth has such a story as Jerusalem ; and these walls which the Fund's excavators have given back to us are almost the only fragments of the past which have heard the whole wonderful tale being told from 2000 B.C. till to-day. One is glad to think that the Government of Palestine has now taken them over as a national monument, so that their safety is assured for the future, no needless precaution when one remembers how near they stand to the stone-thieves of Silwan.

(The recent work of the Jewish excavators in uncovering further remains of what appears to be Agrippa's " Third Wall," on the north side of the city, must be noted. The probability seems to be, in view of these discoveries, that the site of the Church of the Holy Sepulchre must have lain within the Second Wall, and that, therefore, the claim of the site to have been the scene of the events of the Passion and Resurrection of Our Lord must be abandoned. But it will be well to suspend judgment on a question so important until fuller information is available).

CHAPTER XIV

EXCAVATION AMONG THE TELLS OF PALESTINE

THE second section of the work of excavation in Palestine is that which deals with the " Tells " which are dotted over the land. It was the famous Survey of the Palestine Exploration Fund which first emphasised and directed interested attention to these survivals of ancient days, of which there may possibly be something like two hundred within the limits of the country. What, then, is a Tell, and how does it come to be formed ? It is a mound, but a mound of a kind which is only found, in its perfection, in the Near East. " The conditions for the formation of a tell are peculiar to the East," says Dr. Bliss ; and while this is not absolutely true, it is true in the main, and quite sufficiently so for our purpose. Actually there are Tells in our own country ; but the conditions of life here, and the continuity of occupation on all important sites, have hindered them from attaining the perfect development of the Palestinian specimens. " We have our tells," said Sir Flinders Petrie once, " only we still live on the top of them. Whenever any deep digging is done in the City, we work through 20 or 30 feet before we arrive at the native soil. We are, then, looking through the tell of London. At the top of it we see our modern roads and foundations, and bits of modern plates and dishes ; then layers of dirty black earth and brickbats, perhaps relics of the Great Fire ; below that may be a grey-beard jug, then a bit of Norman zig-zag moulding, next a stray penny of Alfred, and below that a bit of Saxon walling patched up from Roman tiles. Then we come to the massive walls of Roman tile and

318

concrete, and pieces of Samian ware, and, below all, perhaps, a bronze sword of the ancient British warrior. And
what has made up all this depth of accumulation in the
last 2000 years ? We see it to be mainly dust, earth, more
or less organic matter, and the fragments of successive
buildings, the ruins of each of which were levelled the one
after the other to make room for the next structure."

In the East, however, and especially in Palestine, with
which we are dealing, the conditions were somewhat
different, and much more favourable for the formation of a
genuine Tell, whose mound-like quality does not need to
be explained to you, but it is apparent at a glance. The
early Palestinian town was generally built upon a hill, for
purposes of defence ; but not upon too high a hill, because
that would make access too difficult and probably complicate the question of the water supply. Therefore, the first
and lowest element of your Tell will be in most cases a
natural hill of no great altitude. On its top, there perhaps
originally existed some natural caverns in the limestone
rock, and these were enlarged and occupied by the first
inhabitants, Neolithic men, Horites, if you like to give
them a Scriptural name. The next step was the building
of houses, which were rudely constructed out of undressed
stones, set in mud mortar. Age and weather gradually
brought about the downfall of these poorly built houses,
and when they fell, the survivors of the disaster, or the
successors of the victims, picked out the useable stones
from the heap of debris (they did not trouble about the
dead bodies), trampled down the mud and small debris,
and built the new house on this new level, which would be
somewhat higher than that of the fallen house. Thus,
under the new house, there would be one thin stratum in
which would be embedded fragments of the potsherds and
utensils belonging to the previous occupants. By the
constant repetition of this process for many centuries, the
final level of the last stratum of house rubbish might be

many feet above the lowest stratum, or the rock on which
the little place was first built. Meanwhile the streets, or
rather alleys, between the houses are not to be conceived
of as gradually deepening gorges between houses which
were steadily rising above them. Not in the least, for the
cleanly habits of the Amorite, or whatever he might call
himself, necessitated a cleansing department, and the method
of operations consisted in simply throwing the family
refuse of each house out into the street in front of the door,
there to rot, and breed smells and disease, until it was
finally trampled down and incorporated in the stratum
which formed the roadway ; and thus the level of the
streets steadily rose *pari passu* with the rise in the level of the
houses. By the gentle persistence of this attractive method
of rising in the world, the level of a town might be, as in
the case of the ancient Lachish (Tell el-Hesy), raised about
five feet in a century ; and the final result might be, as in
the same case, that in the fourth century before Christ the
eleventh city of Lachish stood on the top of a steep hill
120 feet above the stream at the foot of the mound, and
that nine other Lachishes intervened (in a state of com-
pression) between it and the first Amorite city, which, in
its day, was only sixty feet above the brook.

The next stage is the coming of the Romans ; and the
Romans bring security, law, and order. It is no longer
necessary to live on the top of an awkwardly steep hill, lest
you should find when you awake in the morning that your
throat has been cut during the night ; and besides, having
doubled your height in the world, it is now a long job for
the women to go down to the brook for the water which is
needed, not for washing, but for cooking. The trouble
to the women would not have counted in the least, but it
was a nuisance to have one's own meals delayed. So, as
it was now safe to live at a lower level close to the water,
the inhabitants of the city migrated, and built a new city
down on the plain ; and, in a comparatively short time,

the deserted village on the hill-top (scarcely " Sweet Auburn " from any point of view, least of all a sanitary one) gradually tumbled down and was smoothed down by rain and wind to a pretty uniform level. The wall of big stones which had formed the defence of the late stronghold hindered the materials from being washed down the hillside by the rainstorms, acting as a kind of retaining wall, much to the advantage of future archæologists ; and thus the resulting Tell had the flat top, which is the regular characteristic in Palestine of a mound which has been raised by artificial accumulation, and which contrasts so curiously with its steeply sloping sides.

Here, then, you have an arrangement which seems admirably fitted to all the desires and purposes of the archæologist. The mound, by its form, proclaims from afar its character as the site of ancient habitation, and underneath its mantle of earth it preserves in the most obliging fashion strata representative of every age of its own past. It should seem that nothing could be simpler than the excavation of such a repository of ancient history, manners, and customs. Of course, the book of the city's story will have to be read backwards, because excavation has naturally to begin at the top, which is the end of the story, so to speak ; but there is no serious difficulty in this, as the thing is known, and, besides, this is how most people read their stories, anyhow. Actually, however, the job is never so simple as it would seem from such a statement of the position ; the untidy and inconsiderate habits of the earlier inhabitants often seriously complicating the orderly arrangement of the strata. The excavation of a Tell has been compared to the cutting down through the successive coats of an onion ; but while the comparison is not inapt in some respects, the onion is usually much tidier and more obedien. to the laws of orderly growth than your old Amorite cityt Theoretically, the order of discovery in a Tell should be something like this. First, at the top, there should be hard,

x

322 Excavation among the Tells

clinking Maccabæan potsherds, and coins, perhaps of
Antiochus Epiphanes, to remind you that before the coming
of the Romans, Maccabæan and Macedonian were fighting
for the land as men have fought for it from time immemorial.
Beneath this stratum will come ruder and softer pottery,
sometimes stamped on the handles of the jars with some
curious figure, and the Hebrew words meaning " For the
King." There will be no coins ; and you will realise that
this is the period of Persian supremacy. A little deeper
down, and we shall find the relics of the days of Hezekiah,
or Ahab, or Solomon ; " and we shall see a vivid picture of
the civilisation, or rather of the non-civilisation, out of the
heart of which the ancient prophets arose, to revolutionise
man's knowledge of his Maker." Then will come a very
scrubby and poor remnant, representing what has been
called " Israel's Iron Age," though Israel knew no iron
until after it had passed away—the period of the Judges.
Beneath it, a thicker and perhaps richer, though still inartistic, stratum tells of the Amorite days, and you learn
enough of them to be glad that the Hebrew, though by no
means a pattern of decency and kindliness, did at least do
one good thing, when he made a tolerably clean sweep of
" the iniquity of the Amorite."

I have paraphrased Dr. Macalister's description of the
succession which may be expected during the excavation
of a representative Palestinian Tell ; but it must be remembered that that is the ideal section of a mound, and
that the actual work is complicated and often obscured by
all the chances of war, change of taste, and a thousand other
happenings. A city may be stormed, sacked and burned ;
and while the resulting bed of ashes will give an indication
of this chapter of the place's history, the destruction by the
conqueror's hand, and the scarcely less worrying reconstruction, will have seriously complicated all the stratification of your mound, and that not even uniformly over the
whole area, which would not have been so bad, but

capriciously, and in patches. Again, the growth of population at one stage may result in the occupation of an area
which had not been built on in previous days ; and, consequently, at that point you will have houses of a definite
period lying at a much lower level than the houses around
than which were built at the same time, but on the higher
level resulting from previous occupation. These are but
two examples out of many of the difficulties which complicate the interpretation of the results of excavation upon
any site in Palestine which has been occupied for a length
of time, and render the work of the excavator one requiring
not only an almost infinite patience, but also an intimate
knowledge of all the characteristics of human handiwork
in the periods concerned, which will enable him to separate
the true from the apparent in the stratification with which
he is dealing.

It would be quite useless to attempt to give an account
of the work which has been done at all the Tells in Palestine
which have been the subjects of excavation in recent years.
Remarkably interesting results have been attained by the
excavations at Tell el-Hesy (Lachish), which were the first
of the kind, and where, after Professor Flinders Petrie had
surveyed the site, and established the general sequence of
events on it, the subsequent excavations were carried out
by Dr. Bliss, at Tell es-Safi (Gath), Tell el-Judeideh (un-
identified), Tell Zakariya (Azekah ?), and Tell Sanda-
hannah (Moresheth, the home of the prophet Micah), at
Tell Taanak (Taanach of Deborah's Song), at Tell
Mutasellim (the ancient Megiddo), which is now undergoing
a second attack by the Oriental Institute of the University
of Chicago, at Tell el-Jezari (Gezer), at Jericho, and at
Ascalon on the Philistine Plain, Ain esh-Shems (Beth-
shemesh), and Beisan (the ancient Beth-Shean or Beth-
Shan) ; while the site of Samaria, the rival capital to
Jerusalem, has been explored by the Harvard Expedition,
under Dr. G. A. Reisner, and Sir Flinders Petrie has

returned, during this last winter, to the old Philistine sites which he was the first to survey in 1890, and has been excavating at Gaza. ￼From all these it will be enough if we choose two representative sites for brief study ; and the two which we choose are Gezer, on the edge of the Judæan foot-hills, 16¾ miles south-east of Jaffa, and Beth-Shean, at the angle where the valley of Jezreel breaks down to the Jordan Valley.

Of these two sites, the first-named occupies a comparatively insignificant place in the Hebrew story, only coming into view for a moment in the early history of the Conquest of Palestine when its king, Horam, ventured out with a detachment of his townsfolk to help his brother-sheikh of Lachish against the invading Hebrews, and ended by wishing he had stayed at home ; for " Joshua smote him and his people, till he had left him none remaining " : and a second time under Solomon, when Pharaoh of Egypt (possibly Sheshenq or Pinezem) captured it, and gave it to his daughter, who had married Solomon, as part of her pin-money. It is prominent again for a little while in the time of the Maccabees, when it was captured by Simon Maccabæus ; but on the whole, all through, its importance is of a secondary order. On the other hand, the excavations which were carried out on the site of King Horam's old town in 1902–5, and 1907–9 by Dr. R. A. S. Macalister, on behalf of the Palestine Exploration Fund, while they did not complete the unveiling of the place, only three-fifths of the total area being dealt with, have been universally regarded as one of the best examples extant of how such work should be carried on, and the three bulky volumes in which their results are embodied are one of the classics of excavation literature.

The attraction of Beth-Shean is more manifest. Long before Biblical times, it was a great Egyptian fortress ; but its Biblical importance comes in the time of Saul, when the first king of Israel lost his life in the battle of Mt. Gilboa,

which, as the excavations have taught us, was an incident
in the unsuccessful campaign conducted with a view to
wrestling the great fortress of Beth-Shean out of the hands
of the Philistines. The armour of Saul and his gallant sons
was dedicated in the Temple of Ashtoreth at Beth-Shean
by the victors, and their bodies were hung upon the walls
of the fortress as a sign to the surrounding tribes, just as
the body of one of the vanquished Syrian chiefs was sent
by Amenhotep II to far-off Ethiopia, there to be hung on
the walls of Napata, and to fill the hearts of the negro tribes
with dread of the long arm of the Pharaoh. David must
have avenged the defeat by the capture of the place, which
suffered storm, as the excavations show, about this time.
In the seventh century B.C., the Scythians, in their great
raid, established a settlement on the site of the old stronghold, which accounts for the name of Scythopolis which
was given to it by the Greeks. Under this title, it was the
capital of that community of ten cities which we hear of
in the Gospels as the Decapolis. In the fourth century A.D.
the city saw the building of a great Christian church, in
which, apparently, was the tomb of the first bishop of the
town, St. Patrophilus ; but in A.D. 637 it fell into the hands
of the Moslems. When the Crusaders came, they recognised
the importance of the old stronghold, in its dominating position, and projected a great settlement ; but the unhealthy
nature of the neighbourhood forced them to abandon their
site and build their fortress eight miles or so to the north,
where, on a height nearly 1300 feet above the level of Beth-
Shean, they reared the great fortress of Belvoir—" Kaukab
el-Hawa," " Star of the Wind," as the Arabs far more picturesquely called it, from its lights shining out upon the windy
height—the last stronghold to fly the banner of the Cross
in the disastrous rout when Saladin swept the country in
A.D. 1186–88. Altogether, as one can see, Beth-Shean has
had a most chequered and interesting history, far more so
than Gezer. Dr. Macalister has called it " one of the prize

sites of Palestine," and so far the results of the work of the expedition of the Museum of the University of Pennsylvania, under Dr. C. S. Fisher, seem to be justifying the title.

We turn, then, to give a brief summary of the story of Gezer, as revealed by Dr. Macalister's work there ; and instead of reading the story backwards, as the excavator had to do, we can take advantage of the fact that his work, in the meantime, is completed, and begin the tale at the beginning. We have already seen some of the reasons which complicate what should otherwise be the orderly succession of strata in a mound. These reasons were operative even at Gezer, which in many respects ought to have been an ideal town in respect of stratification, having been deserted at the Roman period, and never again occupied. Siege, sack, and reconstruction in ancient days, however, had contorted the coats of the great archæological onion with which Dr. Macalister had to deal, with the result that it had far more coats at one point than at another, and that the succession of the coats was confused here and there by artificial interference. Thus at one point the accumulation of debris above the bed-rock was 16 to 17 feet thick, and contained from 3 to 6 strata ; at another point it varied much more, being from 5 to 23 feet thick, and involving strata which numbered variously from 3 to 7 ; at a third point a maximum was reached of 40 feet, with 8 successive strata of building showing.

Excavation showed that the first occupation of the bare limestone ridge, which in after days became the base of the gradually rising mound, must have been complete round about 3000 B.C. ; but we are not to imagine anything in the shape of a culture comparable to that which we have seen existing in Babylonia or Egypt at this period. In Babylonia, at this time, the Sumerians were already rearing the great ziggurats which have dominated the imagination of mankind ever since ; in Egypt the Pyramid-builders were more than matching, in everlasting stone, what the Sumerians were doing in crumbling brick : but things were different in Palestine. Here, at the very beginning, we get the most forcible illustration of that cultural poverty of Palestine, which is the marked feature of the land all through, and under all races, though the difference is seldom so conspicuous as at this earliest stage. The men who formed the first colony on the hill of Gezer were Troglodytes, Cave-men, who drove out the wild beasts which they found inhabiting the caves in the limestone rock of the ridge, and enlarged the dens to suit their own needs. The resultant dwellings varied from mere cells, 8 to 10 feet square, to complicated and tortuous collections of rooms, united by winding passages. Some of the caves had as many as ten chambers, and several separate entrances. Generally, the roofs were low, a height of more than 7 feet being quite exceptional ; and this, together with the evidence of the few human remains which have survived, goes to show that the Cave-men of Gezer were a small race, probably of not much above five feet in height, but sturdy and thick-skulled.

Their culture, if you can call it by such a name, was of the rudest kind. One cave showed a few scratchings which are the only attempts at art that have come down to us from this race ; but they are pathetically rude and futile, and cannot for a moment bear comparison with even the poorest specimens of the work which the men of the Reindeer Age have left to us in the caves of France and Spain. Their pottery was of the poorest quality, and this, with a few flint implements, rounded pebbles heaped together for throwing at the wild beasts whom they had dispossessed, and here and there an amulet in slate or bone, made up the whole furniture of their dwelling. They have left traces of their religion in a " High-place " of rock surface, cup-marked, and associated with caves, into one of which a channel runs from the rock above, presumably to act as a channel for the sacrificial blood, thus offered to the dark god of the Underworld. The animal offered in sacrifice may have been the pig, judging from the fact that pig-bones were found in the cave at the foot of the channel just mentioned. It is possible that in this religious custom of this primitive people whom the Semites exterminated we may trace the tradition which made the Semite, particularly the Hebrew Semite, regard the pig as unclean, and abhor the very idea of using such an animal in sacrifice. The second Isaiah speaks of " a people which remain among the graves, and lodge in the monuments ; which eat swine's flesh, and broth of abominable things is in their vessels " ; and it is conceivable that here, even at so late a date, we have an echo of the ancient tradition of the foul lives and religious rites of the most ancient inhabitants of the Land of Promise.

Five hundred years later, the Cave-men, Horites, if we care to use what seems to be their Biblical name, were a thing of the past. The invading Semite, in the shape of the Amorite, had swept them out of existence ; and by the end of another five centuries, say about 2000 B.C., the Amorite stronghold on the hill is an old-established fact, with its strong wall, 20 to 30 feet high and 13 feet thick, built of big stones bedded in mortar of mud. The wall is pierced by the town-gate, an opening of about 8 feet broad, between two solid towers of brickwork. It is closed at night by great slabs of wood thrust home between stone supports. Inside the walls, the houses were crowded closely together, and the narrow and filthy alleys between them must have reeked with all manner of foul odours. Dr. Macalister tells us that under the Turkish regime " the smell of a (Palestinian) village could be perceived nearly half a mile off " ; in all probability the range of an Amorite town's odours was longer still. The marked prevalence of disease, as revealed by the bones found during the excavations, shows the unhealthiness of the conditions of life, and supplies a corrective to the sentimental folly that maunders about the " good old days."

The most remarkable thing in Amorite Gezer, as revealed

by the excavations, was the water-supply. We have seen
how the Jebusite fortress of Jerusalem secured access to
its solitary spring by means of the striking piece of rock-
cutting known as " Warren's Shaft." Gezer possessed a
piece of work not inferior to this, in the shape of its Water-
tunnel. A keyhole-shaped entrance gives access to a huge
arched passage, 12 feet across and 23 feet high, hewn out
of the limestone rock by means of flint tools. Following
this gallery, which slopes downwards at an angle of about
30 degrees, you descend by a staircase of 80 steps to a depth
of 90 feet below the surface level. Here a strong spring of
water rises in the midst of a great natural cave, 80 feet by
28. However low we may rank the Amorites in civilisation,
and all the evidence goes to show that we may rank them
very low indeed without doing them injustice, it has yet to
be remembered to their credit that they carried out this
remarkable engineering feat as far back, apparently, as
2000 B.C. " Carried out," for it has been suggested that,
as the excavations have revealed evidence of strong Egyptian
influence in Gezer at this period, the chances are that the
planning of the work was due to Egyptian engineers.

At all events, we may be pretty sure that whoever planned
and executed the water-tunnel there was one thing that the
Gezerites did not do with the water when they had it ;
and that was, use it for washing either themselves or their
clothes. The evidence reveals in them the most absolute
indifference to what all civilised races have always regarded
as the very commonest essentials of decency in life. In
more than one of the cisterns which supplemented the tunnel
as sources of supply, were found the bodies of unfortunate
beings who had evidently overbalanced themselves when
drawing water, and found a watery grave. Dr. Macalister
piously remarks, " We can but hope that the water was never
used again ; certainly the bodies were never taken out."
If such things were done in the green tree, what would be
done in the dry ; if the Amorite was indifferent to the

presence of a deceased relative in his drinking water, was he likely to care for any other decency of life whatsoever ?

The most striking feature of the old Canaanite town appears to have been its High-place. This was marked by a row of ten great unhewn stones, set upright in the midst of an area of irregular shape, measuring about 150 feet by 120. The seventh stone is of a different rock from the others, and has been brought from a distance, as no such formation exists in the neighbourhood. A groove running round the middle of it suggests that it has been dragged to its present position by a rope fastened round it. The probability is that this seventh stone (the lucky number) is the spoil of some successful raid upon another city, possibly Jerusalem, as the rock formation in question exists there, in which the High-place of the conquered town was rifled, and its sacred stone carried off to grace the sanctuary at Gezer. The Moabite Stone records a similar case of later times, in which Mesha, King of Moab, dragged the " Ariel of Dodah " from Ataroth, and set it up before Chemosh, his god, in Kerioth. Instances and examples of the sort of rites which were practised at the High-place of Gezer were forthcoming abundantly during the course of the excavation of the sacred area, and they were of a character which has been summed up in the words, " beastliness and blood." Human sacrifice, especially the sacrifice of infants of a few days old, was frequent ; indeed " the whole area of the High-place was found on excavation to be a cemetery of new-born infants." In several places the excavations disclosed a number of bodies piled together, sometimes with indications that some of them had been sawn asunder while yet alive. In one cistern, a " weird charnel-house," as Dr. Macalister justly calls it, the bodies of fourteen men and a girl of sixteen, the latter sawn asunder at the waist, had been heaped ; while in another instance there was evidence that two men had been buried alive, in company with the upper half of the body of a youth, who had also been treated in the amiable Amorite fashion of being sawn in twain. Altogether, Gezer bore abundant witness to what its excavator has called "an Aztec-like disregard of the value of human life," and on its own evidence suggested that the world was well rid of the Amorite and his beastlinesses.

Nor were cruelty and vileness even partially atoned for, as in the case of other races, by any brilliancy in the artistic qualities, such as has often veiled the grossness of some aspects of the ancient life of the East. There was apparently both cruelty and vice in the Minoan culture of Crete ; but at least it was accompanied by such evidences of artistic brilliance as have won apologists for the Minoan in spite of his bull-grappling excesses, and the vile imagination revealed in some of his work. The Amorite of Gezer has no such make-weights to turn the balance of judgment in his favour. At Gezer, as elsewhere, the race with which the essential culture of the land was associated down to the Greek period (for the Hebrews were closely akin to the Amorites whom they displaced) was one of the most inartistic and least susceptible of culture of all peoples of the ancient East. " The general result of excavation," says Dr. Macalister, " so far as pre-exilic religious history is concerned, is to increase our wonder when we read the writings of the Prophets of Israel. That men gifted with a philosophic insight so clear, and with a literary skill so marvellous, should have arisen in a soil so sordid is hardly to be explained otherwise than as a miracle."

The main relic of Hebrew occupation of the site is afforded by the Solomonic towers which were added to the old Amorite wall after its breaching by Pharaoh. These towers were added to in Maccabæan times, probably by the Syrian general Bacchides ; but the Solomonic work is much superior to the hasty repair of later days. Evidence has been forthcoming, in the shape of cuneiform tablets relating to the sale of slaves and a field, of the Assyrian occupation in the time of Manasseh of Judah ; but even at this late date the traditional Egyptian influence was still strong, as is plain from the fact that the governor of the town, who witnesses one of the deeds, bears the name Huruasi, which is a regular Egyptian form.

Gezer's last appearance in history is in the Maccabæan period, when, as we are told in 1 Macc. XIII, 43–48, Simon Maccabæus stormed " Gazara " by means of a siege-engine, expelled its citizens, and placed in the captured stronghold " such men as would keep the law." The excavators were fortunate enough to find the breach in the wall which Simon's ram had made, and the ruins of the castle with which he had closed it, just as Solomon, in earlier days, built " Millo " to close the breach in the Jebusite walls of the City of David. The quaintest incident of the excavation was the discovery, on one of the stones of this Maccabæan castle, of the curse which one of the Syrians who were forced to labour on the building had scratched on it before building it into the wall. The curse ran : " Says Pampras, ' May fire pursue Simon's palace ! ' " One is reminded of the tablet which was found at Lagash imprecating the vengeance of the gods upon the destroyers of the city of Urukagina ; but poor Pampras's well-meant effort has accomplished pretty much the opposite of what he hoped from it, for it was his inscription which enabled the excavators to identify the building which he had wished to see destroyed !

It was in 1922 that the expedition of the University of Pennsylvania, under Dr. C. S. Fisher, began the work which it is still carrying on at the " prize site " of Beth-Shean. The site is a magnificent one. " No traveller who ever visited Beisan," says Dr. Fisher, " failed to carry away a deep impression of its beautiful and majestic situation." The primitive Canaanite stronghold, which may date from anything round about 3000 B.C., rose on the top of a small isolated hill, or rather mound, which still goes by the name Tell-el-Husn, or " Hill of the Fortress," thus keeping the ancient tradition alive. At this point, the Vale of Jezreel

" suddenly drops over a bank some three hundred feet high
into the Valley of the Jordan. This bank, or lip, which
runs north and south for nearly five miles, is cut by several
streams falling eastward in narrow ravines. . . . Near the
edge of the lip, and between two of the ravines, rises a high
commanding mound that was once the citadel of Beth-
Shan." The old Canaanite town, with its walls and towers,
was doubtless confined, as in other cases, to the summit of
the hill ; the later city of Roman and Byzantine times lay
on the lower levels beneath, which are now surrounded, as
they have been for many centuries, by pestilential marshes,
which are now being drained and reclaimed. The old
citadel commands the descent to the fords of the Jordan,
and is the key-site of Northern Palestine as regards its
eastern approaches ; but in spite of its isolation, it was
abandoned by the Crusaders, owing to its unhealthiness—a
feature due to the double reason that it lies 322 feet below
sea-level, and in the midst of the marshes just mentioned.
Dr. Fisher, however, states that the danger of unhealthiness
can easily be guarded against, as the steady work of five
seasons has proved.

The first operation of the explorers was the driving of a
trial trench on the eastern side of the mound, so as to get a
sectional view of the various strata of occupation which were
to be met with. This trench was carried down to a depth of
36 feet without reaching the rock on which the original
settlement must have been based, and in its progress, it
penetrated through debris of all characters, from that of an
Arab settlement on the top, dating from about A.D. 800, to
characteristic Early Bronze Age jars of about 2000 B.C. at
the 36-foot level. " To trace satisfactorily the development
of such a site," says Dr. Fisher, " it is necessary to remove
one by one the various strata, uncovering each as a whole,
and after mapping the details of the rooms and their contents,
proceed to remove it and reveal the stratum next below. In
this manner we had by the end of the third season taken

twenty to thirty feet off the height of the hill and uncovered eight distinct building periods, reaching a brick fortress dating from the reign of Seti I (1313–1292 B.C.). Going down through the floor of one of the chambers of this building, another three feet disclosed the massive walls of a similar structure with a slightly different orientation." Such a description will show the reader better than anything else the extreme care which must be exercised by the modern excavator in dealing with the extraordinarily complicated mass of material which Time has gathered together for his study. He has not only to deal with perhaps nine different ages, as in this case (reckoning the second fort in), but, as he deals with each stratum in turn, he has finally to destroy it, in order to get at its predecessor, the only one remaining undestroyed in the end being the lowest and most ancient stratum. The necessity is as unavoidable as it is regrettable ; but the very existence of such a necessity underlines the need for an absolutely trustworthy record being kept of everything which each stratum contains. Once gone from their original position and surroundings, there is no possibility of reconstituting these ; the work must therefore be done on the spot and at the moment in such a fashion that there can be no question about a single detail arising in the future to create doubt as to the validity of its evidence.

The feature of outstanding interest in the results at this stage of the work was the Egyptian fortress of the XIXth Dynasty. Its walls still stood in some places to a height of 10 feet, and the citadel was built on a fairly regular plan. The material was mud brick, the bricks being of large size, 21 by 14 by 6 inches. Originally the building had been at least two storeys in height, possibly more ; and at the Main Gate the jambs and sill of the gate, great blocks of basalt, were still in position, while in the store-rooms were quantities of fragments of large *pithoi* for the storage of grain and oil—a feature which, however common in the East, reminds one forcibly of the magazines of Knossos, and, as we shall

see, had probably a similar origin. The most interesting
relics found in the fort were two basalt steles, one of Seti I
and one of Rameses II, and a statue, also in basalt, of
Rameses III. The Seti stele, which is the better preserved
and executed of the two, gives an account of a brief campaign waged by the Pharaoh in support of his vassal the
chief of Beth-Shean, who was threatened with an attack by
" that vile one of Hamath " in alliance with the men of
Pella, on the other side of the Jordan. Seti moved to the
help of his vassal, and dispersed the combination of enemies
with supreme ease. The details of the movements of the
Egyptian divisions are of great interest, both as showing
how well flanking movements were understood and provided
against at this early date, how much better a general Seti
was than his vainglorious son Rameses, and how easily and
strongly Egypt held the land at this period. Still more
interesting is the stele of Rameses II, for the one reason
that in the midst of a mass of vainglorious verbiage, such
as Rameses has familiarised us with, there occurs a statement,
which seemed to its discoverers to affirm plainly that the
Pharaoh used Semites in the building of his name-city,
Rameses, in the Delta. " Have we not here at last," said
Dr. Fisher, " that long-sought-for confirmation of the
Biblical record of the labour of the Children of Israel in the
Land of Egypt, when they were forced under task-masters to
' build for Pharaoh store-cities, Pithom and Rameses ' ?
This would definitely establish Rameses II as the Pharaoh of
the Oppression, an old identification that has persisted in
spite of weighty opposition." Subsequent study of the
inscription, however, scarcely bears out the early interpretation of it, and we must wait until a really authoritative
translation of all the Beth-Shean steles is forthcoming—an
event much to be desired.

The statue of Rameses III carried on further still the
evidence for Egyptian occupation, and the excavation of
the northern necropolis of Beth-Shean, lying along the

northern bank of the river Jalud, yielded a large number of
curious terra-cotta sarcophagi, exhibiting a combination
of Egyptian influence with Mediterranean. These sarcophagi
dated roughly from 1200 to 1000 B.C., and " were clearly
the sepulchres of some body of foreigners having close
affiliation with Egypt. A natural conclusion is that they
were mercenaries whom we know to have formed part of
the Egyptian army as early as the reign of Rameses II,"—
a conclusion which is confirmed by the fact that on his
stele Rameses states that he prepared a splendid burial-
place for his soldiers. The pottery shows that these men
were of the Ægean race which had dominated the Mediterranean area of which Crete is the centre, so that, if they
were not actually Cretans, broken men from the ruined
empire of the Cretan Sea-Kings, as they may very well
have been, they were at all events of the same stock. In
other words, they belonged to the race which in the reign
of Rameses III was one of the main supports of the Sea-
Peoples in their attack on Palestine and Egypt—the Pulesti
or Philistines.

We are therefore being gradually led on to a view-point
which is of extreme interest in itself, and from which we
can see clearly through a problem which once seemed
obscure. Saul and his sons fell in battle with the Philistines,
say somewhere about 1020 B.C., on Mt. Gilboa, close to
this very spot. But what were the Philistines, whose
League had its strongholds on the Maritime Plain far to
the south and west of this, doing at the eastern end of the
Plain of Esdraelon ? We have learned now from the
excavation of Beth-Shean that as early as the reign of
Rameses II there were numbers of mercenaries in the
Egyptian service, who may perfectly legitimately be described
as Philistines, for they were of the same race, in garrison
at the fortress there. Their occupation continued until
after the death of Rameses III (1167 B.C.), and probably
for a considerable time after that event. But after the death

of this great Pharaoh, the hold of Egypt on Palestine grew steadily feebler, and we may imagine, with a high degree of probability, that within a century of the great king's passing this strong outpost of Philistine stock ceased to yield allegiance to Egypt, and allied itself with its brothers of the Philistine League. Thus Philistia was provided with a strong post on the flank of its deadly enemy of Israel, and it is no longer difficult to account for the presence of Saul's army or that of the Philistines at Mount Gilboa. Saul was bent on securing Israel a fortress which, in hostile hands, was a perpetual thorn in the flesh to Israel, and, standing where it did, a perpetual hindrance to unity ; the Philistine army was there to help the Philistine garrison in Beth-Shean and to raise the siege, if a siege had been begun.

The result of the fight for Beth-Shean we have all known since our childhood, and the story of the disaster is one of the most beautiful and tragic of Hebrew narratives. When Saul and his sons had fallen, and the Hebrew army was scattered, the triumphant Philistines naturally placed the spoil of their victory, human and material, in the temples of the gods who had given them their triumph, 1 Samuel xxxi. 10 tells us that " they put his armour in the house of Ashtaroth and they fastened his body to the wall of Beth-Shan." 1 Chronicles x. 10 gives a similar story with a slight variant. The Philistines, it says, " put his armour in the house of their gods, and fastened his head in the temple of Dagon." The expedition has unearthed the remains of four Canaanite, or perhaps it would be more correct to say Canaanite-Philistine temples on the citadel-hill of Beth-Shean. The oldest dates from the Tell el-Amarna period (1375–50 B.C.) The next is the reign of Seti I (1313–1292). The two latest are from the reign of Rameses II (1292–25 B.C.), and were doubtless built by him for the use of his Philistine mercenaries. Of these two temples, one was originally dedicated to the warrior god Reshpu or Resheph, and the other, the northern one, to the warrior-goddess Ashtoreth (of whose

Y

name the common form Ashtaroth is merely the plural). Both these gods, although frequently worshipped in Egypt, were native to Palestine, and no doubt, when the Philistines asserted their independence of their former master at Beth-Shean, they continued the worship of the two familiar divinities, though it is likely enough that they called their Baal or Lord by their own name of Dagon rather than by the less familiar one of Reshpu. Ashtoreth would remain as the Baalath or Lady, with her name unchanged, and her house could quite legitimately be called the " house of their gods " as the goddess is so often spoken of in the plural, and has so many forms. Thus the slight variations in the accounts of Samuel and Chronicles are accounted for simply and completely by the results of excavation. Saul's armour was offered as a trophy before the shrine of Ashtoreth, which was also " the house of their gods " when you think of the goddess as Ashtaroth, while his head was offered in the temple of Reshpu-Dagon, and his body fastened to the walls of the citadel as a warning to all the enemies of Philistia. All the Beth-Shean finds have been, as was hoped they would be, of great value and interest ; perhaps the most interesting of them all, so far, is the ruined shrine, still astonishingly preserved, before which the armour of the vanquished King of Israel was hung, and the flower vases and other cult objects with which it must have been sur-rounded. Philistine occupation of Beth-Shean cannot have lasted long after this triumph. The possession of this key-position was vital to the Hebrew Kingdom, and doubtless David stormed it at an early period of his reign, as he did with Jerusalem in the south, though we have no Biblical record of the fact. The work of the expedition, however, has given us direct evidence of the fact. l " The sack of the citadel," says Dr. Fisher, " was thorough. Everywhere the mud brick walls were baked red in the terrific heat ; especially in the northern portion where the oils and grain in the store-rooms supplied abundant fuel for the flames.

Here the bricks from the falling walls and the beams from the roof had filled corridors and rooms to a depth of over three feet with a mass of debris burned as hard as rock and as difficult to remove."

Thus, as the excavations at Jerusalem yielded us an example of David's siege-practice in the south, so those at Beth-Shean have given us a similar example of it in the north, and in both cases he appears to have been pretty thorough, as might have been inferred from his record at Ammon. Some of the other results of the work at Beth-Shean have been scarcely less notable than those described—notably the discoveries in connection with the early Christian churches on the site, and the Bishop's house, with the striking mosaics found in both places. But the work on this great mound, though it has already lasted long, as such things go, has still a long way to go before the exploration of the site is complete, and we must content ourselves with such details as bear directly on Scriptural incidents and problems. Speaking of this expedition, Dr. Macalister has remarked, " This work at Beisan . . . is being carried out on the sumptuous scale which seems to be possible only to American excavating parties. In such a site anything may come to light ; there is no limit to its possibilities." It is good to close with such an estimate of future possibilities from such an expert ; but the remark which precedes the estimate is one of whose truth our nation should surely be a little ashamed. One has to admit its truth ; but why should adequate provision for the advancement of our knowledge of the past of our race be limited to American excavating parties ? Britain and France led the way in excavation, both in Egypt and Mesopotamia, and we have the men still thoroughly competent to do the work if they are furnished with the means. Mr. Woolley, in command at Ur, is one of our own. But in the meantime we prefer, it seems, to spend our money on things more important than knowledge, and it takes, as we have seen, a stupendous effort to raise

the paltry five thousand pounds which were needed for the
work at the City of David and of Our Lord. By and by,
perhaps, we shall wake up to the significance of the opportunities which we are missing, when wiser nations have
carried off the prizes which we were too foolish to seek
for.

Index

341

The Mayflower Press, Plymouth. William Brendon & Son, Ltd.
1927

STUDIES IN MODERN MUSIC

By Sir WILLIAM H. HADOW, M.A.
Hon. D. Mus. Oxford, Durham & Wales,
A Member of Council, Royal College of Music.

Volume I. BERLIOZ, SCHUMANN & WAGNER
With an Essay on Music & Musical Criticism, & Four Portraits.

Eleventh Edition. 5s. nett each. *Also a Library Edition,* 8s. 6d. nett.

"One more bit of advice is necessary. READ NOW, IF YOU HAVE NOT READ IT BEFORE, THE OPENING ESSAY IN THE FIRST VOLUME OF SIR HENRY HADOW'S 'STUDIES IN MODERN MUSIC,' in which the main characteristics of beauty in music are clearly defined. Nothing could assist you better in the task of 'arranging your emotions' and obtaining a glimpse of the reasons experienced music-lovers have for describing works as beautiful or the reverse."—Extract from "Musical Taste & How to Form It," by M. D. Calvocoressi.

"The first attempt towards laying the foundations of a specific method in musical criticism is Hadow's ("Studies in Modern Music," London: Seeley, Service & Co., First Series), who disengages the four main principles—vitality, labour, proportion and fitness—from the existence of which estimates of musical works can be arrived at."—Extract from "Dictionary of Modern Music & Musicians."

Volume II. CHOPIN, DVORAK & BRAHMS
With an Essay on Musical Form & Four Portraits.

Eleventh Edition. 5s. nett. *Also Library Edition,* 8s. 6d. nett.

"The development of form is described with MANY BRILLIANT TOUCHES and with complete grasp of the subject, and the book, which will probably be considered to be EVEN BETTER THAN THE FORMER WORK, is most heartily to be recommended to all who wish to attain the highest kind of enjoyment of the best music."—*Times.*

PREHISTORIC MAN & HIS STORY
A SKETCH OF THE HISTORY OF MANKIND
FROM THE EARLIEST TIMES
By Prof. G. F. SCOTT ELLIOTT
M.A.(Cantab.), B.Sc.(Edin.), F.R.S.E., F.L.S., F.R.G.S.,
Author of "A Naturalist in Mid-Africa, &c., &c., &c.

Demy 8vo. With 70 Illustrations. 10s. 6d. nett.

"In addition to a marvellously wide range of information, the author is A MASTER OF THE ART OF POPULAR EXPOSITION."—*Aberdeen Jnl.*

"Professor Scott Elliott has contrived to condense all the recent discoveries which bear upon the problem of prehistoric man."—*Outlook.*

"AN ADMIRABLE AND THOUGHTFUL SURVEY. Professor Scott Elliott has A DELIGHTFUL STYLE, WHICH WILL MAKE HIS BOOK VERY POPULAR."—*Pall Mall.*

"We could pile up adjectives to express our appreciation of this delightful work, and of the broad-minded way in which this great anthropologist tells us of the conclusions he has come to."—*Fishing Gazette.*

SEELEY, SERVICE & CO. LIMITED

11/01